365 MEDITATIONS FOR MEN

To LeRoy,

With deep gratitude for your friendship to the Harnish family across the years.

Peace

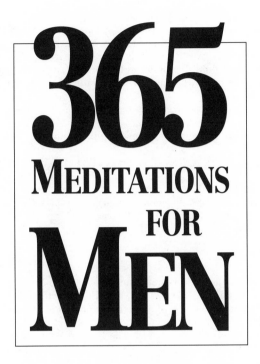

365 MEDITATIONS FOR MEN

M. R. Howes, Editor

James A. Harnish • Kel Groseclose • Vance P. Ross
Robert H. Lauer • James W. Moore • Paul E. Miller
J. Ellsworth Kalas • John Killinger • Walter Kimbrough
Martin L. Camp • James R. King Jr. • Bruce Fish • Tim Philpot

DIMENSIONS
FOR LIVING
NASHVILLE

365 MEDITATIONS FOR MEN

Copyright © 1998 by Dimensions for Living

This book is printed on recycled, acid-free paper.

Library of Congress Cataloging-in-Publication Data

365 meditations for men / M. R. Howes, editor . . . [et al.].
    p.   cm.
   ISBN 0-687-07680-3 (pbk. : alk. paper)
   1. Men—Prayer-books and devotions—English. 2. Bible—Meditations.
 3. Devotional calendars. I. Howes, M. R. (Mary Ruth)
 BV4528.2.A18   1998
 242'.642—dc21   98-28159
                                                             CIP

99 00 01 02 03 04 05 06 07 — 10 9 8 7 6 5 4 3 2

MANUFACTURED IN THE UNITED STATES OF AMERICA

CONTENTS

INTRODUCTION

The fact that you have picked up this book means that you do not fit the stereotypical view of men held by many—that men are not interested in spiritual things or in meditation on a daily basis.

Nor does this book fit a stereotype. These 365 daily meditations will not give you a mere pat on the back, or just a nice spiritual boost—though you *will* receive encouragement and inspiration. You have in your hands a ringing call for reality, a challenge to be a strong man of faith—in your family, in your church, in your community.

Thirteen talented male writers have come together to reflect on key themes of interest to today's Christian men. Each writer explores one topic for four weeks, providing an entire year's worth of encouragement and instruction for a man's spiritual journey.

All thirteen writers call on you to act, to put your faith to work. They challenge you to become leaders, mentors, models for others, to make a difference in your world. One of the recurring themes is that Christian men are called to enter God's army, to join in the battle between good and evil.

At the same time they challenge you not to get so busy, so active, that you never learn what quietness and silence can do to renew your life and rejuvenate you for service.

The writers talk about what it means to be real men—to be both kind and tough, to be vulnerable, to give and forgive, to be able to handle both success and failure. They offer you the companionship of the Scriptures, as well as lessons from their own experience, and provide support and counsel for coping with problems like discouragement or fear. They call you to excellence, and at the same time remind you of the love and patience of our Savior Jesus Christ, who understands failure and doubt and is confident of your perseverance and ultimate triumph. They point you to the Holy Spirit, who provides the power to live the Christian life.

Other characteristics of real men, these writers suggest, are that

- they are men of vision;
- they are men of prayer;
- they are willing to ask for directions (did you know that not asking for directions is "a terminal male disease"?);
- they are willing to wait for results;
- they learn from others, including children;
- they never give up on people;
- they are willing to work out disagreements;
- they have an inner fire;
- they give themselves.

The writers who share their faith and experience in *365 Meditations for Men* believe that today's men—that you—are hungry for a deeper relationship with God and are ready for a new beginning.

So welcome to this new year.

M. R. Howes, Editor

ABOUT THE AUTHORS

Martin L. Camp, a native Texan, decided to be a lawyer when he was fifteen. A graduate of Southern Methodist University Law School, for the past twenty years he has been a member of Texas-based law firms, including a three-year-stint as partner resident in Kuwait. He is a member of the Church of the Incarnation, Episcopal, in Dallas and is the founder of Christian Men in the Law. The father of three children, Eric, Leigh, and Haydon, he is the author of *Why Alligators Don't Have Wings*, a book for children, as well as *Life on the Highwire* (Abingdon, 1997), a book for men.

Bruce Fish is a freelance writer and editor who lives in Bend, Oregon. He and his wife, Becky, are the authors of *A Moment With God for Caregivers* (Dimensions for Living, 1998). Before taking up writing full-time, he spent thirteen years in retail management, including five years each with Waldenbooks and Sherwin Williams. He has over thirty years of experience as a teacher, small group leader, musician, and lay leader in local churches and parachurch ministries.

Kel Groseclose lives in Wenatchee, Washington, with his wife, Ellen, and four cats. They are parents of six grown children who are scattered around the country, and he says he has the most beautiful grandchildren in the world. Kel is a United Methodist pastor serving the Wenatchee First United Methodist Church as minister of congregational care. He enjoys digging in his small garden, writing in a journal, playing the fiddle, watching sports on television, and eating Rocky Road ice cream.

James A. Harnish, a native of Pennsylvania, has pastored churches in Florida for more than twenty-five years and is currently the senior pastor of Hyde Park United Methodist Church in Tampa, Florida. He is the author of nine books, including *God Isn't Finished with Us Yet* and *Men at Mid-Life: Steering Through the Detours*. He and his wife, Marsha, have two grown daughters, Carrie Lynne and Deborah Jeanne. In addition to his passion for preaching and ministry, Jim enjoys University of Florida football games, relaxing in the Florida sun, and playing a "mediocre game of tennis"!

J. Ellsworth Kalas read the Bible through for the first time when he was eleven years old, and it has been a key factor in his faith and daily life ever since. He pastored United Methodist churches in Wisconsin and Ohio for thirty-eight years before becoming the Beeson Senior Pastor in Residence at Asbury Theological Seminary in Wilmore, Kentucky. His daughter is a French professor, and his son is a United Methodist minister. He is the author of a number of books, including *The Grand Sweep* and *The Ten Commandments from the Back Side*. He and his wife Janet live in Lexington, Kentucky.

John Killinger, writer, teacher, and minister at large, is president of the Mission for Biblical Literacy, based in Athens, Georgia. He has taught at numerous institutions, including Vanderbilt University, and his pastorates include First Congregational Church in Los Angeles and First Presbyterian Church of Lynchburg, Virginia. During the summer months he serves as minister of the Little Stone Church on Mackinac Island, Michigan. He is the author of more than sixty books, including *Raising Your Spiritual Awareness* (Abingdon, 1998). He and his wife, Anne, have two grown sons. Besides spending time with his wife, he enjoys walking, reading, and going to the theater.

Walter Kimbrough, a native of Atlanta, has been in the ministry for over a quarter of a century and is now the senior pastor of Cascade United Methodist Church in Atlanta. His ministry has been characterized by evangelism, pastoral care, and teaching, and he has been very active in community affairs. A noted Bible study teacher, workshop leader, and motivator, he received the Denman Award for Excellence in Evangelism in 1988. He is the author of *Nothing Is Impossible* (1992). He and his wife, the former Marjorie Lindsay, an author and university professor, have two adult sons, Walter Mark and Wayne Martin.

James R. King Jr., a United Methodist minister and pastoral counselor, pastored churches in Alabama and California before being appointed to the Wesley Foundation at Tennessee State University. He has served the Tennessee Conference in many capacities, and is now District Superintendent for the Murfreesboro District. James and his wife, Margaret, have three children,

Jothany, James R. III, and Robert. In what spare time he has he enjoys reading, playing tennis, and various water sports.

Robert H. Lauer is an ordained minister who has served as a pastor in a number of churches. He has also been a university professor and dean. He now writes and lectures full-time, primarily with his wife, Jeanette. He has authored or coauthored twenty books as well as many articles in academic, religious, and popular sources. He has three children and five grandchildren. He has a long-standing sense of calling to help people deal with the challenges and crises in their lives. In his last pastorate, he and Jeanette began the Stephen Ministry program (a one-on-one lay caring ministry) and formed a number of marriage support groups. A good part of his ministry has involved counseling and small-group support.

Paul E. Miller has served in many capacities in his thirty years in the ministry, including youth minister and minister to children, and has pastored rural and suburban churches. Currently he is pastor of the Asbury United Methodist Church, South, in Columbus, Ohio. His wife, Pat, is also a United Methodist minister, and together they have raised two daughters, Angie and Suzy. He enjoys gardening and reading and also consults in conflict management and children's spirituality. He coauthored *Having the Mind of Christ: 365 Days of Spiritual Growth Through Scripture, Meditation, and Practice* (Abingdon, 1996).

James W. Moore is a native of Memphis, Tennessee, and pastored United Methodist Churches in Tennessee, Ohio, and Louisiana before becoming senior minister of St. Luke's United Methodist Church in Houston, Texas. He has written, directed, and hosted both weekly television shows and seasonal specials, as well as a weekly radio show, and is the author of many books, including *Yes, Lord, I Have Sinned, But I Have Several Excellent Excuses* and *When You're a Christian, the Whole World is from Missouri*. He and his wife June have two grown children and two grandchildren.

Tim Philpot, president of Christian Business Men's Committee International, based in Chattanooga, Tennessee, has been an active member of CBMC since 1978. A native of Lexington, Kentucky, where he lives with his wife, Anne, he has been a trial lawyer for more than twenty years. In 1990 he was elected to the Kentucky State Senate, and he was reelected in 1994. For many years he was a serious amateur golfer, participating in the 1983 British Amateur Open. He has traveled extensively all over the world, and his most recent trips for CBMC International have included the Ukraine as well as Ethiopia, Kenya, and other African countries.

Vance P. Ross, a native of West Virginia, served as pastor of Simpson Memorial United Methodist Church in Charleston, West Virginia, before joining the General Board of Discipleship in Nashville, Tennessee, as director of congregational revitalization. He is senior pastor of First United Methodist Church in Hyattsville, Maryland. Besides serving on a number of commissions for The United Methodist Church and community boards and agencies, he is an avid basketball fan and coaches grade school community teams and junior high church teams. He also enjoys reading, jazz music, and listening to sermons. He and his wife Pamela have three children, Krystina, Alyssa, and Bryant.

1

REAL PRAYER
FOR REAL MEN

James A. Harnish

Week 1, Sunday   **Do Real Men Really Pray?**

Read Psalm 1.

A vintage Norman Rockwell painting from the cover of *The Saturday Evening Post* magazine is set in a blue-collar coffee shop. One working man holds a newspaper, as smoke from his cigarette drifts to the ceiling. Another leans over his coffee, a cigarette dangling from his lips. In the foreground, a third man holds a cigar. It was a time when smoking was an unambiguous indication of manliness. They all stare with curious respect at a tiny lady in a quaint straw hat and a little boy in a white shirt who, with bowed heads and folded hands, pray over their soup.

The painting's cozy reverence conceals a disturbing cultural assumption, namely, that real men respect prayer, but only gray-headed ladies and little boys practice it. You are among a growing company of men who are breaking that cultural stereotype as you develop a personal discipline of prayer.

The psalms are the biblical center for a life of prayer. They were written by real people who discovered the real presence of God in real human experience. In the psalms they have left "not monuments, but footprints. A monument only says, 'I got this far,' while a footprint says, 'This is where I was when I moved again' " (Wiilliam Faulkner, quoted by Eugene Peterson, *A Long Obedience in the Same Direction,* Downers Grove, IL, 1980, p. 17).

I invite you to follow the footprints of the psalmists as we discover what it means for real men to experience real prayer.

O God, teach me the reality of prayer. Amen.

13

Read Psalm 8.

I was intrigued by a May 15, 1994, *New York Times* review of a collection of poems by Amy Clampitt entitled *A Silence Opens.* The reviewer said that Clampitt's poetry went "to the extreme edge of the sayable" and that "this edge-of-language position is exactly where religious experience begins." That is where real prayer begins, too.

On a recent trip our family arrived in the Great Smoky Mountains National Park after dark. Early the next morning I stepped onto the deck of our rented condominium, which was cantilevered over the edge of the mountainside. The chill in the air and the sight of the rising sun combined to take my breath away. The sky was crimson. A white mist wafted over blue-tinged ranges that folded over one another into infinity. A silence opened in me that took me to "the edge of the sayable."

The eighth psalm reflects an "edge-of-language" experience. It erupts with a shout of astonished praise that soon dissolves into speechless reverence. Before a heaven-measured awareness of God's greatness, the only appropriate response is, "What is man, that you think of him; / mere man, that you care for him?" (v. 4 TEV). Real prayer begins when we realize the bigness of God and the littleness of our own existence.

When was the last time you found yourself at "the extreme edge of the sayable?" How would you translate that experience into prayer?

O Lord, my Lord, take me to that edge-of-language place where I am left in awe of your greatness. Amen.

Week 1, Tuesday   **The Voice in the Thunder**

Read Psalm 29.

It's probably a male thing, like clicking the cable remote control. All I know is that while my wife feels God's presence in the beauty of flowers, I'm drawn to God through the power of the thunder.

As a child, I would sit on the front porch to watch the rain of a summer storm flow like a sheet of glass down over the canvas awnings. As a college student, I remember a hot summer night when I tracked the movement of lightning as it circled the hills of Pittsburgh. As an adult, I watch in awe as the dark line of clouds and rain sweep across the Gulf of Mexico. I hear the thunder, and I am drawn to its power.

The verbs of Psalm 29 are filled with raw, naked power. The voice of the Lord thunders over the waters, breaks the cedars, flashes in fire, shakes the wilderness, whirls the oaks and strips the forests. No wonder all who hear shout, "Glory!" To hear the voice of the Lord is to be astounded by God's awesome power.

There are times for the "still small voice" of God (1 Kings 19:12 RSV), but it will be the same voice we hear in the thunder with the volume turned down. How have you heard the voice that speaks in the thunder? When did you feel like shouting, "Glory!"?

O God of thunderous power, give me a deep sense of your strength, which will overwhelm my weakness. Amen.

Week 1, Wednesday   **Lifeless Idols or Living Power?**

Read Psalm 135.

When I stepped into the office of a pastor/friend in South Africa, I was surprised to discover a drawing of the Lincoln Memorial hanging on the wall. At first glance, it seemed strangely out of place, half a world away from Washington, D.C. But as I watched his witness in the struggle with apartheid, when I felt the surging hope for freedom among his people, as I sang and prayed with people in Soweto, I began to understand why Lincoln was there.

Years later, after freedom came to his country, that friend met me in Washington and we climbed the steps of the Lincoln Memorial in silent reverence. We gazed into those compassionate, marble eyes. We read the words of the Gettysburg Address which are carved into the wall. We looked across the Tidal Basin at the Jefferson Memorial and then walked through the new memorial to FDR. These are all silent reminders of the ideas to which we are called. I remembered the drawing in his office, and I remembered that we will become like the idols we honor.

Far too often, "the idols of the nations are silver and gold" (v. 15). The materialistic gods of his culture and ours are without breath: lifeless, cold, impersonal, unfeeling. In contrast, this psalm praises the living God of divine compassion who liberates people from bondage.

What ideals are shaping your life? Are they consistent with the compassionate character of the God who sets people free?

O God, may my life be shaped by my worship of you. Amen.

Week 1, Thursday   **Power to Lift the World**

Read Psalm 18:1-19, 25-33.

Danish philosopher Søren Kierkegaard wrote, "The Archimedean point outside the world is the little chamber where a true supplicant prays in all sincerity—where he lifts the world off its hinges" (quoted by Martin Marty, *Context*, October 1, 1993, p. 5).

Psalm 18 is attributed to David "on the day when the LORD delivered him from the hand of all his enemies" (NRSV heading). He knew he had been saved through the earth-lifting power of God. He described that power in spectacular, *"Star Wars"* imagery (vv. 7-19). The God upon whom he called was the God of cosmic power, the God whose greatness was beyond his comprehension, and the God whose infinite power was focused into his experience through prayer.

On my first visit to the Trappist monastery of Gethsemani in eastern Kentucky, I asked a typical, hyperactive, '60s social-activist sort of question. It was fine, I thought, to pray, but what were these monks doing to really make a difference in the world? I soon learned how deeply they believe that they are making a difference, not through activity but through faithful prayer, and I have come to believe it, too. It may not be my calling, but I never doubt that it is theirs. In fact, I often feel an inner strength for my active life in the world, which comes from my awareness of their prayerful life of solitude.

Do we believe that real power can be released into our world through prayer? Do we dare to believe that prayer lifts the world off its hinges?

O Lord, hear my cry, and be for me a strong deliverer. Amen.

Read Psalm 139.

Here's a disturbing thought: the all-powerful God we seek is already seeking us. The One we come to know in prayer already knows us. Prayer is not our way of finding God but the discipline by which we allow ourselves to be found.

I cannot read the 139th Psalm without hearing the words of Francis Thompson in "The Hound of Heaven."

> I fled Him, down the nights and down the days;
> I fled Him down the arches of the years;
> I fled Him down the labyrinthine ways
> Of my own mind; and in the mist of tears
> I hid from Him, and under running laughter.
> Up vistaed hopes I sped;
> And shot, precipitated,
> Adown Titanic glooms of chasmed fears,
> From those strong Feet that followed, followed after.
> But with unhurrying chase,
> And unperturbed pace,
> Deliberate speed, majestic instancy,
> They beat—and a Voice beat
> More instant than the Feet—
> "All things betray thee, who betrayest Me."

Thompson could not outrun God. Finally, he surrendered and heard the One who pursued him say,

> "Ah, fondest, blindest, weakest,
> I am He Whom thou seekest!"

Psalm 139 invites us to prayer that is both frightening and wonderful. How does it feel to know that God knows you so well? What part of your life do you attempt to hide from God? Will you allow yourself to be found?

Search me, O God, and know my heart, . . .
and lead me in the way everlasting. Amen.

Read Psalm 84.

My Dad couldn't carry a tune with a handle on it, but Mom gave me the gift of music. She sang her faith as much as she spoke it, and she taught me to sing it, too.

In the psalms, prayer is the music of the soul. Some psalms reverberate with rolling drums and crashing cymbals. Some march to blaring trumpets. Some flow with the earthy passion of blues and jazz. Others rock with a country beat. Beneath Psalm 84, I hear lush strings: the gentle power of Montovani for one generation, the soothing sounds of Yanni or Kenny G for another. While some psalms resound with lightning and thunder, this one soars with sunshine and bird's song. Hebrew pilgrims sang it on their way to worship in Jerusalem. The joyful soul-longing of their song expresses hopeful expectation as they prepare to experience God's presence in the temple.

The journey wasn't easy. The "valley of Baca"—literally, "valley of weeping"—may be a geographic location or it may be symbolic for a soul-place of sorrow and pain. But the "valley of tears" becomes "a place of springs" and the pilgrim is strengthened along the way because this world can offer nothing to compare to the beauty of the dwelling place of God.

The power we discover in prayer leads to worship. It is music for our souls, which joins the songs of other pilgrims in joyful praise.

What music do you hear in this psalm? How does it strengthen you for your journey? How does it prepare you for worship?

O Lord, my heart and flesh sing for joy. Strengthen me for my journey. Amen.

Week 2, Sunday   **What Makes a Man?**

Read Psalm 2.

Who am I? What inner powers and passions motivate me? What defines my identity as a man?

A humorous answer is offered in what a reviewer for the *Tampa Tribune* (June 15, 1997) called "an ungainly, rollicking . . book," and an "ode to testosterone"—Michael Precker's *The Big Damn Book of Sheer Manliness.* It clears up profound enigmas of male identity such as "What is the all-time manliest film?" *(Spartacus)* and "Who's that chrome woman on mud flaps?" (Mustang Sally, "an untamed American beauty jostling over the open road").

Because God laughs at us (v. 4), we can laugh at ourselves. But if we want a soul-level definition of male identity, the Bible provides a more satisfying answer.

Psalm 2 is a hymn for the coronation of a new king. Amid conspiring nations and power-hungry rulers, the leader of God's chosen people received his identity from the Lord: "You are my son; / today I have begotten you" (v. 7). The central core of his identity was defined not by the world around him, but by the voice of God within him. In the same way, when Jesus emerged from the waters of baptism, he heard the voice of God saying, "You are my Son, the Beloved; with you I am well pleased" (Luke 3:22).

Real prayer takes me into the central core of my personality where I listen for the One who names me as a beloved son and where I allow that voice to tell me who I am.

What passions drive your life? Who tells you who you are?

O God, may my identity be shaped by the awareness that I am your beloved son. Amen.

Week 2, Monday   Into Deep Places

Read Psalm 42.

In a powerful sentence full of strong words, biblical theologian Walter Wink writes: "The fawning etiquette of unctuous prayer is utterly foreign to the Bible. Biblical prayer is impertinent, persistent, shameless, indecorous. It is more like haggling in an oriental bazaar than the polite monologues of the churches" *(Engaging the Powers,* Minneapolis, Augsburg/Fortress, 1992, p. 301).

I love the genuine, human passion of the psalms. They are filled with ruthlessly honest, often uncomfortable, sometimes embarrassing emotion.

When I counsel with a person who is struggling with anger, depression, fear, or resentment, I often offer this pastoral prescription for healing. Begin reading the psalms with an ear for the feelings they contain. Don't get hung up on theology; just feel the psalmist's emotions. When you find one that describes the way you feel, settle in with it for a while. Allow the words to flow through you. With the psalmist, allow your deepest passions to become a form of prayer.

Too often, our ideas of prayer are shaped by cultural images of polite piety that never allow room for our deepest passions. Nothing could be farther removed from the psalms, in which "deep calls to deep" (v. 7) in the real experiences of life.

Will you allow prayer to take you into the deep places of your soul? What will it mean for you to pray as the psalmists prayed?

O God, take me to deep places where I can be ruthlessly honest with myself and with you. Amen.

Week 2, Tuesday   A Psalm for Sleepless Nights

Read Psalm 77.

Are you in the Three o'Clock Club? It's a very inclusive group of folks, we who wake up at 3:00 A.M. with our hyperactive brains spinning around tasks to be done, mistakes we have made, frustrations we have to face, conflicts we have not resolved. As we toss and turn, the problems become larger, more intractable, and more difficult to set aside. I've even been known to click on MTV to give my brain a rest!

When we find ourselves in that club, we are in good company. The psalmists often meet us in that dark night where the "soul refuses to be comforted" (v. 2). This psalm names the questions that haunt our anxiety: Has God's love ceased to be with us? Does God even care?

I am encouraged by the way this night owl uses his insomnia. He calls to mind what God has done in the past. He spends his sleepless hours reflecting on God's gracious action in the journey of his people. He finds in his history the footprints of God.

Some nighttime psalms come to a restful resolution; Psalm 127:2, for instance. This one ends abruptly. Biblical scholars say it is an incomplete fragment of an ancient hymn with its final verses missing. Or perhaps, I like to imagine, the writer finally fell asleep, pen in hand, lost in the memory of the goodness of God.

How do you use your sleepless nights? Can you see the goodness of God in your personal history?

O God, in the sleepless hours of the night, help me to remember your goodness in the past. Amen.

Week 2, Wednesday   Guilty!

Read Psalm 51.

"Guilty!" I cannot imagine how the defendant feels who hears the jury foreman declare that verdict, but I know very well how it feels to hear it in the deep places of my soul. I know the way guilt floods through the whole of my personality. I've experienced the painful awareness of the finger of divine judgment pointing at me with the words, "You are the man!" (2 Samuel 12:7). When I fail to live up to the call of God in my life, my sin is ever before me.

Psalm 51 expresses David's guilt for his affair with Bathsheba and his self-serving murder of Uriah. (You can read the "R-rated" story in 2 Samuel 11–12.) Although our moral failure may not be as dramatic as his, our guilt may be just as bona fide. Real prayer sensitizes us to our sin. It teaches us to pray, "Have mercy on me, O God!"

David's soul-searching prayer leads us through the process of forgiveness. He experiences honest confrontation with his failure (Psalm 51:3) and realizes that his sin is ultimately against God. He acknowledges his need of God's cleansing grace (v. 7) and affirms the joy that forgiveness brings (v. 12).

Have you felt the passionate guilt that David expresses here? How have you faced it? Have you confessed it and experienced God's forgiveness?

Only those who acknowledge their guilt can receive the gift of forgiveness. If God's forgiveness was available for David, it is available for us as well.

O God, have mercy on me! Amen.

Week 2, Thursday   God-Forsaken Prayer

Read Psalms 39 and 22.

Contemporary theologian Jürgen Moltmann is often my soul companion during Lent because his book, *The Crucified God,* contains such powerful insights into the meaning of the cross. Recently I discovered the beginning point of his journey.

In World War II, Moltmann served in the German army. After the war, he was sent to a prisoner of war camp in Scotland. Suffering hopeless despair, with a deeply wounded soul, he felt the burden of shame and guilt for his part in Nazism's destructive power. He had no religious faith, but a British Christian gave him a Bible. Reading Psalm 39, he found language for his feelings. And then, when he heard Jesus' cry, "My God, why have you forsaken me?" from the cross, "I knew with certainty: this is someone who understands you. . . . I felt that he understood me: this was the divine brother in distress, who takes the prisoners with him on his way to resurrection. . . . Christ's God-forsakenness showed me *where* God is, *where* he had been with me in my life, and where he would be in the future" (Jürgen Moltmann, *The Source of Life,* Minneapolis, Augsburg Fortress, 1997, p. 5).

I remember a man who was dying of cancer. He said he felt forsaken by God. When I reminded him of Jesus' words from the cross, the godforsaken Christ became a present reality in his suffering and prepared him to die in peace.

Real prayer is not afraid to go into the darkest corners of human experience because Jesus has already gone there. Have you allowed him to go there with you?

O Divine Brother, go with me to the most godforsaken place of my soul. Amen.

Week 2, Friday   **Crushed and Alone**

Read Psalm 38.

I tried to avoid this psalm. There are so many joyful psalms of affirmation; why spend a day with this prayer of almost unrelenting darkness?

The prayer is rooted in a severe physical affliction, which the writer describes in graphic terms. To make matters worse, his friends and neighbors have abandoned him. He feels as if everyone has turned against him. Like most of us, he turns his suffering in on himself and assumes that he is somehow responsible for it. The only glimmer of hope is that he prays to a God who already understands his deepest longings. He has just enough faith to pray that God will not be far from him and that God will come to save him. That is enough to keep him going for another day.

I tried to avoid this psalm. But then I remembered the face of an AIDS patient who had been rejected by his family. Alone in his anguish, he had no where to turn but to the God who, he dared to believe, still cared for him. I remembered the friend who faced the unrelenting pain of brain cancer and the one who held his hand. I remembered the young parents who watched in helpless agony as their child's life ebbed away.

I could no more avoid this psalm than any of them could avoid their pain. The prayer touches the deepest realities of our human condition and points to the hope of our faith in God.

O God, do not forsake me! Amen.

Week 2, Saturday   **Honest-to-God Prayer**

Read Psalm 6.

Are you ever dishonest in prayer? If God knows us as well as the psalms declare, the joke is on us if we are less than fearlessly honest about the deepest, darkest realities of our lives.

While hearing the psalms read in a monastery chapel, Kathleen Norris learned the lesson of prayer that is ruthlessly honest and utterly real. "The psalms are unrelenting in their realism about the human psyche," she discovered. "To your surprise, you find that the psalms do not deny your true feelings but allow you to reflect on them, right in front of God and everyone" *(The Cloister Walk,* New York, Riverhead Books, 1996, pp. 104, 92).

I was a college student when I began to learn this lesson in a sophomoric way with two of my classmates as we tried talking to God the way we talked with each other in the dormitory halls. Resisting anything like the reverence of bowed heads or folded hands, we sprawled on our beds and "prayed" with none of the pious language we had been taught in Sunday school. Looking back, I suspect God was more humored than impressed by our crass and downright vulgar attempt at casual conversation with the Almighty.

Fortunately for us, God is more patient with our honesty than our hypocrisy. My life of prayer has gone far deeper than any of us ever imagined back then, but it was not a bad place to begin.

Can you hear the shocking honesty of the psalms? How will it influence your life of prayer?

O God of truth, let me be honest with you. Amen.

Week 3, Sunday   Prayer as Positive Addiction

Read Psalm 71.

One of the most important lessons he has learned, says psychologist William Glasser, is that "strong people wait a lot." He described the process by which people grow in personal strength as "positive addiction," like runners who eventually reach a "runner's high." It takes time, he warns, and "one has to keep going a long time on faith," "the faith that it is doing them some good. . . . Positive addiction, like all good things in life, is most open to people who have the strength to stick to it" *(Positive Addiction,* New York, Harper & Row, 1976, pp. 8, 50, 51).

A pastor/friend confessed, "It's hard for me to maintain a discipline of prayer, not because prayer is hard, but because discipline is hard." I know what he means. Just as the only path to physical strength is the discipline of exercise, the only path to spiritual peace is the discipline of prayer. I've learned the hard way that to maintain my physical strength, I must get out of bed and meet my friend to run on the Bayshore along Hillsborough Bay. If I am to be strengthened by God's presence, I must keep the discipline of meeting God in Bible study and prayer. There is no other way.

Psalm 71 is the prayer of an old man at the end of a long life of spiritual discipline. His experience confirms the peace and confidence that come from a positive addiction to prayer.

Do you want to discover spiritual strength? Will you follow the discipline of prayer?

O God, give me the desire to keep going in the discipline of prayer, so that I may find strength in you. Amen.

Read Psalm 91.

The late Rabbi Abraham Joshua Heschel stood in the long line of Hebrew faith as a witness of the power of prayer. Brood over his words and allow them to soak into your soul.

> Prayer is not a stratagem for occasional use, a refuge to resort to now and then. It is rather like an established residence for the innermost self. . . . A soul without prayer is a soul without a home. Weary, sobbing, the soul, after roaming through a world festered with aimlessness, falsehoods, and absurdities, seeks a moment in which to gather up its scattered life, in which to divest itself of enforced pretension and camouflage, in which to simplify complexities, in which to call for help without being a coward. . . . For the soul, home is where prayer is. *(Moral Grandeur and Spiritual Audacity,* New York, Farrar, Straus, & Giroux, quoted in *Context,* May 15, 1997, p. 6)

Frankly, I have a bone to pick with Psalm 91. The historical evidence flies in the face of the promise that "no evil shall befall you" (v. 10). I cannot reconcile this psalm with the Holocaust or with the irrational suffering of a host of faithful people. And yet, when I feel my way into these words, I know they describe an inner refuge formed in the soul through prayer, a refuge that is able to sustain us in terrible times. It is a spiritual home that no evil can destroy.

Where is your soul's home? Have you found the shelter of the Almighty for your life?

O Lord, you are my refuge, my God in whom I trust. Amen.

Week 3, Tuesday   **Prayer in the Passive Voice**

Read Psalm 62.

Have you noticed the increasing use of the passive voice in the media these days? No one "makes mistakes" any more. Rather, we say, "Mistakes were made." It's a convenient way to avoid responsibility for our actions by hiding behind the passive voice.

Real prayer, however, knows the best use of the passive voice. E. Stanley Jones, one of the truly global Christians of this century, described the way he surrendered his active thinking to passive receptivity to the Spirit of God. He concluded: "We must learn to live in the passive voice. Only those who do so, know what it means to live in the active voice. The fussy activity of the modern man is not life; it is the nervous twitching of his disordered and starved nerves" *(Abundant Living,* Nashville, Abingdon Press, Festival edition, 1976, p. 226).

Real prayer involves disciplined passivity in which I shut down the hyperactive voices of the world and allow God to come to me in silence. It is not a blank, empty silence that floats in nothingness. It is silence in which I focus my attention on the God who speaks through scripture and is known in Jesus Christ. Christ-centered passivity orders my active life and enables me to live responsibly in the world.

I'm a talker; silence is difficult for me. I always have things I think I need to "do" that get in the way of my need to "be." But I have found that silence is the only way to know the One who matters most.

O God, I wait for you in silence. Amen.

Week 3, Wednesday   Facing Whatever Comes

Read Psalm 138.

Brian Sternberg was headed to the Olympics with a world record for the pole vault when he was paralyzed from the neck down. During rehabilitation, his uncle said, "I wish I could take your place and give you some rest."

Brian replied, "You couldn't do it. I know because I couldn't either, if I didn't have to." Later, when he was asked about his faith, Brian replied, "I want to know that my life is being used fully for the glory of God. . . . I do not want my faith in God to be just a result of my desire to get well. . . . Having faith is a necessary step toward one of two things. Being healed is one of them. Peace of mind if healing doesn't come is the other. Either one will suffice" (James Harnish, *Jesus Makes the Difference!* Nashville, The Upper Room, 1987, p. 43).

Brian's words remain with me as a witness to the difference real prayer makes. He never denies his desire to be healed. But beneath that genuine, human desire, there is a trust in God that enables him to face whatever comes.

I've faced it in my own life, when I prayed for healing that did not come. I've faced it in the lives of others. Along the way I have learned that sometimes prayer releases miraculous power that fulfills our human desires. Sometimes it doesn't. But real prayer always cultivates a trust in God, which produces inner peace to face whatever comes.

O God, increase the strength of my soul that in you I may find peace. Amen.

Week 3, Thursday   Prayer for the Workaholic

Read Psalm 131.

I am a workaholic. I inherited the addiction from my father. But I'm making progress dealing with my addiction.

The key to my healing is grace: the unearned, undeserved, unrepayable love and acceptance of God. Grace means that my value is ultimately dependent not on what I accomplish but on who I am. I am loved, not because of what I have done, but because of what God has done for me. Grace means that I can take the risk of being real because I know the source of genuine forgiveness. Grace frees me from the performance trap to live joyfully and freely as a son of God.

God's grace is unearned, but my awareness of that grace is in direct proportion to my discipline in prayer. In silence and prayer, I receive the gift of grace, which, like the manna God gave the children of Israel in the wilderness, is good for about one day at a time. In prayer I experience God's forgiveness for the ways I blow it. In prayer I find inner direction for the work I do. In prayer I find the calm of inner peace.

Psalm 131, which the New Revised Standard Bible calls "Song of Quiet Trust," paints a beautiful picture of what it means to be held in God's grace like a baby in its mother's arms. All our needs are taken care of, we are protected and loved and at peace.

O God, you calm us, holding us in your arms like a mother. Give me the gift of your grace for this day. Amen.

Read Psalm 116.

In her book *No Ordinary Time* (New York, Simon & Schuster, 1994), Doris Kearns Goodwin tells the story of Franklin and Eleanor Roosevelt during World War II. "Amid tumultuous events abroad, turmoil in Congress, and trouble at home," she writes about FDR, "he remained relaxed, good-humored, and self-assured" (p. 419). His amazing stability was rooted in the way he renewed his energy by returning to his home at Hyde Park, where he refused to work until after noon and indulged in restful jaunts through the countryside and relaxed conversation with friends.

By contrast, Goodwin describes the way Adolf Hitler "diminished his strength through overwork. . . . In time, Albert Speer argued, Hitler's tendency to overwork left him 'permanently caustic and irritable,' unable to absorb fresh impressions, unwilling to listen to criticism" (pp. 419-20).

It would be far too simplistic to say that Hitler lost the war because he never took a day off and Roosevelt won because he did. And yet, the truth in many of our lives is that we are defeated, not by the magnitude of our responsibilities, but by our lack of rest.

I have been there: overworked to utter exhaustion, with all my resources spent and all my energy gone. I don't want to go there again. The leaders I respect the most are those who carry huge burdens very lightly because they know how to relax, to laugh, and to be at rest.

Where do you go to relax, rest, and laugh? Have you been to your own "Hyde Park" lately?

Return, O my soul, to your rest,
for the Lord has dealt bountifully with you. Amen.

Read Psalm 122.

The Songs of Ascents (Psalms 120–134) are a collection of psalms that were sung by pilgrims on their way to worship in

Jerusalem. Because the Temple mount was the highest point in Palestine, travelers were ascending, gaining altitude, most of the way. But the title is also figurative, describing our soul-journey into God's presence. Psalm 122 celebrates the joyful anticipation people found along the way as they prepared to give thanks in the temple and pray for peace.

I knew nothing about the geography of Palestine when, as a kid in Sunday school, I memorized: "I was glad when they said unto me, Let us go into the house of the LORD" (v. 1 KJV). I've sometimes wondered if they taught us that verse in a futile attempt to ward off days when I would not be "glad" about going. It didn't work! That's true not just for kids. Honest adults ask, Do I really need to go to worship? Does going to church make me glad?

Eugene Peterson turns the "customer satisfaction" approach to worship inside out: "Worship does not satisfy our hunger for God—it whets our appetite. Our need for God is not taken care of by engaging in worship—it deepens" *(A Long Obedience in the Same Direction,* p. 52). The Hebrew pilgrims found their gladness along the way and took it with them to worship. No wonder they were glad when they arrived.

Does worship whet your appetite for a deeper life of prayer? What will it mean for you to go gladly to the house of the Lord?

O God, give me gladness for my journey toward you. Amen.

Week 4, Sunday   **A Song for My Life**

Read Psalm 103.

Real prayer culminates in an offertory of praise.

On my first morning in Nairobi, Kenya (which my body thought was night!), I rolled out of bed and walked to All Saints' Cathedral. By the time I arrived, the only seat was directly behind one of the stone pillars that supported the Gothic structure. Unable to see, I soaked in the sounds of traditional Anglican chants and gospel songs to an African beat. I felt strangely alone, and yet strangely at home. The offertory hymn was by Joseph Addision, the eighteenth-century writer who scanned the horizon of his own life and sang:

When all thy mercies, O my God,
   My rising soul surveys,
Transported with the view, I'm lost
   In wonder, love and praise.

Unnumbered comforts to my soul
   Thy tender care bestowed,
Before my infant heart could know
   From whom those comforts flowed.

When in the slippery paths of youth
   With heedless steps I ran,
Thine arm, unseen, conveyed me safe,
   And led me up to man.
Through every period of my life
   Thy goodness I'll pursue;
And after death, in distant worlds,
   The glorious theme renew.

My mind flew back across the years in a rapid review of the amazing way in which God had brought me to that moment. I had to stop singing to catch a huge lump in my throat as I sang the prayer of praise for God's mercies in my life.

O Lord, I bless your name for your goodness to me! Amen.

Week 4, Monday   Fullness of Joy

Read Psalm 16.

As a Benedictine prioress, Joan Chittister's life is radically different from mine, but I identify with her definition of prayer as "a chance to sit down and reflect on something more important than getting out today's mail. . . . The function of prayer is to give expression to the signs of joy and hope you see. It's the place to count your real joys" (Joan Chittister, "A Sign and a Choice," *Sojourners*, June 1987, p. 19).

As I have learned to pray with the psalms, Psalm 16 has become the central song of my soul. Tracing the trajectory of my life from childhood in the hills of western Pennsylvania, through college and seminary days in the Bluegrass State of Kentucky, to the unique communities I've served in the Sunshine State, I rejoice in the way the lines of my life have fallen in pleasant places. Along with its normal collection of hardships, hurts, and pains, it has been a journey of joy in the presence of God's faithful people.

Counting the real joys of the past, I rest secure in God's goodness in the future. I am assured that whatever lies ahead, the Lord will lead me in "the path of life." I know that in God's presence there is "fullness of joy" and, in the end, there will be "pleasures forevermore."

Can you see God's goodness in the lines of your life?

O Lord, help me to keep you before me that I might follow you in a journey of joy. Amen.

Week 4, Tuesday   Joy in the Morning

Read Psalm 30.

One of the joys of a long-term pastoral appointment is the opportunity to be with people over the long haul and watch the way God transforms their mourning into dancing.

John was more than just a neighbor, a fellow Rotarian, and a part of my congregation: he was my friend. When he faced surgery to remove the malignant tumor from his brain, I prayed for his healing. It is an understatement to say that when he died, "I was dismayed" (v. 7). For all of us who loved him, it was a long, dark night of painful tears. But none of us could begin to probe the depth of the pain of the wife and four young sons he left behind.

As their pastor and friend, I was with them when he died. I walked with them through the night of sorrow, confusion, and anger that followed his death. But I was also there when the morning of joy arrived. I was there to perform the ceremony when she remarried, and I was there to celebrate the gift of new life on the day her new son was born.

Through it all, we never stopped praying. Although our prayers were not always answered in the way we might have chosen, we lived together and prayed together long enough to see mourning turned into dancing and tears of sorrow transformed into tears of joy.

Real prayer may not give us what we want, but ultimately it promises to give us joy.

O God, I bring you my mourning, trusting that you will turn it into dancing and that I will awake to the morning of joy. Amen.

Week 4, Wednesday   A Song for the Eighth Inning

Read Psalm 9:1-10.

Tim Crews was a college athlete with big-league aspirations when I baptized him, received him into the church, and performed his marriage. He went on to pitch for the L.A. Dodgers and was playing with the Cleveland Indians when he was killed in a boating accident.

When I met Dodger pitcher Orel Herscheiser at the funeral, I remembered Tim's favorite story from the '88 World Series. In the bottom of the eighth inning the Dodgers were behind. The crowd was hostile and the going was tough when Herscheiser came to the mound. The world watched as he stepped back from the mound, looked up into the sky, and seemed to be talking to himself. He went on to win the game. In the locker room, a reporter asked what he was doing out here. Herscheiser said he was singing a hymn. Later, Johnny Carson asked what the hymn was. Right there on *The Tonight Show,* Herscheiser began to sing, "Praise God from whom all blessings flow." It left Carson speechless!

Sooner or later we all face the eighth inning with the pressure on. When everything is stacked against you and you wonder if you have the strength to go on, do you have inner faith, nurtured by a consistent pattern of prayer, to sing a psalm of praise? Can you find in praise the strength to hang in there and to win the game? Real praise strengthens us for the long haul and keeps us going when the going is tough.

O God, I will sing a song of praise to you not only in the good times, but especially in the tough eighth innings of my life. Amen.

Read Psalm 90.

I found the picture by surprise in my daughter's apartment. It was tucked inside an album my mother had given to her.

The black-and-white snapshot has turned brown, but the picture is still clear. My newly married parents are standing at the foot of the reflecting pool at Bok Tower, in Lake Wales, Florida. He was stationed in Orlando during the war and wears his army uniform. She wears a vintage '40s cotton sundress. They were visiting what was then one of Florida's major attractions. My mother had dated the picture on the back: "June 18, 1944."

My wife and I celebrated our twenty-fifth anniversary on June 14, 1994. In fifty years, a lot has changed in Florida. Most tourists choose the technological excitement of Disney World over the quiet beauty of Bok Tower. My dad died in 1980. His grandchildren are now the age my parents were when the snapshot was taken. But Bok Tower is still there.

My wife and I drove to Lake Wales and had our picture taken on the same spot where my parents stood five decades before. We framed copies of the old print with the new one and gave them to our daughters. Who knows? Fifty years from now our grandchildren might have their pictures taken there, too.

Time passes on. Our days fly away, just as the psalmist said. The one thing that remains unchanged, generation to generation, is the everlasting faithfulness of God. That is the best gift we can pass on.

O God, your faithfulness and your steadfast love have never failed. I put my trust in you and will tell of your greatness to the next generation. Amen.

Read Psalm 73:21-28.

I'm a lousy tennis player, which means that I know enough to know when someone is good. Arthur Ashe was really good; not only good as a tennis champion, but as a man. His death from AIDS stunned the world, but it also demonstrated how a man can face his death with dignity and faith.

In his memoir, *Days of Grace,* Ashe named two things that were sustaining him in his dark hours. One was reading the Bible. He had been raised in the church and had read the Bible since childhood but, not surprisingly, he said, now it was more appealing to him than ever. The second was music. All kinds of music: Beethoven, Dizzy Gillespie, Eric Clapton. But the music that moved him the most deeply was the music of his youth: Black gospel. He described the way music linked him with his past, with his spiritual roots, and most directly with God. "I know," he wrote, "that I turn my back on God only at my peril. This I shall never do" (Arthur Ashe, *Days of Grace,* New York, Alfred A. Knopf, 1993, p. 285).

Reading his story, I felt as if I were listening to the psalmist who asked, "Whom have I in heaven but you?" (v. 25). It is the trusting cry of a man who has been stripped of everything except the essential character of his own life and his assurance of the presence of God. It is faith that is shaped by Scripture and expressed in music—in psalms that become the songs of the soul.

How will you face your death? Are you prepared to face it with a psalm?

O God, whom can I turn to but you? You are my strength and my portion forever. Amen.

Week 4, Saturday   Like a Tree

Read Psalm 1.

We end where we began, with the words of Psalm 1 and the promise that real men, blessed men, happy men, men whose lives are strengthened through prayer, "are like trees / planted by streams of water, / which yield their fruit in its season" (v. 3). Out of my experience with the psalms, I offer these personal words from my prayer journal:

O life-giving God, whose power surges through the whole creation, I want to grow like a tree. Not like a weed, Lord, or an overnight kudzu vine, but like a strong, healthy tree which will be around for the long haul. I want to grow like a tree, Lord, patient enough to grow slowly, but always growing, always sinking deeper roots and stretching wider branches, always wanting to grow higher into the sky. Like a tree, Lord, which can hold its own when the hurricane blows in from the Gulf.

One day, Lord, the tree will fall. It will have been here long enough. Even sequoias die. That's okay, Lord. No tree lasts forever. But may my tree fall because it has lived its life fully, richly, deeply, drawing everything it could from the soil and giving back life to the rest of creation. May the fruit of this tree be a source of life for others.

Lord, I thank you for the soil in which you have planted me. This is where I want to grow. Like a tree beside the waters. Amen.

2

LIVING THE BALANCED LIFE

Kel Groseclose

For everything there is a season, and a time for every matter under heaven.   *—Ecclesiastes 3:1*

I inherited several toys that were my father's when he was a lad. There's a pearl-handled pocket knife he used to whittle willow stick whistles; a small cast-iron wheelbarrow he loaded with rich Idaho soil where he grew up; and my favorite, a hand-carved wooden top. Crafted by a skilled person, the top is nestled inside a box hollowed from a tree branch. These treasures are safely tucked in an antique family cupboard. When I wander by and look inside, I occasionally can't resist the urge. I take out the top and with a quick twist of my fingers give it a spin. It's almost perfectly balanced and can go for nearly a minute on a smooth surface. Fashioned almost one hundred years ago, it has not lost its ability to bring me joy.

Balance is a wonderful desired quality, for humans as well as tops. Our divine Creator wants us to live in balance:

There's a time for work, and a time for recreation;
a time to be with others, and a time to be alone;
a time for family, and a time for self;
a time for physical activity, and a time for the spiritual;
a time for giving, and a time for receiving;
a time to talk and a time to be silent;
a time to care for possessions, and a time to serve people.

When we fail to maintain our inner balance, we begin to wobble and lose our equilibrium. But when we're balanced, our

---

lives will be a joy. So it's important to check our balance regularly, to make certain we're living the full life God wants for us.

Dear God, give me the wisdom and the will to live a healthy, balanced life, and the courage to make changes. Bless me with a sense of wholeness. Amen.

Week 5, Monday   **Don't Pray for Patience**
                                      Unless You Mean It

Be patient, therefore, beloved, until the coming of the Lord.
—James 5:7

Years ago, when I was newly married, I prayed for patience, because problems and pressures were getting to me. I wasn't coping well with the adjustments of becoming established in my profession or with the responsibilities of living together with a spouse. I prayed with much determination and zeal—but I should have been more careful, because God gave me exactly what I asked for. He didn't just hand me patience at once, nor did it come beautifully gift wrapped. In the space of eight years, he sent us six children, each one sweet and adorable but also very normal, active, and growing.

I forgot that patience isn't one of the gifts of the Spirit. It's a fruit that requires human participation and perspiration. The only way we can become more patient is to have it tried. And believe me, even the most loving, gentle children soon learn how to put their parents' patience to the test. I produced an even more abundant harvest of patience when they reached their teenage years.

That has happened in other areas, as well. I prayed for success and was given more work to do; for increased wisdom and was challenged to study harder; for financial security and was called by God to give more generously to others; for comfort and was sent to minister to people who were hurting and in sorrow. Prayer is a powerful resource in our lives to help us find direction and to become true disciples of Jesus Christ. But don't expect God's answers to come in precisely the way you expect. And I suggest you be especially cautious about praying for patience.

Dear God, teach me to pray specifically for what I want, but give me grace to accept what in your wisdom you know I need. Amen.

Week 5, Tuesday   The Power of Laughter

Now Sarah said, "God has brought laughter for me; everyone who hears will laugh with me."   —*Genesis 21:6*

Sarah had to be both amazed and in total turmoil after giving birth to Isaac. She was about ninety years old when this blessed event occurred and her husband, Abraham, was one hundred. You and I would probably laugh hysterically if such a thing were to happen in our lives. Think of being the parent of a teenage son at one hundred and three years of age! (Not to speak of Abraham at one hundred thirteen!) Sarah handled the overwhelming nature of her experience by laughing, and by inviting others to join with her.

Humor is clearly one of the spiritual resources God has given us for keeping our balance, for coping with troubles, trials, and tribulations. And joy of joys, it not only helps relieve the pressure for us, it makes us easier to live with as well. Instead of becoming a cranky old parent, Sarah found a way to rejoice. She laughed, and soon all of her family and friends were laughing with her. This is not to say that finding the humor in situations is always a simple or easy matter. It's an approach to life, an attitude we need to cultivate. We should practice laughing each and every day.

My father was a man of immense good humor. He had an amusing story or a joke to fit every possible human condition. When the end of his life drew near and we could no longer care for him at home, we had the ambulance take him to the hospital. As the attendants wheeled him into the room, he said, "I'm very disappointed in you. You did a terrible job." Their faces fell, thinking he was serious.

"Yes," he continued, "this was my last trip on this earth and you didn't flash the lights or blow the siren." Then he laughed and soon we were all laughing together. It was a very healing moment.

Sometime today, take a laugh break. Smile at a co-worker. Giggle with a child. Tell a joke. Share a funny story about yourself. And at least once when you pray, chuckle out loud.

Week 5, Wednesday   Persevere in Prayer

Rejoice in hope, be patient in suffering, persevere in prayer.
—Romans 12:12

I am often the person who prays out loud in our church's Sunday worship services. In preparation, I read the Scriptures for the day, study the sermon title, and scan world events for anything I should include. This is in addition to reviewing the joys and concerns of the congregation. Then I prepare the prayer. Usually I don't write out a complete text. I simply jot down a general theme, specific names, or main ideas. I like my prayer to have a measure of spontaneity and freshness, too. On some Sundays I feel as though I've prayed effectively, even eloquently. On other Sundays I seem to stumble through our prayer time and am relieved when it's finally over. And sometimes I just seem to go through the motions. At least I'm faithful in my Sunday morning praying, which is more than I can say about the rest of the week.

Prayer is a major power source for people of faith. It brings calmness in the midst of turmoil, comfort in our sorrow, hope in times of disappointment, clarity in times of confusion, inner peace in times of upset and worry. So why do I so often forget to use it? Do I think God only listens if I prepare carefully, use big words, and talk in complete sentences? I have an idea that God's favorite prayers are those of children, which are short, direct, honest to the point of bluntness, and always from the heart.

I halfway expect the Almighty to break into one of my Sabbath prayers to ask who I think I'm impressing. To be profound in our praying is far less important than to persevere.

O God, help me remember to pray today: to praise and thank you, to tell you all my problems, to lift the needs of others before you, and to share my whole day with you. Amen.

> *This is the day that the LORD has made;*
> *let us rejoice and be glad in it.*
> *—Psalm 118:24*

An important spiritual quality in juggling life's many demands is maintaining a positive attitude. I received a wonderful reminder of this truth from our two-year-old granddaughter, Ashley.

It had been a long winter with heavy snows, and my heart was yearning for the arrival of spring. Then one morning I woke up and looked out the window—onto more than three inches of snow! I put on warm clothing, got out the shovel, and started to work. But I wasn't happy. I grumped with every shovelful I moved. Then Ashley arrived for a visit. She insisted we let her play outside. Grandma found a coat, knit hat, and mittens so Ashley could "help" Grandpa.

I was still complaining about my sore back. Would warmer weather ever arrive? I wondered out loud. Then I heard Ashley's voice. She was throwing handfuls of snow into the air while exclaiming joyfully, "Yes! Yes! Oh, yes!" Periodically she'd pause, look around at the trees with their mantle of snow, lift her face heavenward and say with childlike conviction, "It's a new day!"

I quit my whining immediately and began to see the world through the eyes of a two-year-old. Suddenly everything appeared fresh and beautiful. It was indeed a new day filled with the promises and possibilities of God. I offered a silent prayer of thanksgiving and before I knew it, the sidewalks and driveway were done. Not only that, my back muscles weren't sore at all.

O God, help me to keep positive and hopeful in the midst of the challenges before me, and in everything to have thankful hearts. Amen.

Week 5, Friday   **Keep Open to the Spirit**

Listen! I am standing at the door, knocking; if you hear my voice and open the door, I will come in to you and eat with you, and you with me.   *—Revelation 3:20*

There's an old saying that goes, "If you don't feel as close to God as you used to, make no mistake about which one of you has moved." In our busy lives, we don't mean to ignore the presence of God's Spirit, we just drift away. We become preoccupied with our own affairs and with the demands of the moment. We forget to pray. We neglect our study of the Bible. We wander away from regular worship with the Body of Christ. We don't intentionally set out to do so. It just happens a little at a time. We get side-tracked by the small duties of the day. The complexities of life crowd out the simple but eternal message of the gospel.

Then when Christ comes to the door of our heart to gently remind us of our need for him, we're not listening. We're not ready to answer, or we're making so much noise as we hustle about that we don't hear his knock. The football game is on too loud; we're too busy making our own lists of things to accomplish; we're trying to decide what to buy next or how to pay for what we've already got.

Thank goodness, Jesus is patient and persistent with us. The knock will come again. The invitation will be offered once more. When we respond by opening ourselves to him, he gladly enters, to join in the common, everyday stuff of our lives as well as the spiritual. So keep listening for his knock.

Holy Spirit, keep my mind alert and my heart open to your presence in my life. May I respond immediately every time you try to get my attention. Amen.

Week 5, Saturday   **The Courage to Be Yourself**

> *Be strong, and let your heart take courage,*
> *all you who wait for the Lord.*
> *—Psalm 31:24*

One sweltering summer afternoon, something small and brightly colored caught my attention in the corner of a huge parking lot. On closer inspection, I discovered a single petunia poking through a tiny crack. Buried beneath tons of asphalt, the seed had somehow found a fissure, sufficient soil for its roots, and enough moisture for sustenance. From then on, every time I used that lot, I paid close attention to the flower's progress. I enjoyed its cheery blossoms well into the autumn season.

That petunia demonstrated the courage and inherent power hidden within every seed. It served for me as a testimony to the determination of all living things to fulfill their God-given destinies. It also gave me courage to keep going during a particularly stressful time in my life, when I was feeling alone and a little sorry for myself. Facing struggles at work and a bit of turmoil at home, I could feel the weight of the world pressing down on my small, weak shoulders.

The petunia came into my life as a gift from God. It reminded me that the Creator gives my life hope and promise. With the power of faith in my soul, I can flourish in the most unlikely places and the most difficult circumstances. The Spirit of God is a constant presence in my life, enabling me to blossom abundantly no matter where I am or how great my problems may seem.

I can still see those delicate pink and white petals waving to me in the afternoon breeze, reminding me of God's love in Christ and inspiring me to have courage.

O God, when I am feeling alone and weak, give me courage to keep going. Fill me with your love and help me to "bloom where I am planted." Amen.

Week 6, Sunday   Hush, and Listen to the Spirit

Be still, and know that I am God!
I am exalted among the nations,
I am exalted in the earth.
                    —*Psalm 46:10*

I admit it: I talk too much. There's nothing wrong with being sociable, but once in a while I need to be quiet and listen. I especially need to be still in order to experience the presence of God in my life. The world around me is becoming a noisier and more hectic place, so I must intentionally seek out times to find peace within.

One of my favorite words in the English language is *hush*. I like both how it sounds and what it means. To be hushed reminds me of reading in a huge library or being in church during silent prayers. I think of a mother rocking her baby and whispering,

"Hush, don't you cry." It's what everybody says if you talk too loudly at the movie theater during a dramatic moment.

When you're overwhelmed by life's demands, hush, and invite God to calm your anxious spirit. When you're tense or angry, hush, and let God settle your feelings. When you must make a difficult decision, hush, and listen for the Spirit's wisdom. When sorrow comes to visit, hush, and allow God to comfort your heart.

In the normal, daily rush, a brief pause or a moment's hush can be God's opportunity to refresh your tired body and renew your weary soul.

Slow me down, Lord, when I get moving too fast. Tell me to hush when I'm too busy that I may hear your word and really listen to those I love. Amen.

Week 6, Monday   All Things Hold Together

He himself [Christ] is before all things, and in him all things hold together.   —Colossians 1:17

The more commitments and responsibilities we have, the more pushes and pulls we experience. Our spouse and family need our attention and energy. The workplace expects a major investment of our time. Friends want to be with us. The house or apartment must be cleaned and kept in good repair. The car has to be serviced every two thousand miles. There are taxes to be filed and bills to be paid; birthdays to remember, plants to water, pets to feed. The list never seems to grow smaller. New duties simply get added.

Somewhere in this swirl of activities, there's supposed to be time for ourselves: a few moments to read the newspaper, watch a game on television, take a nap, write in a journal, or do nothing. When I get pulled and tugged until I'm so bent out of shape I look like an emotional pretzel, I often remember this text from Colossians. I repeat over and over to myself, "In Christ all things hold together." It always helps.

God created this incredibly complex universe and holds it together. The planet Earth hurtles through space and revolves rapidly, yet it is in perfect balance with the sun and all other heavenly bodies. It is a very reassuring thought when I feel as though I'm about to come apart that "in him all things hold together." Praise God, that includes me and my life!

O God, when the pushes and pulls of this world are too great for me, hold me together with your eternal power in Christ. Amen.

Week 6, Tuesday   Will You Have the Soup or the Steak?

It is better to eat soup with someone you love than steak with someone you hate.   —*Proverbs 15:17 TLB*

Suppose you sat down at your table in the restaurant and when you looked at the menu, there were only two entrees: bean soup with a beloved friend or filet mignon with someone you could hardly stand. Which would it be? Are your taste buds more important than your inner feelings? Is it more important to be seen by the right people or to build long-lasting relationships?

What we value shapes our lives. Values determine how and where we spend our time, with whom we associate, where our paycheck goes, and the things to which we make commitments. Followers of Christ are called to embrace a different set of values than those of the world around them. We are asked to put people and their needs above our own material comforts; to value integrity more than popularity; truth before outward success; kindness and compassion more than stocks, bonds, or bank accounts.

When our values are in order, that is, when they're aligned with the biblical principles of humble servanthood laid out by Jesus, we are productive people in the deepest sense. We may or may not become wealthy or famous, but we will be content. We'll have the assurance that, in the eternal picture, we're pleasing God and fulfilling God's will.

Personally, a perfect meal for me would be a big bowl of potato chowder in the company of a dear friend, or a burger and fries with a grandchild.

O God, I thank you for both soup and steak; but far more than these, I thank you for loved ones and friends. Amen.

But seek ye first the kingdom of God, and his righteousness; and all these things shall be added unto you.   —Matthew 6:33 KJV

I have a way of pleasantly ignoring my spouse when I'd rather not do what she'd like me to do. Let's say I'm watching my favorite mystery show on television and she asks me to take out the garbage. First I pretend I didn't hear her. Then when that fails, I mumble, "Uh-huh," as though I actually intend to take action, which, of course, I don't. Finally, I promise to fulfill her request during the very next commercial.

It's not the best approach to building trust and improving communication in one's marriage. Fortunately, I've been blessed by a very understanding and forgiving wife. She's put up with me for over thirty-five years. When it comes to the spiritual realm, however, trying to pull such stunts with God is a far more serious matter. There are some things we need to attend to in a timely fashion; and our relationship to God is at the top of that list. We can, if we choose, postpone listening for God's voice. We can ignore God's wishes for our life. We can go our own way and say to our Creator, "I'll get back to you one of these days."

But this is the spiritually backward way of doing things. First we are to seek God's will. We are asked to put God's kingdom at the top of our list. Then, and only then, will everything else fit into place. As the old hymn says, it's up to us to "trust and obey."

"Trust and obey, for there's no other way to be happy in Jesus, but to trust and obey."

Week 6, Thursday   **Keep Your Eyes on the Prize**

The kingdom of heaven is like treasure hidden in a field, which someone found and hid; then in his joy he goes and sells all that he has and buys that field.

—Matthew 13:44

My wife has a gift of being able to sort out good noise from bad noise. When our six children were younger and still at home, our house was an active place. There would often be assorted cousins and neighbor kids underfoot as well. I could never understand how she could do it, but in the midst of what seemed like total chaos, my spouse would sit in her rocking chair reading a novel. "How in the world can you concentrate?" I'd ask.

"I only listen for the important noises," she'd reply. "You know, those that tell me somebody's hurt, that they can't solve an argument on their own, or that our little one is getting into the cookie jar again." It helped that our home was child-proofed. Nevertheless her ability amazed me. When I was around, I heard everything and was soon a basket case, plus all the kids eventually ended up across the street at a friend's house.

Even if God put the most wonderful spiritual treasure right in front of me, I'm afraid I might not notice it. I often let the trivial events and minor irritations of each day distract me, when I should be focusing on the treasures God offers: beauty, laughter, inner peace, and power. God wants you and me to live this way, with our eyes focused on Christ, from this day forward.

Help me, O God, to concentrate on the joys of this day and on the love you offer; and give me the courage to stick to it. Amen.

Week 6, Friday   **With Sighs Too Deep for Words**

The Spirit helps us in our weakness; for we do not know how to pray as we ought, but that very Spirit intercedes [for us] with sighs too deep for words.   —*Romans 8:26*

Sometimes even God doesn't know what to say. Or maybe it's that God understands words just aren't enough when the hurt is too great or the pain too much. There are moments in life when no matter how verbally gifted we may be, words simply cannot explain what's happened or repair the damage.

The Spirit has a wonderful variety of other images to express God's love for us. We are held in God's hands; protected by clouds to shade us by day and keep us warm at night; safely gathered beneath the bosom of a mother hen; led beside still waters and through the valley of the shadow of death; lifted high to soar on eagles' wings.

This is one of the most tender biblical images: God's Spirit sighs over us. Just as we human parents often sigh in weariness and in wonderment when trying to cope with our children, so apparently does God with us. I like it. It tells me I am loved profoundly by my Creator; that God goes with me into the depths of my soul.

God understands there are times when words aren't necessary. And so do we. A smile is what's needed, or a touch on the shoulder, a handshake, a hug, or shedding a few tears together. Love is always to be shared with the beloved. Perhaps sighing is the most beautiful and genuine prayer of all, a precious gift of the Spirit.

O God, quiet my anxious spirit and let me feel your love as close as a parent's sighing. And give to me a ministry not only of words but of presence. May my love truly touch another's heart this day. Amen.

Week 6, Saturday   **Sacred Spaces and Places**

They went to a place called Gethsemane; and he said to his disciples, "Sit here while I pray."   *—Mark 14:32*

As a small boy I had a number of special places where I felt cozy and secure. I loved to sit on the front porch during a summer evening storm while lightning streaked and thunder rolled across the darkened sky. A small stream meandered through a cow pasture behind our house. There I explored for tadpoles, sent tiny bark boats on grand adventures, and dabbled my toes in the cool water. Sometimes I snuggled in the crook of an ancient cottonwood tree, safe beneath a canopy of green leaves.

These wonderful places afforded me sacred spaces where I was free to be a child, where I felt close to creation, where I could reflect on the goodness and joy of being alive. Decades later, I still need holy places where, like those disciples of old, I can be alone with the Master. There's the old maple tree in our front yard against whose massive trunk I have often leaned for support. I've also made the inside of our car my personal sanctuary. I listen to "my" radio station and have private conversations with myself and with God. I weed in a tiny plot I call my garden, or walk among its plants.

We humans need room in which to learn, grow, be in touch with our deepest feelings, and let the Holy Spirit speak to us. You and I may not be able to sit with our Savior in Gethsemane, but we can enter sacred places where the touch of God's love is very real.

Jesus, my Savior, invite me to go with you today into a place apart. Even if it's just for a few moments, be close to me and assure me that I am your beloved child. Amen.

Week 7, Sunday   The Spiritual Discipline of Waiting

> *It is good that one should wait quietly*
> *for the salvation of the LORD.*
> *—Lamentations 3:26*

I have a difficult time waiting quietly. I tend to grumble under my breath, drum my fingers on the steering wheel of our car, or fidget in the grocery store line. I not only become tense and cranky, but I lose valuable opportunities for spiritual growth. My complaints have never shortened my waiting time by even one second. They're basically wasted energy.

Why don't I use these enforced pauses in my life for creative purposes? I could just as easily offer a silent prayer of thanksgiving for having the resources to own an automobile. I could praise God for providing the basic necessities of life. I could rejoice in the blessings I have, rather than fuss about the minor irritations I encounter. God gives me the opportunity to use waiting in a positive way, as special moments of each day in which to enjoy the beauty around me, to center my thoughts and settle my soul, to take delight in people.

The other day as I stood in a long line at a fast-food restaurant, I grew ever more impatient. People ahead of me couldn't decide what to order. The employees seemed to be moving in slow motion. Then I took a deep breath and asked the Lord to calm my spirit. A peace settled over me and I noticed the sweet smile of an older gentleman ahead of me. I giggled to myself as a young mother tried to wipe catsup out of her toddler's ears.

And before I knew it, it was my turn. By then I'd forgotten what I intended to order, so as I quickly scanned the menu board again, I prayed for patience for the people behind me.

Dear God, remind me that waiting isn't something to endure but can be an opportunity to grow spiritually: to pray, to hum a joyful song, to remember a kindness done, or to extend a hand of friendship. Above all else, help me to wait quietly for your salvation. Amen.

Week 7, Monday   Calmness in the Midst of the Storm

> *The LORD is my light and my salvation;*
>   *whom shall I fear?*
> *The LORD is the stronghold of my life;*
>   *of whom shall I be afraid?*
> *   —Psalm 27:1*

I was a young clergy person still damp behind the ears. I was getting a handle on the administrative duties of the church and felt fairly competent with Sunday mornings and preaching sermons. But conducting weddings and funerals was almost unbearably stressful. The pressure to perform them without making even the smallest of mistakes was more than I could handle. I began to experience panic attacks halfway through these important rituals. My mouth would keep working while my brain could only tell my body to keep breathing.

Then during one particularly stressful funeral service, when I was nearly a basket case before it even began, God gave me a calmness within. It's now almost thirty years later, but I still remember the moment. I was reading a selection of scripture verses when the words of Psalm 27:1 spoke to my own heart. It was as though a light had been turned on inside my brain. I realized that God's presence was truly with me; that I was not alone. I had been trying to minister to others using only my human training and wisdom. No wonder I was fearful and afraid.

To this day I still quote Psalm 27:1 in every funeral I conduct, and I say it with conviction. I also use it in other stressful situations. I still need to be reminded regularly that "the Lord is the stronghold of my life."

Today, O God, give me the assurance that I am not alone. Especially when the pressures of life are great, calm my anxious spirit and let me trust in you completely. Amen.

Week 7, Tuesday   **The Importance of Being a Team Player**

We, who are many, are one body in Christ, and individually we are members one of another.   —Romans 12:5

In the days of our youth, many of us participated in some kind of group activity. It may have been in athletics, debate, a school band, or an orchestra. But we were part of a team. We learned how to work together: to support and encourage each other, to cover for each other's mistakes, to fail or succeed together. Then we grew up and became adults; and somewhere in the process we decided we had to become competitive in finding jobs, choosing mates, earning money, and getting ahead in life. Forget teamwork. We have to make our own way in the world.

This assumption has turned many of us into very lonely people. Beyond our immediate family, we don't know whom to trust. Well, there's a wonderful alternative and it's called the church. This is a team that reaches back into history and will continue for time and eternity. It's not a perfect team. It has its share of squabbles and disagreements. But when it comes to our spiritual journeys, it's by far the best thing available.

No matter how strong we may think we are, how confident or how successful, we need other people. As Christians we belong to Christ and therefore to each other, and are called by God to help each other along the way. The community of the faithful, flawed as it is, is where we most effectively discover God's will, serve the world, and learn to love one another.

It's good, O Lord, to know that I am part of a team, that I have a place to belong—your church. Help me to be a good team player. Amen.

I am doing a great work and I cannot come down.

—Nehemiah 6:3

Many decades following the destruction of Jerusalem by the Babylonians in the sixth century B.C., Nehemiah came to survey the ruins and to design the holy city's restoration. He was skilled at his craft and was also an able leader. He enlisted the help of the city's residents, and within approximately six months the wall was rebuilt, and Jerusalem was on its way to recovery. He did, however, experience opposition. The governors of neighboring provinces tried to distract him from completing the project. They preferred Jerusalem to remain weak and vulnerable. On at least five different occasions Nehemiah's detractors told him to stop working so hard. "Take a break; ease off," they said.

"I am doing a great work and I cannot come down," Nehemiah replied. He was convinced of the importance of the project, and he knew its success depended upon his vision and leadership. He felt in his heart that he was following God's will.

Though twenty-five hundred years have come and gone since Nehemiah's time, it is still essential for us, like Nehemiah, to have a clear vision of who we are—God's dearly loved children—and what God wants for our lives—to be God's representatives to the world. Such a vision keeps us going when the days are long and the work is discouraging. Trying to be obedient to God's will also gives us focus and direction, and provides a strong inner confidence even in the midst of conflict.

O God, give me a specific work to do for you, and then give me the resolve and dedication to do it well and faithfully. Amen.

Week 7, Thursday   **In Praise of Kneeling**

O come, let us worship and bow down,
  let us kneel before the LORD, our Maker!
                    —*Psalm 95:6*

One of the problems many of us have in maintaining a disciplined prayer life is that we don't or can't hold still long enough.

We're a people on the go, constantly hustling about trying to complete our lists of duties. God is with us in the swirl of activities, but we also need to spend time in quietness when we listen for God's still, small voice.

I have recently rediscovered an old-fashioned but effective method of doing just that: getting down on my knees. It's not quite as easy for me as it used to be. Perhaps it's my age, or maybe it's my lack of practice. But my knees do actually bend. From that physical position I find I'm much more spiritually receptive. Though that makes me nearly two feet shorter, my soul seems to rise to new heights.

The simple act of kneeling produces in me a childlikeness. I feel humble and am able to admit more readily my need for God's help. Would that I knelt more often! Sometimes in my stubborn human pride, I lock my knees to keep from kneeling—until the sheer weight of my burdens brings me to the ground.

Kneeling is the proper stance for pulling weeds in the garden, scrubbing floors, searching for lost socks in the corner of your closet, for proposing marriage—and for praying. I commend it to you as a way of refreshing and renewing your communication with your Creator.

Gracious God, when I'm acting as though I'm tough and totally self-reliant and can take care of everything myself, invite me to kneel humbly before your presence that I may receive an extra measure of your grace. Amen.

Week 7, Friday   First Be Reconciled

So when you are offering your gift at the altar, if you remember that your brother or sister has something against you, leave your gift there before the altar and go; first be reconciled to your brother or sister, and then come and offer your gift.

—Matthew 5:23-24

They were both wonderful men. The problem was they were products of two very different worlds. Axel was old-country, a Swede through and through. Henry embodied the styles and values of present-day America. That would have been fine, except they were both leaders in the same small congregation, the New England church I served as a student pastor. Conflict had long been simmering and a break had finally occurred. They were no longer speaking to each other. People had chosen sides and the church had split down the middle.

We invited a beloved pastor who'd been there some years before to conduct a series of evangelistic services. On the final evening, the preacher gave a powerfully moving sermon. With trembling voice, he asked the church members if they were reconciled to each other; and if not, to do so right there and then.

Henry and Axel rose from their pews on opposite sides of the sanctuary, met in the middle aisle, and with tears in their eyes embraced. Their lives and the lives of the congregation were never the same again. Henry, Axel, and the rest of us still had our disagreements. But there was a new spirit of sweetness and cooperation in that place.

Having enmity in our hearts, holding grudges, and hanging on to bitterness are destructive to our physical and spiritual health. God asks us to be reconciled to one another and, through Christ, gives us the motivation and the power to do so.

Forgiving and accepting God, by your Spirit make me a loving, accepting, and forgiving person. Give me the grace and strength to seek for reconciliation. Amen.

Week 7, Saturday   One Step at a Time

> *Therefore the word of the LORD will be to them,*
>   *"Precept upon precept, precept upon precept,*
>   *line upon line, line upon line,*
>   *here a little, there a little."*
>   *—Isaiah 28:13*

I am a master of the mighty pronouncement. When our children were in their formative years, I often issued lofty statements of how they should and should not behave. They mostly ignored me or reminded me that I was their father, not their preacher, and that they weren't my congregation. I gradually discovered that a few words gently spoken were far more effective.

I also am skilled at making lists ten times longer than I can possibly accomplish. On a day off, my expectations are sometimes so lofty that disappointment and frustration are sure to follow. I try to do more than is humanly possible.

The same is true in my spiritual life. I may set unreasonably high goals for myself: to read the entire Bible in two months; to go to every church meeting they hold; to be the biggest pledger in the congregation; to make my family perfect in every way.

Hold it! Hold it! That's not how God deals with me. God takes me by the hand and patiently walks with me step by step. God is happy when I make a tiny bit of progress toward loving and serving him. Steady growth in faith is more pleasing to God than a once-in-a-lifetime spectacular spurt. May I strive to be as patient with myself as the God of infinite compassion is with me.

O God of everlasting kindness, help me along the way day by day. Guide my every step, even those that are short and halting. Remind me that enduring spiritual growth usually happens "here a little, there a little." Amen.

Week 8, Sunday   The Waterfall of God's Grace

But where sin increased, grace abounded all the more.
                                                    —Romans 5:20*b*

One of my favorite images of God's grace comes from author Annie Dillard. She writes that you and I stand outside holding our little cups, waiting for God's love to fill us, expecting God to act. Suddenly God's Spirit comes upon us, and it's a gusher; it's like standing under a mighty waterfall. We anticipate just enough grace to meet our immediate needs. Instead God gives us grace upon grace and lavishes his love on us. We get drenched, soaked, inundated by joy.

Perhaps you and I would prefer to worship a god who gives less abundantly and who might therefore demand less of us. But the God of the universe is extravagant! God didn't create a tiny bit of beauty. Everywhere we look, from the sky above to the earth beneath our feet, we see God's glory and majesty. We have been blessed with music and art, with a marvelous variety of languages, with a wonderful collection of brothers and sisters from many lands and of many races. We are rich indeed.

When you and I anticipate meager gifts from God, when we assume that our Creator deals with us according to minimums, we are in for a surprise of major proportions. Each and every day of our lives, God's blessings are poured upon us. So put your little cup away and get out the buckets and the tubs. There's a waterfall of grace just around the corner.

God of grace and God of glory, pour your power and wisdom and joy all over me. Drench me with your Spirit through and through. Fill me with your love. Amen.

Week 8, Monday   **Life Is What We Make of the Interruptions**

I am confident of this, that the one who began a good work among you will bring it to completion by the day of Jesus Christ.
—Philippians 1:6

In today's hectic world, sometimes we wonder if we'll ever get to complete a project with all the interruptions we must endure. Unsolicited phone calls come just at mealtime; cute school children selling pizzas or candy ring the doorbell; the delivery truck arrives noisily moments after a fussy baby was put down for a nap; an emergency occurs at work on your day off; or an emergency at home happens on a busy day at work. An interruption interrupts other interruptions.

Interuptions are part of our human condition and have been so since day one of creation. The biblical record is filled with accounts of people being interrupted. Noah dropped everything else when he received a stormy weather report from the Almighty. A burning bush radically changed Moses' plans as he tended sheep in the wilderness. A birth announcement from God drastically altered the comfortable old age Abraham and Sarah had anticipated. Daniel's life took a sudden turn in that lions' den. Several disciples went immediately from plain old fishing to fishing for people's souls. Saul got quite a jolt when God interrupted his trip to Damascus. He also got a new name.

Not all interruptions, of course, come from God. Most are of the irritating variety, the kind that try our patience rather than grow our faith. But even the frustrating kinds can be viewed as opportunities in disguise, as reminders of who's in charge of our lives. We make our plans but God always has the power to interrupt us and send us in a new direction.

Eternal God, help me to deal patiently with life's many interruptions; but when the interruption is from you, dear God, give me an open mind to know it and a gracious spirit to receive it. Amen.

Week 8, Tuesday   Only God Can Make Death Beautiful

The bodies we have now embarrass us for they become sick and die; but they will be full of glory when we come back to life again.
—1 Corinthians 15:43 TLB

The children clustered around the storyteller at the front of the sanctuary for their special moment in worship. As was her custom, she reached into her paper bag to pull out the object lesson for the morning. It was October and the bag was stuffed with autumn leaves: bright crimson from vine maple, golden ones from a birch, and a marvelously bright collection from several other trees. The person sitting next to me on the pew gently poked my ribs and whispered, "Only God can make death beautiful."

I'd never before thought of autumn in quite that way. I confess I didn't hear much of the sermon that followed because I kept reflecting on the truth of what I'd just heard. Somehow the Creator can take our most painful, difficult, tragic events and transform them into positive, even joyful experiences. I don't know how God does it. But by faith I know it happens.

The prospect of death can make us anxious and fearful. It can produce in us a timid lifestyle, a hesitancy to take creative risks or to love fully and unconditionally. But let us take heart from God's creativity. For me, as I approach the autumn of my life, I can strive to make my heart and mind and soul riots of magnificent color, knowing that my caring, my commitments, my faith can be beautiful. I may not be much to look at outwardly, but I pray that my inner life will be a blessing to others and a joy to behold.

57

Help me, O gracious God, to put my trust in you and to have the assurance that my future, no matter what happens, will be beautiful because of your eternal love and goodness. Amen.

Week 8, Wednesday   Rooted and Grounded in Love

I pray . . . that Christ may dwell in your hearts through faith, as you are being rooted and grounded in love.

—Ephesians 3:16-17

I have always enjoyed vegetable gardening. When I was a boy, my father would save me a small corner in his plot. He would help me prepare the soil and offer advice regarding my selection of seeds. From then on, it was my garden to tend. I took my work quite seriously. The carrot, beet, and lettuce rows were often crooked but each tiny plant received tender loving care. I was excited when the shoots first broke through the ground. And I would often rise early in the morning to see how much they'd grown during the night.

I've never become a master gardener but I still get much satisfaction out of planting, tending, and harvesting my plot beside our garage. Nothing tastes quite as delicious as tomatoes or cucumbers fresh from your own garden. Over the years I have learned that young plants are vulnerable to weather conditions, weeds, and insects because they have shallow root systems. I recall how sad I felt as a lad when a seedling would wither and die from the scorching summer sun.

So it is with our inner, spiritual lives. Until we are firmly rooted and deeply grounded in God's love, the pressures of the world may be our undoing. The stability of our faith depends upon a solid foundation in God's Word, having an active prayer life, worshiping regularly in the congregation of God's people, and serving others as Christ's disciple. Then no matter how stressful the times, we will be productive members of God's kingdom.

Nurture my spirit, O God, with your love; remove the weeds in my life by your forgiveness; and keep me ever growing and fruitful, not for my sake but that your will may be done. Amen.

For the Holy Spirit, God's gift, does not want you to be afraid of people, but to be wise and strong, and to love them and enjoy being with them.   *—2 Timothy 1:7 TLB*

My father was a Will Rogers type of person, the kind who never met a stranger, who was always friendly and accepting. He wore a smile constantly. In fact, when I needed discipline, he never raised his voice. He just stopped smiling and that's all it took. I knew I had better straighten up immediately. He had a story or a joke to tell anybody who would listen. They didn't seem to mind even when he'd repeat the same one over and over. They'd laugh as hard as they did the first time. Dad truly loved and enjoyed people, pure and simple.

I wish he'd passed this gift on to his son. Oh, I like being with people, but it doesn't come as naturally to me. I have to work at it. It's a value well worth the effort. I figure if I keep trying, maybe some day it'll be second nature to me. No less an authority than the Holy Spirit wants us to be this way. And if God asks us to be wise, strong, and loving, we can count on God's Spirit helping us do exactly that.

There's so much fear these days. Some of it is well founded. We do need to be alert to possible dangers and aware of potential violence. Yet I refuse to be afraid of everything that moves. I want to love and enjoy people, to be blessed by having friends, to feel good about belonging to a community, and to rejoice in my fellowship with others.

God doesn't expect you and me to be super-extroverts, the life of every party. We are called, each in our own way, simply to love and enjoy people. It's to be our number one priority.

O God, you love and accept me just as I am. May I love and enjoy others as a natural part of my life, and may it be a fun and joyful experience. Amen.

Finally, be strong in the Lord and in the strength of his power.

        —Ephesians 6:10

I enjoy watching sporting events on television—everything from baseball to bowling, from tennis to track and field. I'd be in better physical condition if I was a participant rather than a passive watcher. I do lift a few weights and occasionally shoot hoops on the basket over our garage door. But I've gradually become more and more of a couch potato.

The problem for many of us isn't only our physical inactivity. We've also grown spiritually dormant. Our souls are in hibernation. We've turning into pew potatoes, religious cousins of that more famous couch variety. In the same way that our bodies require proper nutrition and exercise, so our souls need to be fed and to have strenuous workouts. We need to study the Bible and be familiar with its precepts, to sing God's praises with enthusiasm, to kneel in prayer, to join in regular fellowship with our brothers and sisters in the faith. We're called to love God with our whole selves, with heart and soul and mind; and I would add, with our bodies as well. It's important to roll up our sleeves and serve in concrete ways.

Young people today have a saying, "You've got to walk the walk, not just talk the talk." I suggest we try flexing our spiritual muscles by being active, involved Christians. In the process, our communities and world would surely become healthier, better places.

Okay, God, I admit it. I've become spiritually lazy. Do whatever it takes to get me off my "blessed assurance." Challenge my mind, inspire my heart, and give me a faith fit for serving you and for helping others. Amen.

Week 8, Saturday   **Knocked Down but Never Knocked Out**

We are persecuted, but are never deserted: we may be knocked down but we are never knocked out!

—2 Corinthians 4:9 JBP

Life isn't always easy. In fact, it seldom is. We know there were hardships for Paul and the early apostles. But they persisted in proclaiming the good news and did so at considerable risk to their personal comfort and safety. They were loving and kind men but they were determined and tough individuals as well.

In today's world we need to have the same qualities, to be as Jesus said to his disciples, "wise as serpents and innocent as doves" (Matthew 10:16). These times call for strength of character. Raising a family may be more challenging now than ever before in history. The demands upon our energy and resources seem never ending. Relationships face greater stress perhaps than those of any previous generation.

Along with these pressures we still must cope with the old troubles: concerns about health, financial burdens, disappointment, sorrow, and grief. Yet the words quoted above are as valid today as they were when St. Paul wrote them. Life may leave us a little bruised and bewildered, but nothing that ever happens can put us down for the count.

Through the years I've discovered even though I'm short and dumpy, I'm like those very tall and talented basketball players—I can rebound with the best of them! I get my feelings hurt but I recover quickly. I have experienced many losses but I have always healed. God is with us. He's in our corner. God's love and power are forever available. We are not alone! Thanks be to God!

When experiences or events knock me for a loop, O God, pick me up, dust me off, and point me in the right direction. Knowing that you are my constant companion gives me courage to keep going. I entrust my life to you. Amen.

3
BEING A MAN OF VISION

Vance P. Ross

Read John 3:16-21.

What does love mean to you? Is it having a good job? Who are your prime examples of love? The fellows with whom you debate the finer points of professional and college athletics?

Often, this is how men understand love. We would rather not deal with the depth of this emotion. Yet love means so much to us. We crave it. We thirst for it. Sometimes we seek it in nocturnal liaisons of a dangerous kind. We seek it in employment that works us to death. We want the closeness of love, but we seek it in places where it cannot be found.

The most fundamental characteristic of love ought to be someone on whom we can count at all times—someone who will stick by us closer than a brother or sister. There will be times when human beings will fail us. But our scripture text tells us that God's love is the most basic love. In God we have a friend who will be a friend until the end. This friend not only hangs out with us in fun times. This friend died for us, then rose from the dead so that we might be assured that nothing can defeat us. This friend leads us to victory over even the ultimate test—death.

God's love is not "cool" or mere macho showoff. God shows love in a sacrificial way. God's love gives, even to and especially to men. Will you accept the sacrifice?

Eternal God, I see your love in the sacrifice that you have shown us through Jesus. I accept your sacrificial love for me—please make it real in my life. Amen.

Read John 3:16-21.

What have you given today? To whom? Why?

Primary to being a Christian man is the notion of giving. We have an outlook to give to our children. Our experiences shared with them will be invaluable helps as they meet the highs and lows of living. We have the gift of love to share with our women, the tenderness of our hearts and the partnership of our spirits. We have the gift of vocation to offer to the world.

God has called each one of us, and gifted each of us differently. Your gift to the world, through God's fellowship called church, is essential to God's work, which is the changing of our world into God's kingdom.

Too often, men are unaware of how much we have to give. Some of us never hear how talented we are. We never hear that we are called to give what we have, that each of us has something special, something necessary, to give to God's kingdom.

Jesus, the Son of God, is God's gift to you, to me and all the world. In response to God's gift, as a Christian man, what are you giving?

You are a special man. God's special man who can contribute to God's saving act in the world. Ask God to show you how special you are and to help you answer the question, "What do I have to give?"

God of love and of power, I want to give because you have blessed me. Please show me how. Amen.

Read Luke 4:16-21.

What does it mean to say that "the Spirit of the Lord is upon me"? When Jesus read those words from the prophet Isaiah, I imagine that the idea seemed scandalous to his hearers. *How dare he appropriate the words of the prophet as his own?* they must have thought. *Who does he think he is?* I suppose many were irritated by his audacity, his nerve.

Yet, this promise is repeated over and over again. The New Testament is replete with pledges that the Holy Spirit will come upon God's people. We are to await the Spirit's coming, to expect it. When the Spirit comes, power will be given to us to accomplish that which God has ordained for our lives.

Have you disciplined yourself to expect and receive God's Holy Spirit? Are you in prayer on a daily basis? Are you reading the Scriptures regularly? God wants to give you power to be the man that you can be, to save you from the dread of powerlessness. In order to do that, you and I must ready ourselves. We must expect the coming of the Spirit and prepare for it.

Be all that God wants you to be. Expect the Spirit to come upon you. Then be amazed at God's miracle in your life.

God of might and majesty, I give myself to you now in expectation of your Spirit's coming. Work in my heart so that I will be a man of prayer and a man of the Scriptures. I pray this prayer in the name of Jesus. Amen.

Week 9, Wednesday   Proclaim Your Faith

Read Luke 4:16-21.

Your life is a proclamation. Whatever it is you truly believe is seen in your everyday walk and talk. The way you feel about people shows in the way you treat them. You publish your care for your family by the things you do with them. You evince your care for the church by the way you carry out your ministry.

In the synagogue in Nazareth, Jesus outlined in advance his lifestyle and his proclamation. Throughout his ministry the words he read from Isaiah constantly rang true. He comforted the least and the lost. He ate with persons whom others disdained. He released persons from the bondage of guilt by offering forgiveness and friendship even to those considered unforgivable.

Jesus worshiped and prayed often. But it was not a worship found only in the temple. He prayed often in private, sometimes all night, but he was not separated from the rest of the world. Jesus let his life speak as powerfully as the holy words of Isaiah. He not only read from the Scripture and heralded its truth, but each day he lived its truth.

As a follower of Jesus the challenge before each of us men is to let our lives proclaim what our mouths profess. With his Spirit upon us, we can do it. God wants us to do it. As God's men, let us declare that we will be Spirit-led, vision-driven agents of salvation.

O Great God, I want to live my life in a way that pleases you, that is a reflection of your holiness. Give me the courage to keep living this way. I pray in the name of Jesus, Amen.

Week 9, Thursday   You Are Not Alone

Read Psalm 46.

Thanks be to God! We are not alone. There is no burden that we need to carry by ourselves. God is our strength, a very present help in trouble.

This psalm of strength and defense in times of attack is a vitally important one for all men today. Many men feel attacked by our culture and politics and find it easy to become despondent and angry. Because of sins like sexism, racism, child neglect, and aggressive behaviors, a man can feel battered for things he truthfully has not caused.

Yet if we men told the truth, we would admit that these attitudes give us benefits. We can gain certain advantages at the expense of others. But when women and children, for instance, cry out and blame us for unfair treatment, our manhood becomes less than popular and our caring for women and children seems an unfair burden.

How do we face these times with dignity and holiness? Can these troubles be addressed without our becoming bitter, disagreeable, even threatening to those who only want fairness?

If we remember that God is our refuge and strength, we can make it. God will not only give strength to endure what seems unfair, God will give us creative solutions to address the issues. We can be saved from bitterness and hostility and move into the strength and dignity only God, in Christ, can provide.

Remember, today, no matter what, you are not alone!

God of community, give me strength to bear the burden for this day, even if it seems misplaced or unfair. Because you are with me I know that I can see today's problems through, and overcome them by your power. I pray in Jesus' name. Amen.

Week 9, Friday   God Is Your Refuge and Strength

Read Psalm 46.

Trouble is a great equalizer. Every one of us encounters situations that are difficult for us to cope with. What do we do?

We must read the psalmist's declaration with eyes of faith to realize its massive power. "Therefore we will not fear, though the earth should change" (v. 2). If the very foundations on which all life depends are altered, the writer declares that God will still be his strength. Nothing is going to take away his reliance on his God.

A dear friend of mine called to say that trouble had him down. He felt that he was going to lose all that he had—why, he would not say. No matter what I said to him, he couldn't, wouldn't accept that I loved him. He wouldn't believe that God loved him, that even though the earth had changed and he was in terrible trouble, he was loved.

Somehow, God broke through to his battered and bruised soul and he placed his trust in the Lord. He now pastors a small church, has a wonderful wife and a darling son. For a moment, he was ready to kill himself—but God's presence gave him victory.

Are you at a low point in your life? Do you want to give up, to throw in the towel and say forget all of this? Know, dear brother, that the God of the ages and the universe is especially looking out for you. Whatever the issue is, whatever the shortcoming is, you can make it. You are not alone. God's people, God's followers, and God Almighty are for you and with you.

Hang in there today. God is *your* refuge and strength. Know that and be blessed.

Persevering God, give me this day the will to stay with you. Help me to believe that I can handle anything because you are with me, and give me the courage to act on my belief. I pray and believe through my Savior, Jesus Christ. Amen.

Read Isaiah 6:1-8.

There are times when we are awestruck at God's deeds. The majesty of the stars, the birth of a child, a miraculous recovery from illness—such glimpses and experiences remind us that the God of the universe is awesome.

How do you stack up before this awesome God? Isaiah was overwhelmed when he was given a vision of God in his heavenly glory. We can easily see the trivial, even sinful, nature of our pursuits when we compare them with God's majestic deeds. That is what makes this passage from Isaiah so important for us men of today. Isaiah was given his vision so that the Divine Drafter could make known an amazing request: "Whom shall I send, and who will go for us?" (v. 8). It was a crucial request because Isaiah's people were being threatened by their lack of faith. They needed a word from God and an example of living faith.

Brother, know that God is asking the same thing of us today. So many boys do not know how to become good men. So many women and girls do not know what a good man looks like. The lives and souls of a people today are at stake. God has shown us his glory in Jesus Christ. And as in the days of Isaiah, our Lord is asking this historic question yet again: "Whom shall I send, and who will go for us?"

The question is put to you again this day. Are you answering the call? Are you willing to say yes?

God of love and power, open my eyes to see you and my ears to hear your call. I know that there is no call greater than yours, no mission more important than yours. Empower me to say with courage and conviction, "Here am I Lord, send me!" I pray in the name of your Son, Amen.

Week 10, Sunday   **Confess Your Sin**

Read Isaiah 6:1-8.

One of the tragedies of today's religious community is our failure to realize that we are sinners saved by grace. Many of us believe that anything we do is all right, that the grace of God means, in contemporary vernacular, "it's all good." We have been seduced by the idea that thinking or acting in ways that hurt no one else absolves us from moral and ethical culpability. Many of us believe that whatever we do, our tenderhearted God will make it all right after a while.

God wants us to correct this misguided notion. The God of mercy is also a God of justice and judgment. Men need to tell this truth anew, not to stand in judgment but so that God's people might seek forgiveness and betterment. It is the confessed sinner who is assured of God's pardon. When we admit a need for mercy, God's grace begins to work his miracle in us. When Isaiah confessed his sin, fire from God's altar cleansed him.

Have you yielded yourself to the Lord for forgiveness? When we are able to say, "Woe is me! . . . for I am a man of unclean lips, and I live among a people of unclean lips," we will be ready to be the spiritual leaders God calls for and needs.

Let us confess our sin to God this day. Then we can lead others to do the same.

Merciful God, I admit my faults and sins to you. Cleanse me and assure me of your pardon, that I may be the Christian leader you wish for. I pray in the strong name of your Christ. Amen.

Week 10, Monday   **Trust in the Lord**

Read Proverbs 3:5-6.

One of my favorite songs of the faith is "I Will Trust in the Lord." It conveys a complex commitment in the simplest way. Until breath leaves my body, I will commit myself fully to God Almighty. Nothing else will take God's place. No one else will compete for my unflinching loyalty. That is the beginning and ending of the writer's faith.

Some years ago, I visited the former Soviet Union. Late one evening I stood out in the darkness, looking up at the stars strewn in noble array across the sky. I thought of Mama True, my grandmother. *She can see the same stars and sky that I see right now!* I thought, too, of all those who suffered under Communist domination, and I remembered all the imprisonments and murders of Christians. For a few brief moments I was scared. Then I remembered Mama True again and the thought came: *I can go anywhere as long as I know she is there, at home praying for me and loving me.* Mama True was my strength, my supporter, my fortress.

Mama True died in 1985. I was devastated at first. I had never really considered her death a possibility. It took some time for me to realize that I could no longer depend on her presence, her strong personality and loving prayers.

Gradually through the years, God has shown me that I need not depend on her that way. Rather, I depend on the One who made her, who made you and me. God has been with me since then across highways and byways. Across the seas and skies, I have known God's presence with me. That has been invaluable. My salvation from fear depends on God alone.

Sing it today, dear brother. "I will trust in the Lord, 'til I die"! Watch the difference it makes in your day.

O Lord, you are worthy of all my trust. Help me to remember it and live it. In Christ's name I pray. Amen.

Week 10, Tuesday   **Ask for Direction**

Read Proverbs 3:5-6.

I have a problem with asking for directions on a trip. It seems a waste of time and effort to stop and ask someone else how to get where I want to go. I always figure, however irrationally, *I can find my way myself!*

Female friends of mine have called this a "terminal male disease"! Many a brother has taken his family on many a wild goose chase because he refused to ask for directions.

Why are so many families in turmoil today? Why are communities in an uproar all over the world? Perhaps it is because the men in our communities are suffering spiritually from this "terminal male disease"! Prayer, Scripture reading, regular giving, fasting, receiving the Eucharist—all ways in which we ask for God's direction—can easily fall by the wayside for men in today's culture. The leadership God wants to see in Christian men will always suffer if we fail to seek guidance from God through use of the spiritual disciplines.

The writer of these verses from Proverbs tells us that we do not have to travel crooked roads. If we will seek the Lord's guidance wherever we go and for whatever we do, our paths can be made straight. There is no reason to stay lost—or become lost in the first place. We can seek the owner of the eternal compass and our direction can be made sure.

On this day, seek the Lord especially in prayer. Ask God to show you the way you should go. Be sure that God will!

I want your guidance this day, Lord, in all that I say and do, so that I will walk in your way. I pray in Jesus' holy and righteous name. Amen.

Week 10, Wednesday   Trust God's Working

Read Exodus 2:1-10.

One of the fascinating revelations of the Bible is the weakness found in the barbaric. The paranoia of oppressors is a continual theme, as is the downfall of the oppressor. The story of Moses from Exodus is one of the first to demonstrate these themes, and one of the most amazing. When the slave masters of Egypt found their land teeming with the enslaved Israelites, they were afraid of an uprising or a revolt. They came up with a solution that would, they thought, keep the money flowing and the slaves under control: genocide. Kill the men and the women will be helpless.

But the power of God is not subject to this greedy kind of human restraint. The God of our salvation cannot be controlled, especially by apprehensive tyrants. Moses escapes death through a mysterious grace that teams Moses' mother, his sister, and Pharaoh's daughter. Like the graceful waters of the Nile, this man-child moves with a smooth and powerful ease from a certain death to a lifestyle paid for by the very king who would have destroyed him!

Is there a threat looming over your life? Is something or someone threatening your work? Know that the God who protected and nurtured Moses is ready to do the same for you. God is moving at this very moment on your behalf. You may not see it now. It may seem hard to believe. But it is so. You can receive it and believe it, right now. I pray that you will.

God of power, today I will put my life in your hands, knowing that you can give me victory. I thank you in advance, through Christ, Amen.

Week 10, Thursday   **Thank God for the People in Your Life**

Read Exodus 2:1-10.

Have you thanked God for the persons who have blessed your journey?

Think back over your life. There have been people who believed in you, who saw something special in your life and told you. They saw your potential, your possible impact and talents, so they gave whatever they could to let you know that you are special. You are not where you are just because of your talents and gifts. You are here because God gifted you with these precious persons.

Moses had a mother who believed he should live. The love that physically nurtured him to birth would not allow Jochebed to see him easily destroyed. Moses had a birth sister who believed that somehow he should live. The government said no, but the love God put in Miriam's heart helped her resist the murderous laws of that day. Pharaoh's daughter believed he should live. Down in her soul God placed a hunger for life, for nurturing life, and she disallowed the extinguishing of the life of this Hebrew boy.

God placed people in your life who believed in your life. People who stood up for you and would not let you be extinguished. Have you thanked God for them? Have you called and thanked them recently? Take the time to do it—perhaps right now. God blessed you to be here, to be who you are, through them.

Thank you, God, for each person along the way who helped me to make it. I name them now before you: _____ , _____ , _____ ; and I ask your blessing on them. Amen.

Read Exodus 2:11–3:4.

Passion, the heat of emotion, can be destructive. Today's story from Exodus illustrates this vividly. Moses sees a Hebrew being victimized. Reacting heatedly to the injustice, he takes matters into his own hands to try and change the hostile and evil situation. He "gets hot" over this wrong, but the heat consumes him—and murder is the result.

It is very easy to allow heat to consume us. Rage in the midst of wrong, desire when starved of affection, hostility when conflicts arise, all can cause us to go over the edge. The need to respond is correct, but the way we respond is wrong.

When injury comes, people who love justice will attempt to stop it. But if we do this on our own, without seeking God's direction, we will often act in a regrettable fashion. We will hurt ourselves, hurt others, and perhaps cause irreparable damage if we have not checked it out through the Spirit. As Christian men, we need to bring our anger to God and check out our proposed actions.

Encountering God in our passion keeps us from harmful reactions. When we seek self-control through the Holy Spirit, we are enabled to do the right thing for the right reason.

Pray today for the power and presence of God's Spirit. If you encounter something that is painful to yourself or others, know that you need not be enslaved by injurious passion. You can overcome. Believe that this day.

O God, help me to control my passions and not to be controlled by them. I pray in Christ's name. Amen.

Week 10, Saturday   **Constructive Passion**

Read Exodus 3:1-4.

Passion, the heat of emotion, can also be constructive. Moses, now a fugitive from Egypt's legal system, encounters a heat different from his own. Moses happens upon a bush that is clearly on fire. This bush differs in that the fire does not burn it up. It is lit but not incinerated. Moses moves closer to behold this remarkable sight. It is from this bush that he will hear his call to ministry. God is the fire in the bush; therefore Moses receives wondrous energy from the bush, not damaging force.

Where we get our heat from is of paramount importance. Not all energy helps us to do the good that God Almighty desires. When we fail to listen for God's voice, the heat that drives us can cause many problems. Death to relationships can easily result. Devastation of ministry can follow.

Our Lord wants us to be passionate. We were given passion so that we might be inspired to work for God's vital and living kingdom. Passion is essential to our giving our very best. But the source for our passion must be God. When we begin with God, no pharaoh, no mountain, no obstacle of any kind can keep us from reaching God's goals.

What is the source of your passion? Consider that but do not stop there. Make sure, when all is said and done, that your passion begins with God.

God of passion, keep me hooked to you. With you as my source, I can be the agent for kingdom-building that you want me to be. Amen.

Week 11, Sunday   Saved from Fear

Read Exodus 4:1-17.

Moses did not know who "the man" *really* was—that the power of the universe was speaking to him.

It was a colossal assignment that God gave Moses from the burning bush. But Moses was reluctant. He offered a grand litany of questions, reasons, and excuses why he was not qualified, not the person for this assignment. Time after time he offered his concerns, hoping that God would take back the call, find somebody, anybody other than him.

For us, too, our pains and panics can greatly inhibit us from working for the Lord. We can wallow so much in our fearful excuses that we become one great fear. For every possibility we claim its opposite. We search for reasons not to do what God asks—but not because we cannot do the task. It just appears so formidable that we forget who is calling us. This is why some men refuse fatherhood. This is why others abandon their rightful place in their communities. Many of our brothers fear the idea of the task much more than they fear the task itself.

Fear is as common as the air we breathe. But fear should not rule us. We need to be saved from our fears. When God speaks, we should have more trust in God than in our fears. Remember, at God's command, Moses defeated the great armies of Pharaoh with a mere staff. There is nothing that can stop you if you listen to and obey the call of God.

Where is God calling you today? Don't dodge God with excuses. As a follower of Jesus, dare to say, "Lord, let's show Pharaoh who 'the man' *really* is—that you are the power of the universe!"

Lord, save me from my fears. Help me to answer your call and trust you to be with me as I live your plan for me. In Christ I pray. Amen.

Week 11, Monday   No Excuses

Read Exodus 4:10-17.

Some of us believe that our reasons for not obeying God are all right. It's okay to delay, to deny, or to ignore God, because God's mercy accepts us and doesn't ask us to struggle. The Bible, however, doesn't support such a view. In fact, it shows us that there are times when the Lord stops us in our tracks to save us from ourselves.

Moses was making God angry here. All of his excuses were getting on God's nerves! God finally asked him, "Who gave man his mouth? Who makes him deaf or dumb? Who gives him sight or makes him blind?" (v. 11 NIV). God is not being rhetorical in these questions. In the vernacular of today's youth, God is about to "get real" with Moses.

It is all too easy when we talk about God's grace to ignore the fact that God will "get real" with us when we refuse obedience. The reality of God's mercy does not do away with the fact of God's demands. When God deals with issues of justice, God will not wait long. History is replete with God's serious movements for right. When the time for justice comes, God will step forward in a "sanctified fury."

It is not prudent, for our world or for ourselves, to delay or disobey God's bidding. God is calling, my brother. Are you stalling?

God of heaven, grant me the wisdom and courage to obey your commands. Let me stand up where you call me to stand, speak up where you call me to speak, do all you call me to do. I pray and believe through Jesus the Christ. Amen.

Week 11, Tuesday   The Listening Ear

Read 1 Kings 9:9-13.

It is imperative to remember where God is. The easiest thing to do, when our world becomes difficult, is to forget that God is with us. We can be so overcome by the powers of the day that we aren't able to see or hear God.

Elijah was in trouble. He had snatched victory from the jaws of defeat by proving God superior to the gods of Ahab and Jezebel. Jezebel was so infuriated that she vowed to have Elijah's life. Despised by the powers of government, Elijah fled for safety, believing that he was the only one left who believed in the one, true God.

One of the seductions of evil is that it deludes us, making us believe that we are alone, the only person on the side of right. We can be so insulated and isolated that we cannot see or hear God's presence, God's support. God does not leave us alone—ever. The divine presence, the Holy Spirit, is always available, always around to give us hope and help.

With what Howard Thurman called "the listening ear," Elijah went out of the cave onto the mountainside. High winds, earth-quakes, and fire passed by with all their terrible awe and power. Then came God in a still, small voice. In the midst of all the force and rage, God was indeed present. Elijah just needed to be in a place and context to hear, not the terror of the natural, but the calming presence of the supernatural.

You are ready now to hear the calming, peace-filled voice of God. Whatever the day brings you will be ready, because you know where God is. God is with you.

Help me in the midst of trouble and the world's clamor to be quiet and listen for your voice, O God. Because you are with me, I know I will not only survive my troubles, but in Christ, I will thrive. I pray in Christ's name. Amen.

Read 1 Kings 19:9-18.

The hope is in the small voice, not the thunder and lightning. Not in the smashed rocks and the splattered buildings. The hope for the world is in the small voice.

One afternoon I forgot my daughter. I was fifteen minutes away from meeting her school bus, and I needed to be there in ten minutes. My son Bryant and I jumped in the car and swooped across the highways at breakneck speeds to reach Alyssa's bus at the appointed time.

When I got there, she was gone! I was scared to death! *Where is my child?* What might my tardiness have done? I was in true agony. I zipped back along the streets to get to my house. There Alyssa was, knocking on the door. She had walked the quarter mile by herself.

"Where have you been?" she said stridently, as I picked her up. Then she cried out, "I was scared, Daddy!"

Have you ever hurt your youngster? Do you know the pain of scaring your precious baby? All I could say in my inadequate way was "I'm sorry, baby. Daddy's sorry."

In a soothing, sweet and sincere voice, my Alyssa said to me, "I know you are sorry, Daddy, but I love you anyway!"

Friend, the voice of love is not found in booming or resounding noises, in boastful words or grand declarations. The voice of love and care is often, in fact usually, heard in the still small voice. Listen for it today. God is calling to you—softly and lovingly.

God, help me to recognize the quiet voice of love, and to hear you speaking in it. In the name of Jesus, Amen.

Week 11, Thursday   **Struggle with Your Friend**

Read Matthew 18:15-20.

Friendship can sometimes be a very fragile thing. When a problem arises, the true mettle of the relationship shows itself, whether it will hold or break. Sadly, when breaks occur, too often they are not mended. This is particularly true for men.

As Christians, we are called to confront problems. We should be overcoming our differences. This is the whole point of Christian love. It is no sentimental goo; Christian love confronts the issues of our relationships with one another. And that is the point of this biblical text. Jesus says that we are to address the issues that separate us. When we do, we provide an opportunity for the relationship to be repaired.

How many friendships have we lost simply because we were not honest enough to admit a misunderstanding? Many men get into fixes with their fellows and then refuse to discuss the problems. We feel it is manly to be independent! It is masculine to act unhurt, to ignore pain, to behave as if we do not have feelings that can be bruised!

Jesus here teaches us how to keep the breaches from occurring in relationships, how to be saved from relational isolation. He begins by telling us to go directly to the brother with whom we are struggling.

How many relationships are broken because we never confront the issue? We never tell our brother that we are angry or hurt. Relationships cannot be mended if we do not own up to the issue.

Dear brother, why not put Jesus' teaching to the test. You will be surprised at what will happen. Most times, people are more than willing to address our concerns. Our brothers want peace as much as you and I do. People do not want trouble. The question Rodney King asked is appropriate: "Can't we all get along?"

The answer is yes! We can get along. Try the Jesus way. See how easy it can be.

Lord, help me to admit my struggle with my friend first to myself and then to him, so that we can be together in you. I pray in Jesus' name. Amen.

Week 11, Friday   **Take Along a Witness**

Read Matthew 18:15-20.

Sometimes my brother disagrees that I have offended him. What am I to do then? The Bible suggests that there is a way to arbitrate disputes even when the disputees disagree. Take along witnesses.

Should we trust that advice? Can we trust it? In this world of suspicion and mistrust, what good is a witness?

A brother and his former friend had become estranged. One day they happened to be together with a mutual acquaintance, and were so obviously angry with each other that the third man asked, "What is this foolishness you are mad about?"

The first man became indignant. "What do you mean 'foolishness'?" he asked.

"Just what I said. What is the problem?"

Continued inquiry revealed that neither of the men knew exactly where the problem originated. They had just stopped talking, and had allowed the silence to continue.

After the three of them laughed at the obvious silliness of their plight, the acquaintance pronounced what each of them knew to be so: "If you don't even remember the problem, how can there really be one?"

Sometimes it takes the view of an outside, loving person to help us see the problem clearly. Often we will be shocked to find that there really is no problem at all. But to get to this point, we must be willing to hear from a Spirit-led, vision-driven Christ follower.

Do you have a rift with your brother? Take along a witness. See what God can do for him and you.

Lord, lead me to someone who truly seeks you through Christ, who can help me justly and fairly arbitrate my disputes with my brother. I pray for reconciliation through Jesus, my Lord and Savior. Amen.

Week 11, Saturday   **Hug Your Brother**

Read Micah 6:8.

Two boys on a basketball team were fighting at practice. They were going at it tooth and nail. Neither was ready to give an inch. The coach walked in, but the boys continued as if he weren't there. He walked over, big burly man that he was, and peeled them one from another.

When they noticed that Coach was doing the peeling, they became meek and mild, although the steam continued to blow from their silent nostrils. They were still fuming, but now it was somewhat controlled.

"Okay, gentlemen," the coach said. "You know the drill. Let's get to it!"

"Oh, no, Coach! Please don't make us do that."

"Do you want to play this week or not?" the coach responded.

"We want to play!"

"Then hop to it."

So stubbornly, they walked, faced each other, still with some defiance.

"Boys, am I going to have to help you?"

"No, Coach," they said, somewhat sadly. Then they hugged, a good, long hug!

Sometimes we need to be saved from our macho attitudes—and it is not contemporary notions of macho that will do it. Loving mercy means to act kindly, to seek redemption, to forgive in times that are not easy.

Whom do you need to hug today? With whom must you share mercy? Be freed from your anger. Go give a hug. It is really a manly act—and good for your team.

Gracious Lord, enable me to hug the one I am angry with. On this day, let me embody the power of mercy in my living and my giving. I receive this gift and thank you for it in the name of Jesus. Amen.

Week 12, Sunday   Be a Model

Read Micah 6:8.

A friend of mine heard about the incident in yesterday's devotion. She thought it was funny, even cute.

"Who was the coach of that team?" she asked. "It sounds like you might know him or her pretty well."

"Oh, just a brother friend of mine," I said, trying to feign ignorance and anonymity before her.

"Well, brother friend, do you hug people when you fight with them?"

"What are you talking about?" I asked.

"You heard me. *Do you hug people when you get in a fight?*"

She did not need to say another word. God convicted me through her words. The justice and love I have been so prepared to lead kids to, that I demand of my basketball players, I have not practiced myself. I was proud of what I was asking of my players, but I could not say that I displayed it myself.

Doing justice, loving-kindness (or mercy), and walking humbly with God is not just a child's enterprise. It must not be something that we expect in others without practicing it ourselves. As spiritual leaders in our homes and communities, Christian men must model the behaviors we expect of others. Our boys learn to be men based on what they see in us.

What kind of modeling are you doing, brother friend? There are boys and girls watching you, learning how to be Christian by what you do. Let's you and me show them, show all around us, how to hug!

Lord of justice, help me to exemplify the mercy and love I expect children to show. In Jesus' name. Amen.

Week 12, Monday   What Do You See?

Read Habakkuk 2:2-3.

The late Senator Robert Kennedy once declared, quoting George Bernard Shaw, "Some men see things as they are and say, 'Why?' I see things that never were and say, 'Why not?'"

What do you see, dear brother? In a world that seems so chaotic, so mad and distraught, what is it that you see?

In the town where I live, the things I see are often disturbing. Such was the article in today's newspaper, which reported the mass murder of four children—by their father! He was so distraught and pained over losing his children and wife through divorce that, to avenge the loss, he killed the ones whose loss caused his grief.

Senseless occurrences like this happen so often that we begin to expect them, even look forward to them for their excitement. But aren't you tired of this? Wouldn't you like to see a different kind of world? A different kind of life?

Will you dare to see, to envision something different? Will you, as a Christian man, venture to be the herald of God's vision, a divine revelation for a new world?

Pray this morning. No matter what the morning news says, no matter how the daily papers recount the day's events, pray for God's revelation. Believe in God's miracle and accept what God wants to say—*through you*. Then write the vision and make it plain for those around you.

O God, I will not despair because of the state of society. Give me a revelation of your vision for me and my community, and I will follow you in joyful obedience and give you the praise, in Jesus' name. Amen.

Week 12, Tuesday   Wait for the Vision

Read Habakkuk 2:2-3.

The revelation will come. It may be hard to see, hard to believe at times, but the revelation will come.

One of my favorite stories is of a man banished with others to an island because of his beliefs. His people suffered oppression of biblical proportions, and this man, viewed by some as a prophet, by others as a messiah, was a special victim. He was incarcerated well into his later years, so that he lost a life with his spouse, the joy of reading to his children, the mere prospect of enjoying the career of his choice.

Then came a glorious day. The oppressors came to release him. They were willing to liberate this man, give him his freedom—but with conditions. If he would renounce some of his views, if he would deny the beliefs that had caused his conviction and banishment, he could be free.

By now he was an old man. His youth was gone, his children were grown and he had grandchildren. Why not take the bait? Why not live freely in his last years? It made sense to accept this prize.

But not to this man. He categorically rejected the offer and he did so with these stirring words: "I shall return."

That man is now the president of the very nation that banished him to a prison island. His name is Nelson Mandela.

Dear friend, if the vision is of God, it will come. When it does, it cannot be stopped.

Pledge today to wait for the vision. As the prophet tells us: "It will certainly come and will not delay" (Habakkuk 2:3 NIV).

God of revelation, enable me by your grace to wait on the vision. As the ancestors of the faith did, help me to believe in you and in the vision. I pray in your Son's name. Amen.

Week 12, Wednesday   Pray for Faith

Read Hebrews 11:1.

There is no more crucial passage in the Bible than this one. The writer gives us a beautiful definition of something that can be neither seen nor felt. Faith cannot be touched or tasted. Its existence cannot be measured, yet its reality can never be ignored or its value negated. The substance of things hoped for is the essence of a Christian man's life. The strength we need to answer God's call on our lives is derived from faith and faith alone. We become who God wants us to be by the power of faith.

It is the life of faith that makes a difference, a fact demonstrated in history. Men like Desmond Tutu, Oscar Romero, Kaj Munk and Medgar Evers have sacrificed comforts and even life itself, to be instruments of God through unswerving faith. They, along with countless other Christian men, deflected calamity and thwarted oppression, conquered disaster and defeated evil by the power of faith in God through Christ. Faith is the most valuable possession of the Christian man.

Men of today's culture must be rescued from reliance on lesser things. Often we become enamored of earthly things that will not give us the spiritual power we need to do God's will in the world. Political power, economic wealth, public stature, military might, job status, and brute strength—none of these can accomplish what is possible through faith. We lose power because we seek it in the wrong things. We try to find substance in what, in the long run, are insubstantial things.

Where do you find your power? There is a power waiting for you. It comes through faith in God through Christ. As you walk through this day, pray for greater faith. It will make you a better man.

God, help me to seek power today in you. Strengthen my faith. In the holy name of Jesus. Amen.

Read Hebrews 11:1.

John Thompson, coach of the Georgetown Hoyas, is reported to keep a deflated basketball in his office. He tells the members of his team that basketball is merely a game, and to place all one's hope on a small piece of leather that can be rendered useless by a mere pin prick is senseless and foolish. He challenges his young men to live more substantial lives than that.

The challenge before you today, as a man of God, is to live a substantial life. Christians have a reality, an essential quality, that the world craves. And we are called to go out into the world. Instead we spend our time in the same way the world does. But video games and computer technology can entertain us only for a while. Cable and satellite television can keep us company only for a few moments. They cannot satisfy us. Nor can they meet the world's needs. Sooner or later, we must confront the world. We cannot run away and hide. We need to build our lives on a solid foundation.

On what are you building your life today? This is a question we must ask ourselves every day. New challenges emerge every morning. How will you meet them? With technology? With entertainment? Or with God's power? In order to successfully live up to what our Lord expects of us, we need to renew our commitment daily, to build only on the solid foundation of Jesus Christ (1 Corinthians 3:11).

Can you say, "My hope is built on nothing less / Than Jesus' blood and righteousness"? Seek the Lord as your foundation and salvation today. Keep putting your faith and hope in him. That is the way to assure a substantial life.

O God, I commit my life to you this day, in order to be part of your plan for the world. Strengthen my faith as I claim victory through Christ. Amen.

Week 12, Friday   **Share Your Conviction**

Read Romans 8:37-39.

The man was overwhelmed with distress. He had lost his wife and three children in a car wreck. Only he had survived. Why did he live? he wondered miserably over the phone to his friend. Why couldn't he protect his wife and children from this tragic death that cut short their lives?

"I caused their deaths!" he cried in suicidal tones. "I deserve to die. What kind of man kills his own family and dares to live?" He was inconsolable.

His friend listened intently. He would break in only to say, "You are my friend, no matter what."

After hours of this heavy-laden conversation, the distraught husband screamed out, "How can you, how can anyone be my friend? I have killed my family."

The friend calmly and confidently replied; "I am convinced that neither death nor life, neither angels nor demons, neither the present nor the future, nor any powers, neither height nor depth, nor anything else in all creation, will be able to separate us from the love of God that is in Christ Jesus our Lord" (Romans 8:38-39 NIV).

Before the telephone call ended, the bereft man knew and accepted the fact that he was not alone.

In the midnight of the soul, sometimes the only Christ others can see is you or me. We may be the God-ordained difference between suicide and security. We are God's gifts, to offer a word of hope to hopeless and broken people. Our witness can save a life. Because you are convinced, share the conviction with one who needs it.

Lord, let me be an instrument of hope this day. Through Christ. Amen.

Week 12, Saturday   "We Are Going to Win"

Read Romans 8:37-39.

My basketball team was down ten points with one quarter left. "This is our game," I told the fellows. "We are going to win."

They looked at me as if I had lost my mind. Whenever we had made a run at the opposition, they had withstood it. They were taller. They were bigger. My guys were sure I had lost my mind.

Victory against the odds is tough for this world. Bets are made based on past performance. Expectations are very high for the "large and in charge."

But consider the Bible. How do we reconcile the stories of Joseph, the Exodus, Samson, David, Elijah, and a host of others with the odds of contemporary culture?

The fact of the matter is that we cannot. The Bible contradicts the notion that the oddsmakers are correct. There is another reality that flies in the face of these ideas. That is what Paul is discussing in our text. We are conquerors, victors in Jesus. There is no one, no thing, that can keep us from that to which God has appointed us. "We are more than conquerors," Paul states flatly.

In the last quarter of that basketball game, we came back and won by three points—and my boys believed they could have beaten Michael Jordan and the Chicago Bulls!

Believe that, in Jesus, you are more than a conqueror today. Then watch the victories begin to roll in!

O God, I do believe that you have won the victory and that with you I am a conqueror over the obstacles that beset me. I claim that victory today and praise you, for it. Through Jesus Christ. Amen.

4
OVERCOMING DISAPPOINTMENTS AND DIFFICULTIES

Robert H. Lauer

     Faith: For Overcoming, Not Avoiding

And this is the victory that conquers the world, our faith.
—1 John 5:4

My mother was delighted when I told her I planned to become a minister. Eventually I discovered that her delight was rooted in the belief that, because I was a minister, God would protect me from all the ills, misfortunes, and struggles that other people endured.

She was wrong, of course. Faith—whether that of a minister or any other Christian—is not a way to avoid adversity, but a way to deal with it. Still, there have been times when I wished my mother had been right. I don't enjoy adversity. I've never faced a difficult time of life with relish, confident that I would gloriously defeat the adversity that threatened my well-being. I face adversity with more sighs and complaints than smiles and poise.

But in retrospect, I can see the truth of the biblical promise. As I have struggled to remain firm in my commitment, my faith has been a tool for overcoming—not merely for coping, but for wresting out a victory.

Even God's creation teaches us this truth. I live near the ocean and have seen the way in which birds face into the wind when they are at rest on the beach. This keeps their feathers in the correct position. If they turn around, the wind will ruffle their feathers. It's only by facing the threat that the birds remain safe and whole.

And it is only by facing adversity, of whatever kind, head-on in faith that we can claim the promise and emerge as victors.

Help me, gracious Father, not to run away from difficulties but, through trusting you, to deal courageously with every problem I encounter. Amen.

Week 13, Monday   Faith Means to Be Faithful

Read Acts 16:16-25.

How can you sing and pray all night after you've been beaten and thrown into prison? A friend of mine suggested that Paul and Silas were too bruised to sleep. Perhaps they were. But they were also affirming their faith in the face of unjust treatment. Their reaction shows us one way to exercise faith when dealing with adversity—remain faithful to God.

Think about other possible reactions. Paul and Silas could have complained bitterly to their fellow inmates. They could have called to the jailor and insisted on their rights. They could have questioned the goodness of God. Yet they chose to sing and pray and worship God in the midst of an unfair situation.

Sometimes that's all you can do to help yourself—wait patiently and continue to be faithful in worshiping and serving your Lord. A man suffered severe burns in an accident. Shortly after that, doctors found a malfunction in his heart that required surgery. He was devastated. At times, he felt abandoned by God. However, like Paul and Silas, he continued to affirm his faith. "That was the hardest part," he told me, "to keep praying and worshiping when God seemed indifferent to my needs. Now I can give thanks to the Lord for bringing me through it all. But at the time, I couldn't even say with certainty that God existed."

Faith doesn't mean you understand or appreciate everything that happens to you. Faith means that you continue to pray and worship and serve no matter what is happening to you.

With your help, O God, I will continue to trust you when things are going badly as much as when they are going well. Amen.

Read Psalm 103.

I had a problem with one of my eyes that caused it to swell and redden for a few weeks. When a friend saw it, he asked me, "How does that make you feel?"

"Vulnerable," I blurted without thinking.

I thought about it later, though. Like most men I know, I prefer to think of myself as able to handle anything that comes my way. Yet things keep coming my way that underscore my vulnerability. Things happen that remind me that I am not as healthy, not as competent, not as pure, and not as confident as I would like to be. And that's good. It's important for me to be aware of my limitations, of the fact that I am not self-sufficient. I can't handle on my own all the challenges and problems that beset me. I need my family. I need my friends. I need experts like physicians and teachers. I need help from strangers when I've lost my way. Above all, I need God.

Psalm 103 is one of my favorite passages because it reminds me that my faith is in the God who is able. I am vulnerable to sin, but he is able to forgive. I am vulnerable to disease, but he is able to heal. I am vulnerable to failure and despair, but he is able to redeem, to satisfy, to renew. Granted, he doesn't always respond to my vulnerabilities according to my preferred time schedule. But he does respond, crowning me "with steadfast love and mercy." So, indeed,"bless the Lord, O my soul."

O God, you who are able, I want to experience for myself the blessings you have promised—salvation, forgiveness, healing, and your steadfast love. I praise you and entrust myself to you. Amen.

Week 13, Wednesday   **Faith in the Justice of God**

When he was abused, he did not return abuse; when he suffered, he did not threaten; but he entrusted himself to the one who judges justly.   *—1 Peter 2:23*

What's the difference between a manager and a leader? According to business literature, a manager does things right, while a leader does the right things. In other words, a manager follows the established rules and procedures, while a leader creatively attains the best.

Is God a manager or a leader? Does he do things right, or does he do the right things? Clearly, Peter believed that God does the right things, for he is "the one who judges justly." We can have faith in his justice even when he isn't following the rules we think he ought to follow. If we made up the rules, for instance, people would not lose their jobs, no one would feel like a total failure, and children would not die. How can God allow such things to happen?

An Australian pastor shared with me the stories of two men in his church who suffered the loss of children. One was very bitter about the death of his only son. He began to doubt God and dropped out of church.

The other man's daughter was driving with her family one day when she spotted a dog on the road. She swerved to avoid the dog, went over an embankment, and was killed. When the pastor went to visit this man, his first words were: "My grandson asked me if God ever makes mistakes. I told him no, God makes no mistakes."

One man reacted to his loss with bitterness. The other reacted as Jesus did when facing undeserved suffering: he "entrusted himself to the one who judges justly."

I thank you, God of justice, that you do things right in my life. Remind me of that when it seems that things are not going well. Amen.

Week 13, Thursday   **Hope: God's Antidepressant**

> *Why are you cast down, O my soul,*
> *and why are you disquieted within me?*
> *Hope in God; for I shall again praise him,*
> *my help and my God.*
> *—Psalm 42:11*

There are two lines in Robert Frost's poem, "The Death of the Hired Man," that epitomize despair: the hired man had "nothing to look backward to with pride, / And nothing to look forward to with hope." In other words, the hired man had nothing meaningful in his past and no prospect of anything meaningful in his future. Actually, you can live with a bleak past as long as you have something to look forward to. However bland or dark or difficult the past has been, you can proceed with joyous anticipation if somewhere on the horizon of your future life there is the promise of a new beginning.

That's why I call hope God's antidepressant. I don't mean that hope is a quick and sure fix for depression, or that hope will vanquish every moment of doubt and despair. But hope sustains you in the darkness and eventually brings you into the light of God's joy. David knew this. When he was depressed, he asked himself why. Although he apparently got no answer to the question, he affirmed his hope in God: "I shall again praise him, my help and my God."

Hope, in other words, is the conviction that God will take care of his children. Hope is the expectation that God will—in his time—lift us out of the valley of depression and into the light of the joy and peace of his salvation. Hope is the anticipation of a future, conscious that we are secure, nested in the hands of the Lord who wills the best for his own.

Father, Jesus promised that nothing can snatch us out of your hands. Nourish that hope in me by your grace so that it may remain strong. Amen.

Week 13, Friday   **Hope Makes Us Farsighted**

Rejoice in hope, be patient in suffering, persevere in prayer.
                                        —Romans 12:12

On a few occasions I have driven through dense fog. It's always disturbing. Fog restricts your vision to what is very close to you. For comfortable and safe driving, I need to see more than the ten or twenty feet ahead allowed by the fog.

Disappointments and difficult times can become a mental fog, restricting our thoughts to the vexing problem at hand. This is one reason that Paul extols hope. Hope makes us farsighted. However oppressive our difficulties, hope is the conviction that God is with us and will deliver us because God wills the best for us.

Hope, in other words, enables you to think about something other than present difficulties. Occasionally, I have counseled someone whose mind is stuck on "woe is me." One man was in a mental fog because he hated his job. All efforts to get him to think about possible alternatives were fruitless. He had no hope. He did not believe that God had something better in store for him. He could only moan about his sorry situation.

"Rejoice in hope." Indeed, cherish hope, so that your mind will not be fogged in by difficult times, but you will be able to trust God for your future. So you will be able to fulfill the rest of Paul's admonition—to be patient in suffering and persevering in prayer. Hope nurtures patience, because you know that your present trial is not endless. Hope drives you to prayer because you know that God has something good in store for you; in prayer, you can thank him and claim his promise.

I look forward, Lord God, to the good things you have in store for me, and I trust your presence with me now. Thank you for the hope you have given me in Jesus my Savior. Amen.

Week 13, Saturday   **Hope and Grief**

But we do not want you to be uninformed, brothers and sisters, about those who have died, so that you may not grieve as others do who have no hope.

—1 Thessalonians 4:13

The death of someone you love is one of the most difficult experiences of life. Grief over that death can last for many years. That is because, first, you are dealing with the pain of your loss. But also you are confronting your own future death.

When Paul told us not to grieve as others do, he was talking about both aspects of grief. The Christian's hope relates to both the painful separation from those you love and the apprehension about your own eventual death. Hope tempers your grief because it reminds you that Jesus has conquered death. (See Hebrews 2:14-15.) Consequently, hope means that the separation is not final. It also assures you that your own death will take place within the context of Christ's love.

I found this true when my mother died. A friend came to visit and offered his sympathy. After a bit, he smiled and said: "I guess one of the things that makes it hard is that you realize you're next."

I thought about that for a moment. "Actually, no," I told him. "My mother's death does not make my own dying more real or more frightening. It makes the thought of it easier because I feel that I have someone to go to, someone who is waiting for me." I was not giving my friend a pious answer. I really felt that way because God's hope was alive within me.

I thank you, Lord God, for the hope of eternal life you plant within me through Jesus Christ my Lord. Keep that hope alive and strong. Amen.

Week 14, Sunday   **It's Tough to Love**

But I say to you, Love your enemies and pray for those who per-secute you.   *—Matthew 5:44*

I was a university dean when my pastor asked me to teach a Lenten series on the fruits of the Spirit (Galatians 5:22-23), a challenge that excited me. Before the series started, I discussed some of my ideas on the first fruit—love—with my wife. She listened carefully without saying anything. Then she said, "What does it mean for you to love your boss at the university?"

That was a disturbing question! The man—I'll call him Dr. Smith—had added considerable stress to my life. Dr. Smith was known throughout the university as arbitrary, self-serving, and ruthless in his pursuit of success. He was unquestionably the most difficult boss I ever had. A few people respected him, but virtually everyone preferred to avoid him.

I've talked to a great many other men about their bosses, and nearly every one of them has worked for a difficult boss. But almost no one has raised the question that my wife raised for me that day: What does it mean to love your difficult boss?

All of us have thought about how to survive the difficult boss. We have all fantasized about the difficult boss's getting his or her due. But the question for the Christian is, How do you love that person?

As I accepted my responsibility to love, my behavior changed. I began to pray for both Dr. Smith and myself as I dealt with him. I resigned from that position before I could fully implement my task of loving, but I have tried to follow it with other difficult people.

It's a tough calling to love someone who vexes you. It helps to remember Jesus' example and command: "Love your enemies and pray for those who persecute you."

Help me, Lord Jesus, to love those who vex me even as you loved those who hated and resisted you. May your love in me enable me to want the best for all others. Amen.

Week 14, Monday   Love Makes Us Tough

Read 1 Samuel 24:1-7.

Saul, the first king of Israel, began his reign well. Yet his military successes transformed him into an arrogant and proud man. Eventually, Saul's growing disregard for both the welfare of his people and the commands of God led to God's rejection of him and the choice of David as his successor.

Saul felt intense jealousy and hatred toward David. He repeatedly tried to kill him. In contrast, when David had an opportunity to kill Saul, he refused to do so: "The LORD forbid that I should do this thing . . . to raise my hand against him; for he is the LORD's anointed" (1 Samuel 24:6).

Yesterday, we noted that it's tough to love. However, when we do love, it makes us tough. It takes toughness of character to resist the temptation to meet irritation with irritation, anger with anger, sarcasm with sarcasm.

David could have quickly ended his harrowing experiences with the king by doing to Saul what Saul was trying to do to him—kill him. Instead, David chose love. Love led him away from retaliation. Love meant that David would continue to face difficult days with Saul. But love gave him the toughness to endure those days. We sometimes think that if we love much, we should be spared from painful times because we have obeyed what Jesus called the greatest of the commandments. However, love is not a way to escape adversity. It is a way to have the toughness to be Christlike in the midst of adversity.

God of love, toughen me with your love that I may be able to love others in the most difficult circumstances. Amen.

Week 14, Tuesday   **Love Isn't Conditional**

> *A friend loves at all times.*
> —*Proverbs 17:17*

"Love never ends," wrote Paul (1 Corinthians 13:8). Or as the book of Proverbs puts it, "A friend loves at all times" (17:17). As I reflect on these two statements, I am personally challenged to respond. I don't find it very difficult to love when I'm dealing with lovable people or when things are going well in my life. It's the difficult people and the tough times that severely test my capacity to love.

But I am called to love difficult people, and I am commanded to love in difficult times. Love doesn't depend upon the worth of the people or the ease of the times. After all, neither my sins nor my circumstances can quench the love that Jesus has for me. If I, who am loved so much, can't love someone I find odious, and if I can't love when I am enmeshed in painful circumstances, then I'm not yet loving with the love of Christ.

True love isn't conditional. Though I may often fail, I will strive to love all people and to love at all times. I want others to see God's love filling me and overflowing into them. I want it to be apparent that no adverse situation can stem the flow of love from my being. Like St. Francis, I pray to be made an instrument of God's love. I want to live in such a way that people can say of me after I have died: "He was greatly loved, and he loved greatly."

I give myself to you, Father, to be your channel of love. Deliver me by your grace from all those temptations and barriers that would block the flow of love. Amen.

Week 14, Wednesday   **Love—and Loving—Lifted Me**

> *Better is a dinner of vegetables where love is*
> *than a fatted ox and hatred with it.*
> —*Proverbs 15:17*

When I was a young Christian, my church frequently sang with gusto a rousing hymn, "Love Lifted Me." You could see smiles come on people's faces as they sang, "When nothing else could help, love lifted me." I suspect that many of them had experienced the truth of those words in their own lives by encountering God's love in some valley of despair.

Love is uplifting. That is true in two different ways: to receive love is uplifting and to give love is uplifting. Most people can recall a time when the love of God or love from some person lifted them. I hope you have had these kinds of experiences.

A man struggling in the bitter aftermath of a divorce desperately felt the need for help, and came to me for counseling. His wife had abandoned both him and his young son. For more than a year he tried to keep his personal anguish under control in order to provide a good home for his son. Eventually, he began to feel good about himself, about his parenting, and about life and the future. Looking back on that year, he said he had been so angry that he could have slipped into some kind of self-destructive way of life. But his faith and his responsibility for his son forced him to keep going until he felt whole again. Love—from Christ his Lord—and loving—caring for his son— lifted him.

Lift me by your love, O God, that I may know the uplifting experience of loving.

Week 14, Thursday   No Quick Fixes

Be still before the LORD, and wait patiently for him;
do not fret over those who prosper in their way,
over those who carry out evil devices.
—Psalm 37:7

An ad for aspirin touted its ability to work faster than any other brand. That's appealing. For most of us, the question raised by any kind of pain or problem is how and how quickly can we get rid of it? David's counsel of patience is not easy to accept. But many other biblical passages also urge patience in the face of various kinds of tribulations and struggles.

Patience doesn't mean inaction. It does suggest, however, that there may not be a quick fix for problems. We are never promised a detour around or a shortcut through tough times.

> But now thus says the LORD . . . :
> When you pass through the waters, I will be with you;
>   and through the rivers, they shall not overwhelm you.
>
> —Isaiah 43:1-2

God promises to be with us, not to show us a quick way out.

The search for a quick fix can be spiritually damaging. A man struggling with a long-term illness was advised by a fellow Christian to "just ask Jesus to deliver you."

"I have asked Jesus," the man told me, "and I'm still struggling. I know now that there is no quick fix for me. I don't need someone to tell me that if I only ask Jesus in faith he will heal me. I need someone to support me, pray for me, and remind me of God's presence."

Jesus, Lord, nurture patience in me that I may wait upon you, trusting your love and knowing that you are with me in whatever is happening in my life. Amen.

Week 14, Friday   Love Is Patient

Love is patient; love is kind; love is not envious or boastful or arrogant or rude.   *—1 Corinthians 13:4-5a*

Love is patient. I wonder why patience was the first quality of love that came to Paul's mind. Perhaps, like me, he found it difficult to wait for the results of his loving. When I try to love someone in a Christian way—in a way that enhances that person's well-being—I want to see a quick return on my efforts. But of course, it doesn't always happen that way. I have been working with one man for over five years, supporting him in a difficult situation and encouraging him to take action that would set his life on a different course. For five years, he has returned with some regularity for support. And for five years, he has done nothing to alter his situation.

Happily, most people respond more quickly than he has. As of this writing, I'm disappointed that my work with him has only enabled him to hang on in a wretched situation. I had hoped that with my loving support he would have long ago begun a new chapter in his life.

Love is patient. Okay. I'll keep loving and waiting. How long, Lord? In my impatience I raise the question. But I don't really need an answer. I just need patience.

Patiently, Lord Jesus, you abide with me through all my stumblings and failings; grant me the patience to do likewise with those who need my love. Amen.

Week 14, Saturday   Waiting Patiently for Wholeness

. . . so that you may not become sluggish, but imitators of those who through faith and patience inherit the promises.

—Hebrews 6:12

For many men, one of the most difficult tasks of life is achieving a sense of spiritual wholeness, of feeling—as an old hymn puts it—that "it is well with my soul." We can find encouragement in the fact that the writer of Hebrews identified faith and patience as two qualities important to inheriting the promises of God. Those promises include, as Jesus taught us (John 10:10), both abundant life now and eternal life with God. In other words, faith and patience are both integral parts of achieving spiritual wholeness.

Faith as a tool of reaching wholeness is easy to understand. But why patience? Because wholeness doesn't come easily and it doesn't come quickly. You exercise patience, therefore, when you make the following covenant with God:

> I will continue to believe in you and follow you no matter what is happening in my life. I don't like some of the things that happen to me. I don't understand some of them. But when those things happen, I will remind myself that I am your child and you are my God, that I am nested in your hands of love. And then, O God, I will patiently wait upon you as you lead me to the fulfillment of your promises.

Forgive my impatience, Lord God, and continue to lead me to spiritual wholeness by the power of your Spirit. Amen.

Read Proverbs 31:10-12.

"More precious than jewels." In my experience, that's what most men want—a mate whom they can treasure beyond anything else on this earth. It can happen. But it doesn't happen simply because you are a Christian and you marry a Christian. More than one Christian has been sadly disappointed by a marriage that failed.

Today and for the next three days I want to reflect on one of the tools that is crucial for helping you avoid such a disappointment: openness. To be open doesn't mean that you are transparent, that you bare all or are an "open book." It does mean, though, that you are honest about the way you think and feel and that you share your thoughts and feelings.

One reason men are disappointed with the quality of their marriages is that they don't open up and share their feelings with their wives. A man who had a hard time doing this told me that his wife helped him by encouraging—and occasionally even prodding—him to talk to her. "I made a wonderful discovery," he said. "As I talked to my wife about some of my deepest feelings, it did more than make her feel closer to me. I felt closer to her as well."

We serve a Lord who told us that he has made known to us "everything that I have heard from my Father" (John 15:15). His openness with us is a model for our openness with each other.

Jesus, help me to follow your example of openness as I relate to those I love. Amen.

Read Matthew 8:5-13.

If we were to stand in the presence of Jesus, I believe we would all feel as the centurion did in today's scripture—unworthy. How could anyone not be overawed by the Son of God? I also believe that Jesus would respond to each of us as he responded to the centurion—he would bless us in accord with our faith.

Indeed, he does bless us in accord with our faith. The stronger my faith, the more blessed I feel. For that reason, I have often uttered the same prayer as the father of the sick son that Mark's Gospel tells us about: "I believe; help my unbelief!" (Mark 9:24).

I don't feel completely comfortable with that prayer. I'd like to be able to say that I have never been disappointed with my spiritual progress and that my faith is and always has been unwavering. Yet that isn't true. And God knows it isn't true. So part of my openness with God is acknowledging my doubts and praying for grace to have an ever firmer faith.

Openness is difficult. It is also liberating. It's wonderful to be able to share openly with God my own spiritual limitations. For then I hear his reassuring word that I am forgiven. And so once again "I press on toward the goal for the prize of the heavenly call of God in Christ Jesus" (Philippians 3:14).

Lord Jesus, I believe. Help my unbelief, that I may grow into your likeness and be your good and faithful servant. Amen.

Week 15, Tuesday   **Openness with Friends**

Bear one another's burdens, and in this way you will fulfill the law of Christ. —Galatians 6:2

Some men think they have to bear their burdens on their own—it's part of being a real man. Others think that all they need is to let God take over their burdens. But the Bible teaches that an important part of dealing with our burdens is sharing them with one another. We are not called together in a church in order to put on a happy face and pretend that everything is great because we are all Christians. We are called to support one another.

At a men's retreat, four of us gathered to chat one evening. I knew that one of the young men had been struggling both in his career and in his love life. In the relaxed and open atmosphere, he began to talk about his problems. For perhaps two hours, we sat around and listened and encouraged him. At the end, he acknowledged that it had been a transforming experience. He went on to make a career change and to settle some matters in his love life.

By sharing his burdens with trusted friends, he found relief and insights that enabled him to set out on a new course. You don't want to share your burdens with everyone, of course. But let someone you trust share a part of your load. You both will be richer for it.

Let me willingly bear the burdens of others, O God, as well as willingly let others share my own burdens, that I might fulfill the law of Christ my Lord. Amen.

Week 15, Wednesday   **Openness with Other Christians**

Read Matthew 18:15-17.

Disappointments with fellow Christians happened early in my Christian life. I'm not talking about disappointment in the sense that I am better than others, but in the sense that Christian people acted in a way that fell dramatically short of my expectations. I remember the first time it happened to me. I was a teenager and a new Christian. I saw another member of my church in a store and went over to him expecting to be greeted warmly as a fellow believer. Instead, I received what seemed to be a cool and indifferent "Hi, Bob."

It seems trivial, but at the time it unsettled me. Subsequently, I have been unsettled by such things as Christians angrily hurling insults at each other in church business meetings and pastors making caustic remarks about other pastors.

What do you do when you are disappointed with a fellow Christian? Jesus said to confront the person openly. Paul illustrated the point by being open and frank with the churches: e.g., "My little children," he wrote to one church, "for whom I am again in the pain of childbirth until Christ is formed in you, . . . I am perplexed about you" (Galatians 4:19). The alternative is quiet resentment, and I've practiced that too often. I have found that only in open discussion is there healing for my disappointment and the hope of restoration in the relationship.

Resentment somehow seems more natural than openness, Father, but grant me the strength to be open with those who have disappointed me. Amen.

Read 2 Corinthians 1:23–2:4.

Have you ever been discouraged as you tried to serve your Lord? You're unusual if you haven't. A friend of mine became so discouraged with drawn-out, wrangling committee meetings that he no longer attends church. It's easy to get discouraged when people don't behave or respond as you think they should.

Such discouragement is nothing new. Paul felt it over and again because of the conflict, divisions, and immorality in the churches. Yet in the midst of discouragement we hear his call to persevere: "If we endure, we will also reign with him" (2 Timothy 2:12).

Whenever I think of perseverance in the face of discouragement I think of a Japanese pastor who told me of his first efforts to minister to Japanese people in the United States. He began his work in a midwestern city, distributing pamphlets to Japanese families about a worship service to be held for them. On the appointed day, one man showed up. The pastor waited, but no one else came. Finally, he said to the man that they would sing. "Unfortunately, I can't sing," the pastor told me, "and he couldn't sing either, so we gave up singing." The pastor then preached his sermon. And the one man in his congregation fell asleep!

But the pastor persevered and eventually built a Japanese Christian congregation. He knew that our calling is not to carve out success, but to be faithful in service. God will provide whatever success is needed.

Jesus Savior, you persevered for me unto the cross, and God raised you from the dead. By your grace, I will keep on serving you in my situation, no matter how difficult, trusting you for the outcome. Amen.

Week 15, Friday   **Persevering in Helping Others**

Read Exodus 17:1-7.

How often, do you think, was Moses ready to chuck his responsibility as Israel's leader and give up on the contentious group of people he was trying to help? Can you imagine what it was like to devote your life to helping people only to have them get so angry that they almost stone you to death?

Trying to help others can be exhausting, frustrating, and discouraging. Mother Teresa knew discouragement and urged other Christians not to give in to it. If you get discouraged, she wrote, "it is a sign of pride because it shows you trust in your own powers" (*Total Surrender,* Ann Arbor, Servant Publications, 1985, p. 119). It's difficult not to get discouraged, she noted, because we all want to reap success from our efforts to help others. But you must leave the success to Jesus and persevere in your efforts. Your job is not to make things right in people's lives. It is to give what support, guidance, or help you can so that God can make things right.

If you persevere in helping others, you will know the joy of serving God. At the end of his life, Moses remembered not the agonies but the victories. He blessed the people and rejoiced with them over God's grace:

> Happy are you, O Israel! Who is like you,
>   a people saved by the LORD,
> the shield of your help.
> > —Deuteronomy 33:29

I want to minister to others as you ministered, Lord Jesus. Help me to persevere and to leave the results to you. Amen.

Week 15, Saturday   Persevere in Overcoming Bad Habits

I have learned to be content with whatever I have.
> *—Philippians 4:11*

Paul was not always content with whatever he had. He wrote to the Corinthians that "a thorn was given me in the flesh, a messenger of Satan to torment me, to keep me from being too elated" (2 Corinthians 12:7). Three times he appealed to God to take the trouble away. But it wasn't taken away. Instead, Paul learned that God's grace was sufficient to enable him to deal with it.

Although he didn't lose the thorn, whatever it was, he did overcome another problem—his lack of contentment. Note, however, that it didn't happen quickly. Paul prayed three times, over an unknown period of time, which meant at least two relapses before he learned to be content in spite of having the thorn.

I find this to be a very instructive incident. A crucial principle of growing in grace is that you must persevere in getting rid of old habits, old ways of thinking, old ways of behaving. It took time for Paul to surmount the habit of discontent. It will take time for you to discard the habits you would like to abandon. Keep in mind, however, that perseverance is necessary because you will probably have relapses. Whether the habit is smoking, excessive drinking, obscene thoughts, a quick temper, or anything else, Jesus will give you the power to overcome it, if you persevere in your efforts.

Jesus, Lord, I need your power to enable me to overcome
_____. *Thank you for helping me persevere. Amen.*

Week 16, Sunday   Prayer: Preventive Spiritual Medicine

Rejoice always, pray without ceasing, give thanks in all circum-
stances; for this is the will of God in Christ Jesus for you.
                                                    —1 Thessalonians 5:16-18

There is an old story about a businessman in deep trouble who prayed: "Lord, I haven't bothered you for seven years now, and if you get me out of this, I promise not to bother you for at least seven more."

We laugh at his missing the point of prayer. But who of us hasn't been guilty of a similar attitude? Prayer is not merely a divine aspirin to be taken only when dealing with the aches and pains of life. As we shall see over the next few days, prayer is a key resource in dealing with problems and challenges. But it is also an ongoing relationship with God. If we reserve prayer for only those times when we're in trouble, our prayers may sound as mindless as the businessman's.

We can think of praying as a form of preventive spiritual medicine. The more we pray, the closer we feel to God. The more we pray, the more natural prayer will be for us. The more we pray, the easier it will be to turn to God to help us deal with times of adversity.

"Put on the whole armor of God," Paul counseled (Ephesians

6:11), for we are involved in warfare. An effective soldier goes into battle with familiar weapons. An effective Christian enters the battle of life with the weapon of prayer as a familiar friend. Thus, when the severe struggles come, connecting with God through prayer is as natural as breathing; for, like breathing, we do it without ceasing.

I come to you in prayer now, Father, and ask you to nudge me frequently by your Spirit to remind me of my ongoing need to talk to you. Amen.

Week 16, Monday   **Honest and Submissive Prayer**

Read Mark 14:32-42.

"How do I know what to pray for?" a friend with problems asked me. "Should I just pray that God's will be done? Somehow, that isn't completely satisfying to me."

I sympathized with him. I've struggled with how to pray. It's comforting to know that the disciples also struggled and asked Jesus to teach them how to pray. In his teaching, and in his own prayers, we can learn how to pray about our problems.

It was in the Garden of Gethsemane that Jesus gave us the answer to my friend's questions. Be both honest and submissive. How do you know what to pray for? Pray for what you want, what you would like to happen. That's an honest prayer. It's what Jesus did. He asked the Father, if at all possible, to enable him to avoid the cross. He shrank from the pain and degradation of that end to his earthly life.

How do you know if that's what God wants? You don't. So, like Jesus, you tell God what you want, then tell him that you submit to his will—whatever it is. That's a submissive prayer. For example, you could pray this way: "Father, I need more income. Help me to find a better job. But if, for some reason, I can serve you better where I am, your will be done." Such prayer is satisfying. You are free to voice your desires and complaints to God and then let the matter rest in God's hands.

Father, help me as I pray to be both honest and submissive. I bring you now my desires and complaints, knowing that you love and care for me. But most of all, I want your will to be done. Amen.

Week 16, Tuesday — A Spiritual Swiss Army Knife

Read James 5:13-18.

My daughter always carries a Swiss army knife with her. She tells me that it's a marvelous tool that enables her to deal with all sorts of problems. You just choose the part of the knife you need—to cut, to tighten a screw, to pry something, or even to eat.

I think of prayer as a spiritual Swiss army knife. This passage in James tells why. Are you suffering? Are you sick? Have you sinned? Is there trouble in the land? Whatever the problem, prayer is one of your spiritual tools. But James speaks of different kinds of prayer. Like a Swiss army knife, prayer is not just one thing.

You should pray about your troubles and concerns. However, James also suggests that if you are sick, call for the church elders and have them pray over you. This is a much neglected form of prayer. James says to pray for one another. How often have you asked a family member or friend to pray for you?

When there was trouble in the land, Elijah "prayed fervently." How often has your prayer been not merely words, but words sent to God clothed in intense feelings?

Prayer is a crucial part of dealing effectively with problems. Don't limit its effectiveness by confining it to a single form. Pray yourself. Enlist others to pray for you. And let your feelings be a part of the prayers you offer to God.

Father, give me the courage to ask others to pray for me, and the honesty to be open with you about all my needs and my feelings. Amen.

Week 16, Wednesday — The Pressure of God's Hands

Read Psalm 16.

David begins this beautiful psalm with a plea for God's protection and ends it with a song of praise for the joy of God's presence. I find myself resonating with this psalm. I too feel the need for God's protection, and I have learned that the ultimate in experiencing that protection is the joyous presence of God in my life. After all, if I sense that I am in God's hands, if I experience the caring presence of the Creator of the universe, I am secure.

As Paul put it, "If God is for us, who is against us?" (Romans 8:31). Or as David said in another Psalm (27:1): "The LORD is my light and my salvation; / whom shall I fear? / The LORD is the stronghold of my life; / of whom shall I be afraid?"

A man who was a mentor to me shared the various struggles he had gone through. What had he learned in it all? "There are many pressures on us," he said, "but we also need to feel the pressure of God's hands upon us." It is by our constant, regular prayer that we will feel the pressure of God's hands upon us, because prayer is a way of practicing the presence of God. And with the pressure of God's hands upon us, we are secure, well equipped to deal with all the challenges and problems of life.

As I pray to you each day, Father, help me to feel the pressure of your hands upon me that I may rest securely in you. Amen.

Week 16, Thursday   Serving Is Healing

Read 1 Peter 4:1-11.

Peter wrote his first epistle to Christians who were suffering for their faith. One of the many things he tells them may sound surprising: he urges them to continue to serve others. "Like good stewards of the manifold grace of God, serve one another with whatever gift each of you has received" (1 Peter 4:10). I can imagine some of those who first heard Peter's words responding with dismay: "Serve? That's the last thing on my mind, Peter. I appreciate your words of hope and encouragement, but I don't have the time or energy to think about serving."

This would be an understandable reaction. Suffering of any kind tends to absorb all our attention and strength. It turns the focus inward, not outward. But there is godly wisdom in Peter's words. The people I have known who have dealt best with their suffering continued to serve others in spite of their situations. I ministered to a dying woman who used her last weeks in the hospital to teach and comfort other patients. I ministered to a dying man who left a smile on the faces of those trying to care for him and who used the time to bring a loving and hope-filled closure to his family relationships.

I have known other men who, in spite of personal struggles, continued to serve others and found healing for themselves. They discovered the truth in Peter's counsel, that serving is healing for the server as well as for the one being served.

Even when I am struggling, Lord God, help me to continue to look for ways to serve others, that I may follow the example of Jesus my Savior. Amen.

Week 16, Friday   Serving at Work

Read Acts 18:1-4; 1 Corinthians 9:12-18.

"I know very few people who really love their work," a friend said while complaining about his own job. Actually, I do know a number of such people. Yet I also know a lot who would rate their work as satisfactory but certainly not the most thrilling part of their lives. And I know many who would change their jobs in a minute if a good opportunity arose.

How do you suppose Paul, Aquila, and Priscilla felt about making tents to support themselves? Would they have preferred to use that time to preach and teach? Perhaps. But the work had a purpose other than mere support. In his letter to the Corinthians, Paul pointed out that he worked so there would be no "obstacle in the way of the gospel of Christ" (1 Corinthians 9:12). He wanted no one to claim that he was profiting from his preaching.

Clearly, work was part of Paul's ministry. And that is a Christian way to view work. Your work may be stressful. Your boss may be insufferable. You may be underpaid and overworked. Even so, think of your work as part of your ministry. One man told me that he makes a point of talking to coworkers who are shunned or neglected by others in order to let them know that someone cares about them.

What are you, as a Christian, called to do at your place of work? Remember—serving is healing.

Lord Jesus, how can I serve you through my work? Help me to be alert for the opportunities you present to me. Amen.

Week 16, Saturday   **Use Afflictions to Serve**

Read 2 Corinthians 1:3-7.

The most perplexing question about afflictions is the question of why. Why me? Why now? Why this? But "why" is often an unanswerable question. It is more useful to raise the question of what. What now? What can I do? What purpose will this have in my life?

When the Corinthian Christians were struggling with various afflictions, Paul didn't even raise the question of why. Rather, he told them what would happen: God would console them and they would "be able to console those who are in any affliction with the consolation with which we ourselves are consoled by God" (2 Corinthians 1:4).

What now? Now you will be better able to help others. A pastor told me that one of the most difficult times of his life was when his health broke. He was incapacitated for a long time. Eventually he regained his health and continued his ministry. A few years later his wife told him that since his illness he was much better at helping troubled people than he had ever been. Similarly, a young man who suffered a serious accident told me that, while he couldn't understand why it happened to him, he knew he would be uniquely prepared to help others with similar experiences.

God doesn't *send* afflictions in order to make his people better consolers; he *uses* our afflictions for that purpose. So when you face afflictions, don't get stuck in the impossible question of why. Troubles happen to everyone. The question is, What now, Lord?

Gracious Father, use my afflictions to make me a better and more useful servant of yours. Amen.

5
BEING A REAL CHRISTIAN

James W. Moore

Read Philippians 2:5-11.

Some years ago, there was a young professional baseball player who prided himself in being a great hitter. He knew that he could make it big in the major leagues if he could just get his chance.

For several years, he bounced around in the minor leagues. Then one year toward the end of the season, the major league parent team brought him up to help them as they were in the thick of a heated pennant race.

Finally, this was his chance. But he was promptly put on the bench! Day after day went by, the rookie was itching to bat, to show what he could do, to show the world that he was a great hitter—and he sat on the bench.

Then one day the manager called for the rookie to pinch-hit. This was the dramatic moment he had dreamed of for so long—a crucial game, last inning, score tied, a runner on first base. The rookie's heart pounded with excitement as he stepped into the batter's box. Routinely, he glanced down toward the third base coach—and couldn't believe his eyes! They were giving him the signal to sacrifice! His chance to make a great hit, and he was asked to bunt.

The rookie ignored the signal, took three hefty swings, and struck out. When he returned to the dugout, he was met by a red-faced, irate manager. "Son, what's the matter with you? Didn't you see the signal to sacrifice?"

"Yes, sir, I saw it," said the rookie, "but, I didn't think you meant it!"

"I saw it, but I didn't think you meant it!" Isn't that what we say to God? On page after page of the Scriptures, God says to us, "Sacrifice! Sacrifice! Love others! Lay down your life for others! Sacrifice yourself for the good of the team! Lose yourself! Be self-giving!"

That's what God says to us. That is God's signal to us. But we are not so sure he means it. Well, Jesus showed us that he means it—on a cross!

Teach me, O Lord, how to love and serve you and others as a living sacrifice. In the name of Christ I pray. Amen.

Week 17, Monday   Finding God in Unexpected Places

Read Genesis 28:16-17.

Some of the most memorable moments in the Scriptures tell of surprise meetings with God. Think of Moses, in exile in the wilderness; Jacob, wrestling with his soul; Job, grappling with tragedy, sorrow, heartache, and physical pain; Paul, on a vigilante hunt; Zacchaeus, perched up in a sycamore tree.

A few years ago, some close friends of ours in Tennessee suddenly and tragically lost their youngest daughter, Ellen. She was sitting in the den of their home one Sunday evening, laughing and talking with her mother. Suddenly, without warning, her leg went numb and then her arm. Then she fell back, paralyzed and unconscious. So quickly it had happened.

She was rushed to the hospital where brain surgery was performed. She died the next morning—sixteen years old!

When I got word of her death, I called to express my love, to try to minister to these dear friends. Instead, they ministered to me. Ellen's mother said: "God is giving us strength we didn't know we could have. He is seeing us through this. He keeps reminding us that we got to have Ellen for sixteen years and that she packed more life and love into sixteen years than most people do in a lifetime. We are all right. Don't worry about us because God is with us as never before."

"God is with us as never before." They had found God many

times before in expected places: in church, in the Scriptures, in prayer, at the altar, in joys and blessings and good times. But now he was there with them as never before in the unexpected place of tragedy and sorrow.

Remember how the apostle Paul put it, that nothing at all can separate us from God and his love (Romans 8:38-39).

God is always there . . . even in the most unexpected places!

O Lord, give me the eyes of faith that I may see you, the ears of faith that I may hear you, and the heart of faith that I may feel your presence even in the unexpected places. Amen.

Week 17, Tuesday   When Troubles Come

Read Exodus 14:13-15.

During the War Between the States at the Battle of Shiloh, a Union soldier from Ohio was wounded, shot in the arm. His captain saw that he was injured and barked out an order: "Gimme your gun, Private, and get to the rear!"

The private handed over his rifle and ran back toward the north seeking safety. But after covering two or three hundred yards, he came on another skirmish. So he ran to the east and happened on another part of the battle. Then he ran west and encountered more fighting. Finally, he ran back to the front lines and shouted: "Gimme my gun back, Cap'n. There ain't no rear to this battle!"

Precisely so. When it comes to the troubles of this world, "there ain't no rear to the battle!" We can't really run away and hide.

The only sensible answer is "to trust God and go forward." That's what Moses did when he was trapped at the Red Sea. He trusted God and went forward—and God opened a way. Notice that God didn't lead Moses around the Red Sea or over it or under it. He led him through it! And that's what he can do for us. He can deliver us from our troubles by leading us "through them."

When trouble erupts in our lives, we can remember Moses at the Red Sea. He didn't have all the answers, but he did stay in communication with God. He went forward to do the best he knew to do and he trusted God to bring it out right. We can do that too!

O God, you led Moses and the people not over or under or around the Red Sea but through it. Help me, O Lord, to trust you and go forward, in the name of Christ. Amen.

Week 17, Wednesday   "I Shall Be There!"

Read Exodus 3:13-14.

The great scholar Martin Buber said something toward the end of his life that touched me greatly. He was commenting on that wonderful scene in the book of Exodus where God appears to Moses in the burning bush. Moses asks God, "What is your name?" God answers, "I Am Who I Am."

After studying the Hebrew text for many years, Buber said he had come to the conclusion that we have mistranslated that verse. Instead of translating the name of God as "I Am Who I Am," it should read, "I Shall Be There"!

Isn't that beautiful? The name of God is "I Shall Be There"!

When you have to face the Pharaohs of life, the name of God is "I Shall Be There." When you are scared or lonely or depressed, the name of God is "I Shall Be There." When you face sickness or heartache, or even death, the name of God is "I Shall Be There." When you have to go to a cross, the name of God is "I Shall Be There." When you are laid out in a tomb, the name of God is "I Shall Be There." And when Easter morning comes, the name of God is "I Shall Be There."

Jesus knew it. That's why he was so strong. He knew who he was. He knew where he was going. He knew who was with him. Do you?

Eternal God, I thank you that you are always with me in every circumstance, even when I have to face the difficulties and challenges of life. I pray in Christ's name. Amen.

Week 17, Thursday   Is There Life After Stress?

Read Psalm 23:4.

Dr. Richard Hoffman of New York says that the three major killers of today's culture are "calendars, telephones, and clocks"—the "tyranny of an accelerated life."

What can we do about these killers? How do we cope? Is there life after stress? How do we withstand the onslaught? Here are three suggestions:

1. Travel light. Decide what is really important to you and give your energies to those things. We can't do everything, so we have to decide what really matters and weed out all the rest.

2. Take one step at a time. Do one thing at a time. Live one day at a time. Remember in the old elementary school reader the story about the clock that stopped? It figured out that it would have to tick more than thirty-one million times in one year. Overwhelmed by that thought, the clock just "up and quit" until someone reminded the clock that it wouldn't have to tick them all at once—"just one tick at a time."

Jesus spoke about this in the Sermon on the Mount when he told us, "Do not worry"—about health, food, drink, or the future (Matthew 6:25-34). We need to take life one day at a time, one thing at a time, one step at a time.

3. Relax our souls in God. Jesus' parable of the seed speaks to this (Mark 4:26-29). The idea is to sow the seed the best you can and trust God to bring the harvest. It doesn't matter if the odds are against you. It doesn't matter that things may seem hopeless sometimes. It doesn't matter how bleak the outlook. Don't worry about it. Just sow the seed, and leave the rest to God.

Teach me, O Lord, how to trust you and celebrate your love and grace. Remind me to relax my soul in you. I pray in the strong name of Jesus. Amen.

Week 17, Friday   **Best Friends**

Read John 3:16.

One of my favorite Broadway characters is Tevye from the wonderful musical *Fiddler on the Roof.* Tevye had such a beautiful relationship with God. He saw God as a real force in his life, as an intimate friend with whom he could share his joys and sorrows, his victories and defeats. He told God everything.

Tevye didn't talk to God in pious tones or sanctimonious phrases. He just talked to God like you would talk to your best friend, and he told him just what he thought. Sometimes Tevye would laugh with God and sometimes he would cry. Sometimes he would complain to God and sometimes he would rejoice. But always he told God what he was thinking and he knew deep down in his heart that God was listening, that God cared! For Tevye and God were friends, close friends!

Wouldn't that be the ultimate tribute for someone to say of you, "He and God were 'best friends'?" That's my prayer for all of us today. When our days are finished on this earth, when people think back and try to recall our best quality and the overriding theme of our life, I am hoping that they will remember most that we were best friends with God!

Thank you, Father, that you so loved the world—loved me—that you gave your only Son for me. I offer you my love in return. Amen.

Week 17, Saturday   God's Kinfolk

Read John 13:34-35.

There is a wonderful story about a woman in Birmingham who, on a cold winter morning, saw a little boy standing outside a bakery. It was snowing and sleeting and the little boy was barefooted and had no coat. He was trying to warm himself with the air coming up from the bakery grating.

The woman's heart went out to the boy. She couldn't stand seeing him shivering in the cold. She bought him a nice coat and some shoes and socks. He thanked her and headed for home, but then he turned back and asked her a surprising question: "Lady, are you God's wife?"

She was embarrassed by the question at first, but then she replied, "No, I'm not God's wife, but I am one of his children."

The little boy grinned and said, "I knew it! I knew it! I just knew you were some kin to him!"

Can people tell by the way you live that you are one of God's sons? That's something to think about, isn't it?

Father, help me to live this day in such a way that my kinship with you will be radiantly reflected. I pray in the name of Christ, our Lord. Amen.

Read Matthew 5:7-9; 25:31-46.

Some years ago in a respectable New York residential area, a twenty-eight-year-old woman named Kitty Genovese was attacked, beaten, and stabbed by a man who had followed her home. For some thirty minutes, the man beat and stabbed her as she screamed for help. Finally, she died. After it was all over, police found thirty-eight people who had watched the whole brutal murder process. Not one of them cared enough to act.

Finally, after the girl was dead and the killer gone, someone called the police. Do you know how long it took the police to get there? Two minutes. Two minutes after the call was made, police were on the scene. Kitty Genovese might well be alive today if one person out of thirty-eight had had enough compassion to help, enough concern to call the police. When questioned later, almost every one of the witnesses gave the same excuse: "I just didn't want to get involved!"

There is no such excuse for the Christian.

- Christian love demands that we get involved.
- Christian love demands that we hear the cries of those who are in trouble.
- Christian love will not permit us to close our eyes or look the other way when we see someone hurting.
- Christian love is compassionate, and compassion and action go hand in hand.

You see, the only thing more costly than caring is not caring!

O God, you sent your Son, Jesus Christ, to be the Savior of the world and the Prince of Peace. By the power of your Holy Spirit, put the spirit of mercy and compassion and peacemaking in me, so that I may put Christ's love into action. Amen.

Read Colossians 3:12-14.

I was only twelve years old when my father died. As we stood by his casket that evening, scores of people came by, all different kinds of people. Some were rich and some were poor, some were young and some were old, some were black and some were white, and some were Oriental. Some were professional people, some were laborers; some I knew quite well, some I had never seen before. But they all came, and they all said the same thing: "Jim, your dad was kind to me."

I determined then and there that the best tribute I could pay to my dad was to take up his torch of kindness. From that moment I have tried to be a kind person. I haven't always succeeded, but I have tried, and I am still trying to let my father's kindness live on in me.

Please hold that in your mind for a moment, and remember with me what a kind person Jesus was. We give up on people, we write them off, we conclude that there is no hope for them, we decide that they are beyond redemption. But Jesus never did that. He was kind to the end. He never relinquished his loving-kindness. Even on the cross, he was taking care of his mother and forgiving those who were putting him to death. To the very last, he was kind.

The best tribute we can pay him is to take up his torch of kindness; to love as he loved, to care as he cared, to forgive as he forgave, to live as he lived to the very last—in the spirit of kindness. The best tribute we can pay our Lord is to let his kindness live on in us.

O God, help me to live each day as a tribute to Christ. Continue his ministry of kindness and love through me. I pray in his holy name. Amen.

Week 18, Tuesday   You Can Soothe or You Can Seethe

Read Matthew 5:21-24.

In my opinion, there is nothing more destructive to our spirits than seething resentment. Resentment is a spiritual cancer. It can ruin your life. It can make you sick.

In his book *A Doctor's Case Book in the Light of the Bible* (New York, Harper, 1960, pp. 149-50), Dr. Paul Tournier tells of a woman who was treated for anemia for months without much success. As a last resort, the doctor decided to put her in a sanatorium. A preliminary blood test, however, discovered no sign of anemia. When the doctor himself rechecked her, he also found no anemia.

"Has anything out of the ordinary happened in your life since your last visit?" the doctor asked.

"Yes; something has happened," she replied. "I have suddenly been able to forgive someone against whom I bore a nasty grudge; and all at once I felt as if I could at last say 'Yes' to life!"

The woman's seething had made her ill, and when she stopped seething and soothed the situation, the impact was so great, so powerful, that it changed the physical state of her blood and made her well.

The choice is yours. You can encourage or you can discourage; you can soothe or you can seethe!

Deliver me, heavenly Father, from seething, brooding resentment. Bring me back to the forgiving spirit I see so powerfully in Christ our Lord, in whose name I pray. Amen.

Week 18, Wednesday   Justifying Our Existence

Read Philippians 1:21.

Our lives can be constructive and productive and creative. We can be peacemakers. We can be people who care, who help, who love, who serve, who act with compassion. We can bring healing where there is hurt.

Let me illustrate. In a *Peanuts* cartoon, Lucy decides that Linus has to learn to live without his security blanket. While he is taking a nap, she steals it and buries it in the dirt. When Linus wakes up he immediately misses his blanket and panics. He screams, shouts, pounds the floor, gasps for air, and cries, "I can't live without my blanket!" Then he faints.

Snoopy, the trusty dog, sees Linus's dilemma and rises to the occasion. He sniffs out the blanket, digs it up, and brings it back to Linus, who is relieved and ecstatic. Grabbing the blanket with one hand and Snoopy with the other, he kisses Snoopy, hugs him and pats him and thanks him over and over. The last picture shows Snoopy lying on his back on his doghouse, thinking, *Every now and then my existence is justified!*

Loving others, helping others, ministering to their hurts in the spirit of Christ—these are the justification for our existence.

Help me this day, O Lord, to bring healing where there is hurt, to bring hope where there is despair, to bring the Spirit of Christ to everyone I meet today. I pray in his name. Amen.

Week 18, Thursday   Forgetting What Lies Behind

Read Philippians 3:13-14.

I don't know a lot about boxing, but I know enough to understand two phrases that carry over into other dimensions of life. Recently I heard a former boxer use these two phrases on television about an upcoming fight. He predicted that one boxer, who had been very successful, would lose because, he said, "He has become a fat cat." The other boxer, he predicted, would win because "he is a hungry fighter."

I knew what he was talking about. "Fat cats" are those in any field who, because of their past successes, have become spoiled, lazy, complacent, self-satisfied, pompous, and prideful. The "hungry" are those in any field who are struggling, working, dreaming, reaching, grasping, sacrificing—willing to pay the price for achieving their dream.

Then my mind darted back to the Sermon on the Mount and the words of Jesus: "Blessed are those who keep on hungering and thirsting after righteousness" (Matthew 5:6, literal). And then I recalled the words of Paul in his letter to the Philippians: "Forgetting what lies behind and straining forward . . . I press on" (3:13-14).

We need to forget our past successes and keep looking for new challenges.

By the power and presence of your Holy Spirit, O God, give me the strength and endurance to keep running the race set before me. Put deep within me a hunger for righteousness. I pray in Christ's name. Amen.

Read 2 Timothy 4:7-8.

If it's true that practice makes perfect in music, golf, art, poetry, speaking, writing, even relating to others, it must be true that practice enhances the spiritual graces. If you want to have a good prayer life, there is only one way to do it—you just pray, pray, and pray some more. You have to work at it!

If you want to have a good grasp of the Bible, there is only one way. You study the Scriptures. Study, study, and study some more. Then read the Bible dictionaries and commentaries, and everything you can get your hands on about the Bible. That is the only way to do it.

If you want to be a good churchman, how do you do it? You get in the stream of the church, and you take advantage of all the opportunities it offers. You get involved and participate. You go expectantly, hoping, learning, and living your faith.

How do you become a good Christian? You live it, every day. You practice living the Christian life until you get it right. We either live the faith or we lose it. Every time we say no to Christ, the longer we put him off, the more difficult it becomes to say yes to him. And the more we say yes to him, the easier it becomes to go on saying yes to him and to life.

That's the choice that is open to us, spiritually, in our faith experience. We use it or we lose it!

O Lord, touch me afresh today with your amazing grace and then enable me to respond with a tenacious daily commitment to Christ, in whose name I pray. Amen.

Week 18, Saturday   **The Courage to Change**

Read 2 Corinthians 3:1-3.

In his book *How to Be a Successful Failure* (New York: Atheneum, 1978), Ernest Fitzgerald tells a fascinating story from an earlier time about a young man who was caught stealing sheep. He was charged and convicted. As a penalty, the villagers decided to brand his forehead with the letters "ST" meaning

"Sheep Thief." The brand was a constant source of shame to the young man. Penitent, he asked God for forgiveness to help him overcome his problem, and he determined not to be remembered as a thief. With courage, he began to live in a new way. He constantly performed small acts of kindness for everyone. He was kind, thoughtful, helpful, compassionate, and always dependable.

Years and years went by. One day a visitor asked the people of the village what the "ST" on the man's forehead stood for. Strangely, no one could remember. But, they told the visitor, they suspected that it stood for "SAINT"!

That's something to think about, isn't it?

Thank you, O Lord, for your power to redeem and to change me. Father, make me more like Christ, in whose name I pray. Amen.

Week 19, Sunday   "Outdo One Another in Showing Honor"

Read Romans 12:9-10.

Gary Smalley is one of America's best-selling authors and most popular speakers on human relationships. In one of his seminars, he does a very interesting thing. He pulls out his old violin. It's obviously an antique and also obviously in need of repair. It doesn't look like it could be worth much at all. In fact, it really looks like a piece of junk.

Smalley holds it up high for all to see. "Do you have any idea how much this violin is worth?" he asks. "This may surprise you, but it's actually worth close to one million dollars, because if you look through the opening on the face of the violin, you can see inside some very special words: '1722 Stradivarius.'"

"Ahhh!" responds the audience.

But Smalley continues: "I want you to go home and write on the forehead of your mate the word 'Stradivarius.' Write on the foreheads of your children 'Stradivarius.' Because they are much more valuable than any violin. If you will honor other people like that," he adds, "it will change your life. It's the greatest relationship principle I know of."

Now Jesus would like that counsel! As a matter of fact, he would enlarge it. He would say: "Write the word 'Stradivarius' on the forehead of every single person you meet. Honor them. Value them. Respect them. Appreciate them. Love them."

O God, help me to love the people in my life, and even the people I meet, in the same way that you have loved me in Christ. Use me as an instrument of your love and peace. Amen.

Week 19, Monday   Life Is Too Short for Littleness

Read Philippians 2:1-11.

Pettiness is a spiritual poison. To be petty according to Webster is to be "small in nature, trifling, mean or ungenerous." How often pettiness cuts us off from God, from other people, and from the church!

I am thinking of a man I know in another state who is a fine singer. He has an excellent tenor voice—but he has not sung in church for more than twenty years. Twenty-three years ago, he was active in his church's music program, sang in the choir, and was the church's main soloist.

Then he went to a convention in New York and discovered that some of the large churches in New York City pay their choir members. When he returned home, he gave his church an ultimatum: "Pay me, or I quit the choir!" The church declined his offer and he quit. The choir suffered his loss for a while, but soon enough someone came along to take his place. None of us are indispensable; the church rolls on. But that man has sulked for twenty-three years. He doesn't come to church regularly anymore; when he does, he sits in the congregation with bitterness written all over his face. He is mad most of the time; he is cynical and critical of the church, especially the music program; but people long ago stopped listening to him.

Here is a man who has wasted his talent and who has wasted twenty-three years. Think of what he has missed while making himself miserable through pettiness. Life is too short for littleness, and pettiness is a waste of time, talent, and energy.

Father, by the miracle of your redemptive power, put within me the spirit of magnanimity and forbearance. Give me bigness of spirit through Christ, our Lord. Amen.

Week 19, Tuesday   Seizing the Moment

Read Psalm 118:24.

The great preacher Phillips Brooks was preaching one Sunday morning in his Boston church. About halfway through his sermon, a man in the balcony stood up, came down the stairs, and walked down the center aisle to the front of the pulpit. Dr. Brooks stopped his sermon. "Can I help you?" he asked.

The man said, "Dr. Brooks, I'm so sorry to disturb your sermon, but I had to come down to the altar, and I had to come in this moment. For you see, two years ago, I sat in this church, and I was moved, genuinely touched. I wanted to come down and dedicate my life to Christ and the church. But I fought it off and I didn't come, and I have regretted it ever since. So, I promised God and I promised myself that if I ever felt that way again, I would seize the moment; I wouldn't put it off another second. I felt it again this morning, Dr. Brooks, so I had to do it. I had to come now. It's my time, my moment, and I just couldn't let it pass. I couldn't let it get away from me this time!"

When God calls, don't ignore him. Don't miss your moment. Seize the special moments in life, and celebrate them! Don't let those powerful, destiny moments slip through your fingers!

That's something to think about, isn't it?

Open my heart, Lord, to those special moments in which you break into my routine and challenge me. Through Christ, our Lord. Amen.

Week 19, Wednesday   Remembering to Forget

Read John 8:1-11.

Great men have always known that there are some things you are better off forgetting. The apostle Paul said that he would forget what lay behind him and would press on to what lay ahead (Philippians 3:13-14). He had learned that as wonderful as it is to remember, it is also good sometimes to forget. And it is sometimes good to intentionally remember to forget! Let me show you what I mean.

First, we may need to forget our past accomplishments. Past victories, if we dwell on them, can make us lazy, spoiled, or complacent. It's not healthy to live in the glow of past successes for too long. We must constantly press ahead, looking for new thresholds and new challenges.

Second, we may need to forget our past hurts—hurts that dampen our spirits, drain away our energies, and poison our souls. In other words, don't nurse grievances! Don't give in to self-pity! Don't wallow in heartaches! Put them behind you, and go on with life.

Third, we may need to forget our failures. Remember how the song puts it? "You can pick yourself up, dust yourself off and start all over again." No failure need be final. With God's help we can start over, make a new beginning, try again—and have a new life.

I know, Lord, that I can start over—but not alone! I can't do it without you. Give me, I pray, a new beginning and a new life through Jesus Christ, my Lord and Savior, in whose name I pray. Amen.

Week 19, Thursday   **We Know Who Holds the Future**

Read Matthew 25:14-30.

Some people are afraid of the future. They want as little change as possible.

The story is told about a group of people who gathered at the Hudson River in the last century to see the launching of the first steamship. Out of the crowd one man was heard to say in a cynical tone, "They'll never get her going." But they did. As the ship started up and moved out fast, the same man was heard to say, "They'll never get her stopped."

We are all too familiar with such skepticism.

Some years ago, Dr. Werner von Braun was speaking on the

subject of putting a man on the moon. When his lecture was over, he made the mistake that many speakers make—he asked if there were any questions. Immediately, a man's hand shot up. "Why can't you folks forget about getting people on the moon," he asked, "and just stay home and watch television like the good Lord intended for you to do?"

We are afraid of the unknown. The future has always been threatening to some people. The good news is that we don't have to be afraid because God is with us, God watches over us, and nothing, not even death, can separate us from him and his love through Christ. As the old gospel song puts it: "We know not what the future holds, but we know who holds the future."

Father, even though Jesus told us many times not to be afraid or anxious, I still have trouble trusting you. Help me to do my best today and trust you to bring it out right. I pray in Christ's holy name. Amen.

Week 19, Friday   Things Can Be Redeemed

Read 1 Corinthians 1:22-25.

I'm thinking of John Wesley's study desk. It's on display in his home in London. That same desk once belonged to a bookie. It was designed originally for taking bets, but it was redeemed into a place of spiritual power where John Wesley thought through and wrote down his greatest sermons.

I'm thinking of a little church in the Fiji Islands. They have there an unusual baptismal font, a large stone, deeply stained, with a portion of the top hollowed out to hold the water. It used to be called "The Killing Rock," the place where cannibals once brought their victims for the kill. It is now the place where they bring their babies to be baptized in the church.

Mostly though, I'm thinking of a cross and how the cross, once the emblem of suffering and shame, punishment and death, has been redeemed and now is the symbol of love and victory and forgiveness and life.

Through the power of Christ, things can be redeemed—and so can people like you and me.

Thank you, O God, for so loving the world that you sent your only Son to save me, to change me, to redeem me. I pray in his name. Amen.

Week 19, Saturday   **The Power of Your Influence**

Read Matthew 5:14-16.

Albert Schweitzer was one of the great men of history. He was an intellectual giant, a physician, a prominent Christian theologian, an oft-quoted author, a superb organist, and the world's foremost authority on the music of Bach. Some would have said that Schweitzer had the world at his feet.

However, look at what he did. When he was thirty, he renounced the promise of a great and prosperous European career to give the remaining forty years of his life to being a missionary jungle doctor in Africa. There Schweitzer built with his own hands a hospital and a settlement on the Ogowe River, and paid for medical supplies by giving organ recitals in Vienna, London, and Paris. In his lifetime, he was a crusader for world peace and a winner of the Nobel Peace Prize. He was one of the truly great men of our time. Though he died in 1965, his philosophy, especially his ethical code of reverence for life, of protecting life, is still with us.

Sometimes I have to admit that when I pick up a fly swatter at home and begin to stalk a fly, I think of Schweitzer and his reverence-for-life ethic, and I put the fly swatter down and shoo the fly out of the house!

I like what Norman Cousins said about him: "The greatness of Schweitzer . . . is not so much what he has done, but what others have done because of him and the power of his example. This is the real measure of the man."

Isn't that the real measure of every person? It's not so much what we do, but what we cause others to do. It's what others do because of us.

O Lord Jesus, my life has been changed because of you. Help me to live and serve in the power of your Spirit. Amen.

Read Colossians 3:12-17.

In the early days of the church, a rather strong-smelling incense was burned in the worship services and the aroma would saturate the clothing of those in church. When they left the church, they literally smelled of incense. People could tell by their fragrance that they had been to church, that they had been in the presence of God.

Today, when many churches do not use incense, and those that do are often so large any scent is lost, it is still possible to talk about a Christian's aroma. The fragrance of the totally committed Christian is gratitude—gratitude at all times and in all circumstances—unconditional gratitude.

Have you ever noticed that many of our greatest expressions of thanksgiving have come from people who did not have a lot of material things? Think about it:

David, pursued by King Saul;
Jesus, who had no place to lay his head;
Paul, in chains in prison;
Francis of Assisi, who was voluntarily poor;
Luther, in hiding for his life;
The Pilgrims, hungry, cold, and scared at Plymouth Rock;
Helen Keller, blind and deaf;
Mother Teresa, living among dying beggars.

Unconditional gratitude, gratitude with no strings attached— that was the watchword of their lives, because they knew God was with them. Life was hard, but God was with them. Times were tough, but God was with them. And that was all that mattered!

Thanksgiving in all circumstances—that's the fragrance of life! That's the aroma of a Christian.

O God, how can I ever express in words my gratitude to you for all you have done for me? Help me to live my thanks every day. Through Jesus Christ, my Lord and Savior. Amen.

Read Matthew 6:19-21.

When our son, Jeff, was five years old, he did something in church one Sunday morning that we have chuckled about for years. During the first hymn, the young minister standing next to me on the platform began laughing. "Look at your son," he whispered.

There on the first pew, five-year-old Jeff Moore was holding his hymnal out rather angelically in front of him—with two half-dollars squeezed into his eye sockets! They were held in place by a marvelous, mischievous squint!

Where in the world did he get the half-dollars? was my first thought.

My second was *Isn't that a great parable for life!* Jeff couldn't see the hymnal. He was just holding it out in front of him. He couldn't see anything because of the half-dollars in his eyes.

It happens that way with some people. Money and possessions become blinders! They give all their energy and time and effort to making money, to accumulating wealth, and become blind to everything else.

Of course it's important to make a living. But it's far more important to make a life. It's good to have money and the things money can buy. But every now and then we need to stop and be sure that we don't have blinders on and that we do have the things money can't buy!

Father, you have given me so many material blessings. I ask that I may not be blinded by them. Help me to seek above all your gifts that money can't buy: love, hope, forgiveness, mercy, and eternal life through your Son Jesus Christ. Amen.

Week 20, Tuesday　　　　　　　　　　　　　　**"I Am Here"**

Read Romans 8:31-39.

When Tex Evans first started out in the ministry, he served a church in a small town in Texas. One of his neighbors was a man named Mr. Gentry. Tex Evans noticed that Mr. Gentry worked in his yard a lot and that he always whistled as he worked. He would work with the roses in the front yard whistling away. Then he would move to the side yard and work with his tulips, still whistling. And when he went to the backyard to work in the vegetable garden, he would whistle even louder.

One day at the little store in the middle of the town, Tex mentioned something about the whistling Mr. Gentry.

"Do you know why Mr. Gentry always whistles when he is outside in the yard?" one of the old-timers asked.

"I have no idea," Tex replied.

The old-timer said quietly, "His wife is blind!"

Now Tex understood. Mr. Gentry's whistling was a way of saying to Mrs. Gentry, "I'm out here, dear. Now I'm back here." Or, "If you need me, call me, I'll hear you. I'm not far away. I'm not going to leave you."

In a sense, God is whistling for us today. He never stops letting us know that he loves us and is with us, if we will only listen for his voice. And he calls to us most loudly from a cross.

Thank you, Lord, for your constant love expressed through Jesus Christ who came and died and rose again that I might have life. In his name. Amen.

Week 20, Wednesday   When Someone You Love Dies

Read John 11:25-26.

When someone you love dies, remember the good news of our Christian faith—that God is on both sides of the grave, and nothing can separate us from him. God is there, and that's really all we need to know.

John Baillie underscores this in one of his books. He tells of an old country doctor who made his rounds in a horse-drawn carriage, accompanied by his dog. One day, the doctor went to visit a critically ill patient.

"How am I, doctor?" the man asked.

The doctor replied, "It doesn't look good."

Both men were quiet for a while. Then the man asked, "What's it like to die, doctor?"

As the old doctor sat there trying to think of some words of comfort, he heard his dog coming up the stairs. Then, because the door was shut, the dog began to scratch at the door to get in.

"You hear that?" the doctor said. "That's my dog. He's never been in this house before. He doesn't know what's on this side of the door. But he knows that his master is in here. And because of that he knows that everything is all right.

"Death is like that," he continued. "We've never been there and we don't know what's on the other side of the door. But we know our Master is there. And because of that we know that everything is all right."

God loves us. He cares for us. And he has prepared a place for us and he is there—that's all we need to know. When someone you love dies, remember, our faith teaches us, God is on both sides of the grave.

I thank you, Lord, that Christ is the resurrection and the life, and through faith in him, we can be resurrected, too. I pray in his name. Amen.

Week 20, Thursday   "The Least of These"

Read Matthew 25:31-40.

One of the most remarkable and beloved persons of this century was the dedicated Catholic nun Mother Teresa who died in 1997. She spent her life working among the destitute and dying, first in Calcutta, where she also established a leper colony, and then through other Missionaries of Charity homes in many countries.

Mother Teresa was noted for her magnanimity. When the patients were demanding, irritable, and rude, she never got offended; she just kept on loving them. She possessed a secret that enabled her to forgive and understand and care—a secret that she shared with her Missionaries of Charity and with the rest of us. She made it a spiritual practice to look at every patient as Jesus himself in disguise. Here is the prayer with which she began each day, entitled "Jesus, My Patient":

Dearest Lord, may I see you today and every day in the person of your sick, and whilst nursing them, minister unto you. Though you sometimes hide yourself behind the unattractive disguise of

---

131

the irritable, the exacting, the unreasonable, may I still recognize you and say, "Jesus, my patient, how good it is to serve you." Lord, give me this seeing faith, then my work will never be monotonous. I will ever find joy in humoring the fancies and gratifying the wishes of all poor sufferers. O beloved sick, how doubly dear you are to me when you personify Christ and what a privilege is mine to be allowed to tend you. Amen.

What a difference it would make in us and in our world if you and I could somehow learn this spiritual practice, and relate to every person we meet as if that person were Jesus Christ himself in disguise.

Dearest Lord, open my eyes that I may see you today in every person I meet. Teach me how to serve you in little things as well as in big ones. I pray in Christ's name. Amen.

Week 20, Friday   Where Is Happiness to Be Found?

Read Colossians 3:12-17.

Some years ago in Paris, a handsome and obviously wealthy young man went to see a psychiatrist. "Please help me," he said. "I feel so empty inside. I'm bored to tears. I'm depressed and unhappy most of the time. My life is going nowhere. Please help me."

The psychiatrist, an older man, looked at this young man with a twinge of envy. But then he remembered Grimaldi, the most notorious playboy in Paris and the most admired leader of the Jet Set in France. "I know what you need to do to find happiness," he told the young man. "Go to Grimaldi. He will teach you how to enjoy life. Grimaldi will show you how to be happy. Yes, that's what you need to do. Go to Grimaldi!"

"But, sir," said the young man, "I am Grimaldi!"

Where is happiness to be found? Not out there somewhere! Not in places to go or things to do or stuff to swallow. No, happiness is within! Happiness is a by-product of being in right relationship with God and with other people. It's a by-product of usefulness. It's a by-product of commitment to Christ and his cause. It's a by-product of gratitude, of celebrating every day as God's gift to us.

Heavenly Father, I praise and thank you for all that you have given me. In gratitude I surrender my life to you to find true fulfillment, for Christ's sake. Amen.

Week 20, Saturday   Christianity Is a Lifestyle

Read Luke 9:57-62.

The story is told about a businessman who announced to his office staff one day that he was going on a diet. However, the very next day he arrived at the office with a large coffee cake in hand. "What happened?" his colleagues asked. "We thought you were going on a diet."

"I was," the man replied, "but as I was on my way to the office this morning, I passed by a bakery and saw this incredibly sumptuous-looking coffee cake on display in the window. So I prayed, 'God, if you really want me to have that coffee cake for breakfast this morning, please find me a parking spot right in front of the bakery.' And sure enough, there it was—the eighth time around the block, there it was!"

All of us can laugh at that story, and for some of us who have a sweet tooth it hits home. The truth is that too many of us treat our Christian faith the same way. We say we are committed to Christ, but we also want to go our own way, to keep on with our own lifestyle. But being a Christian is serious business. It is commitment to Christ with every fiber of our being.

You see, Christianity is not merely a set of intellectual ideas, not merely a collection of theological doctrines, not merely a series of philosophical arguments. It is a way of life! It is a constant, daily lifestyle. It is not only a way of believing; it is also a way of behaving. Our Christian faith is not just something we celebrate in the sanctuary one day a week; it is something we live out in the world every day, something we demonstrate and share with others at home, in the office, on the street, on the tennis court, even on a date. It is commitment to Christ with all our heart, soul, mind, and strength.

Through the presence of your Holy Spirit in my mind and heart, help me, O Lord, to do more than just talk a good game. Empower me to live each day committed to Christ, in whose name I pray. Amen.

6
ON THE WAY
TO CHRISTIAN MANHOOD

Paul E. Miller

Now the LORD came and stood there, calling as before, "Samuel! Samuel!" And Samuel said, "Speak, for your servant is listening."   *—1 Samuel 3:10*

At our church's Christmas Eve service, I had just finished reading the story of Jesus' birth from Luke 2. In the moment of silence before going on with the service, I thought I heard a child's voice timidly begin to sing. The whole congregation listened intently as three-year-old Sarah sang, "Happy birthday to you, / Happy birthday to you, / Happy birthday, dear Jesus, / Happy birthday to you." By the time she reached "dear Jesus," Sarah was singing boldly and the power of her voice echoed in the sanctuary. The richness of the experience settled in on us as we sat in silence. A child in her innocence had connected the ancient story to a modern celebration. The birth of Jesus was more than a piece of history. It was a present reality, not only for Sarah but for all of us.

Samuel responds similarly to God's calling in the night. "If God is talking, I should be listening." Indeed, God called Samuel as a child to bear a very important message to Eli, the priest. In his innocence, Samuel did just as God asked him to do. From this humble beginning, Samuel grew to be a powerful leader for God's people.

As we grow older and "mature," we tend to let go of our childlike innocence. Instead of being spontaneous, we become cautious. Instead of listening, we argue. Instead of responding to God, we

---

rationalize away the messages. Sarah helped me regain a bit of the innocence that allows me to hear God speaking to me every day.

O God of surprises, strip away my sophistication so that I might experience you in new and fresh ways. Restore my innocence that I might once again be amazed at all that you do. Amen.

Week 21, Monday   **God Is Revealed in New Ways**

God is spirit, and those who worship him must worship in spirit and truth.   *—John 4:24*

The question for the confirmation class was: Where and how do you discover God? Bradley was the first to answer, "I discover God when I travel and see things that God has made." It did not require much encouragement to get him to share more. He told excitedly of the many trips he had taken with his family. At each spot they visited, Bradley noticed the creative hand of God at work. On their first trip to Maine, he encountered the power and majesty of the ocean. The beauty of glacial streams and lakes captured his attention on a trip to Canada. In the Rockies, Bradley was amazed by the elk, deer, and bear. Everywhere they went, Bradley discovered God in new ways.

When I asked the question of the confirmation class, I had expected to hear other answers: "in worship," "at church camp," "in Sunday school," "reading my Bible," "from leaders in my church." My thoughts ran along more traditional lines. Bradley expanded the limits and encouraged the rest of the class to move beyond "Sunday school" answers.

Sometimes my thinking needs to be jolted. It is so easy to stay in a spiritual rut, giving answers without much thought. But God is spirit and therefore not limited in any way. To really worship God, we must remain open to encountering the divine in all times and places. If we are willing to look with eyes of faith, we will see the Creator reflected in all of life.

Thank you, O God, for all the ways you reveal yourself. Open my eyes and my mind so that I might discover you in new and exciting ways. Amen.

Immediately aware that power had gone forth from him, Jesus turned about in the crowd and said, "Who touched my clothes?"
—*Mark 5:30*

Jesus' question seems absurd. He is in a crowd of people who are pushing against him trying to get closer. And he asks who touched his clothes! Because he felt power go out from him, he is aware that someone has touched him in a purposeful way. Something happened that was more than just the hustle and bustle of the crowd.

Different kinds of touches have different meanings and carry different significances. Some bring comfort and some make us uncomfortable. The intention of the person touching us has a lot to do with how we receive or experience the touch.

Parishioners have frequently commented to me about the fact that when I baptize a baby, the baby is so calm and peaceful. Sometimes the baby has been crying in its parents arms and stops when it is given to me. This change has been so dramatic at times that the congregation has been amazed by it. But it really is not difficult to understand. A baby is very sensitive to the muscle tension of the person holding it. Usually, the parents who are presenting the child for baptism are nervous, anxious that things may not go well. The child picks up this stress and responds in like manner. On the other hand, I have baptized hundreds of little ones and have always been comfortable holding babies. When they sense my relaxed muscles, they relax as well.

It is easy to forget how interconnected and interrelated all of creation really is. I tend to think in terms of our separateness instead of our unity. But we are truly one in Christ and even my intentions have a powerful effect upon others.

Great Physician, heal me with a sense of your arms holding me. And use my arms and my hands to bring a deep and abiding sense of peace to others. Amen.

Week 21, Wednesday   **Fear Will Not Stop Me**

David said to Saul, "Let no one's heart fail because of him; your servant will go and fight with this Philistine." —*1 Samuel 17:32*

Such courage! David was a young boy and Goliath was a giant. Yet, he was not afraid. Remembering all the times that he had fought the wild animals in the night and won, David faced this danger with courage.

Stewart was just ten years old. He had always been a timid boy. Observing was more his style than performing. The very thought of being up in front of a crowd terrified him. But he loved to sing. Because of a friend's encouragement, Stewart joined our children's choir. When it was time for them to sing for a worship service, Stewart began to back out. His stomach started to do all sorts of strange things. "It feels like there are butterflies in there." Putting my arm around him, I confided that I felt the same way every Sunday as I stood to preach. He looked at me with disbelief that slowly changed to acceptance that I was telling the truth. Still trembling a little, he took his place with the choir. After the anthem was over, the smile on his face revealed the pride that Stewart felt. He had done it!

We are not called upon to be fearless. It is part of human nature to feel fear. Sometimes fear saves us from real danger. But sometimes fear keeps us from doing what is good and right. In those moments, it is helpful to admit our fear and then to move on ahead with a courage that comes from knowing that what we are doing is right.

O God of courage, come and dwell in me. I am ready to do what is right. Lead me forward and I will fight the good fight. Amen.

Week 21, Thursday   God Can Use Anything We Offer

There is a boy here who has five barley loaves and two fish. But what are they among so many people?

—John 6:9

When Angie and Suzy were in grade school, the song "We Are the World" hit the popular charts. The music industry was trying to make a difference in the world by calling attention to famine on the African continent. The girls asked why the church couldn't get involved. Rather than trying to explain all that our church was already doing, I simply promised to take their request to the next staff meeting. To my surprise, the senior pastor asked the girls to find three other friends who would be willing to work with them to prepare a special worship service on world hunger.

The children led a Sunday morning worship service based on John 6:9, the little boy's willingness to share what he had. We all sang "We Are the World" and examined our own willingness to share the blessings that we had received. Self-help crafts from various African countries were sold and a special world hunger offering was received. Together, under the leadership of the children, we made a difference in our world.

Sometimes I find myself waiting until I have more resources before moving ahead. But God can use whatever we offer, now. Each of us has something to give, to share, to make a difference in our world. We don't need more to begin. Offer up what you have and let God perform the miracles.

Generous and loving God, you give your good gifts to all of us according to your grace, not our merits. Help me to give generously, like you do, so that I too may experience miracles of multiplication. Amen.

Week 21, Friday   We See Differently with Eyes of Faith

Jesus, looking at him, loved him and said, "You lack one thing; go, sell what you own, and give the money to the poor, and you will have treasure in heaven; then come, follow me."
—Mark 10:21

The rich man did not expect this response from Jesus. Perhaps there was a commandment he could obey more perfectly. But to get rid of his possessions was asking too much. Or was it? Jesus knew the man had placed his sense of security in material blessings. Jesus also knew that these things provide no lasting security. The man was offered the greatest security of all, to become a follower of Jesus. He was invited to see things differently.

Once a year, the children in our church gather for a Liturgical Arts Day. After reviewing the seasons of the Christian year and the symbols appropriate for each, the children are invited to select a season and create their own work of art for that season. Two months later, their art is gathered, matted and framed, and held for display in the church narthex during the appropriate season.

Katie, eight years old, had selected Lent for her project. When she finished her picture and showed it to her mother, she was surprised by her mother's reaction, who did not think a clown was "appropriate" for the Lenten season. But upon closer examination, she noticed the reflection of the cross in the eyes of the clown and the tear running down his cheek. The picture had captured the introspective mood of the Lenten season. It invited all who saw it to reflect upon their own lives, especially in relationship to the cross.

It is important to see life through the eyes of faith. It changes our perceptions of security and gives us new understandings of our journey as followers of Christ.

Precious Savior, show me where I have misplaced my trust. I renew my commitment to be a faithful follower of yours. Amen.

Week 21, Saturday   Transformation Is Always Possible

Then the woman left her water jar and went back to the city. She said to the people, "Come and see a man who told me everything I have ever done! He cannot be the Messiah, can he?"
—John 4:28-29

Jimmy was just four years old but already he had been kicked out of three different preschool programs. He was uncooperative and disruptive to the classes. He came to our preschool already labeled a failure. His parents begged us to admit him and promised to be in regular contact with his new teacher. They would do anything to cooperate if we would just take him.

Jimmy was placed in Mrs. Hiss's class. She had been teaching the four-year-olds in that room for over twenty years. Discipline was never a problem, not because she was a stern person but because she created an environment in which the children wanted to participate. After Jimmy's third day, the parents insisted on having a parent/teacher conference. They were very anxious to know what was happening, because there had been no complaints.

When asked why Jimmy wasn't a problem, Mrs. Hiss replied that she didn't know. When asked what her secret was, she shared that her approach had been the same with Jimmy as it had been with the other children. She lovingly invited him to cooperate and to participate in doing the things that she had planned for the day. He had not created any problem at all for her or the class.

No one, not even a little boy who was kicked out of three preschools, is beyond the transforming power of love. The woman at the well experienced a similar transformation when Jesus accepted her just as she was and invited her to become all that she could be.

God of grace and God of mercy, may I feel your love flowing through my life. Give me the courage to share love with each person I encounter, knowing that it will make a difference in their lives and in mine. Amen.

Week 22, Sunday   God Surprises Us

And suddenly from heaven there came a sound like the rush of a violent wind, and it filled the entire house where they were sitting.
                                                              —Acts 2:2

While the girls were still at home, our family would spend a week's vacation every summer at Lakeside, a United Methodist resort community. It was a safe place and provided tremendous freedom for the girls to come and go as they wanted. Each time we packed a box of toys and games in case it was a rainy week. And we always included a couple of bottles of bubble solution.

The first summer, the girls created a tradition. At some point in the week, they would remove the upstairs screens in the cottage and blow bubbles out the window, waiting for the people walking below to notice. But just as the passersby looked up to find the source of the bubbles, the girls would duck behind the curtains. It was great fun watching the surprised looks. Often people who had been staring at the ground would be suddenly looking toward the sky.

Jesus' followers in Acts 2 were certainly downcast before the heavenly winds began. But in just a few amazing moments a miracle happened. The Spirit came and changed their lives. No longer were they looking down at the ground. Their eyes were lifted heavenward.

Sometimes I need a wake-up call. I'll settle for bubbles or wind or fire. Anything that will lift my eyes beyond the shadows of this earth. When I need it most, the Spirit comes to me.

And, perhaps, people around us need to see bubbles, need us to bring them words of hope, so that they too will lift their eyes heavenward. It is not really that difficult if we remember that we do not perform the miracle. We simply give it an opportunity to happen.

Spirit of the Living God, blow into my life, so that I may see your miracles happening in my everyday life—and pass them on to others. Amen.

Week 22, Monday   Take a Leap of Faith

He said, "Come." So Peter got out of the boat, started walking on the water, and came toward Jesus.
—Matthew 14:29

The country church I served had one of those signs out front that provided space for a saying. It was my job to come up with a clever line for each week. Once I put out the following: "Behold the turtle who only makes progress by sticking its neck out." Sometime later I received a personal letter from a couple who read that sign as they traveled by. They had been debating whether or not to risk beginning a new business. After reading the sign, they took the risk. They were writing to thank me for the word of encouragement they had found on the church's signboard.

Peter stepped out in faith when Jesus invited him to come over the waters. As long as he kept his attention upon his Master he did fine. But when he noticed the wind blowing against him, he began to sink. How like Peter I am. I do fine on this walk of faith until I begin to notice all the negatives around me. If I give a lot of energy to them, they begin to pull me under. I need to learn to take each step in faith.

Angie, our oldest daughter, taught me about faith when she was just four years old. One night, I heard her feet hit the floor as she hopped out of bed in her bedroom just above our family room. Guessing she had had a bad dream, I ran to the stairs to meet her. As she got to the landing halfway down, she saw me standing at the bottom. In an act of absolute trust, she jumped into the air. Luckily, I caught her.

O Jesus, when you call I want to be ready to step out in faith. Keep me focused upon you. If I begin to sink, lift me up. I place my trust in you. Amen.

Week 22, Tuesday   Creation Reveals the Creator

> *The earth is the LORD's and all that is in it,*
> *the world, and those who live in it.*
> *—Psalm 24:1*

The springtime field trip for our church's daycare center always took the children to a nearby state park. The park was filled with huge pine trees, ducks, and lots of water. We timed it right so that the woodland flowers would be in blossom. It was a treat that the whole staff, as well as the children, looked forward to each year.

Billy's first opportunity to go along came when he was four. He was one of those little boys you could never be sure was paying attention. Yet, somehow he always seemed to know what was going on. When we returned from the outing, each child was encouraged to draw a picture of something they had seen during the day. Billy drew the path through the forest complete with the flowers along the way. He proudly presented his picture to his teacher, asking her to write underneath it, "I never knew there was such a beautiful world as this!"

It is so easy for us as adults to live as though God created the world with asphalt, concrete, plastic, and Formica, particularly if we live in the city. We drive past trees, flowers, birds, clouds, sunsets, never seeing them. And then we wonder why it feels as though God is so far away. Billy taught me to notice God's creation and thereby to become more familiar with the Creator.

Creator God, thank you for giving us such a beautiful world. Slow me down so that I will not miss any of its daily miracles. Amen.

Afterward Moses and Aaron went to Pharaoh and said, "Thus says the LORD, the God of Israel, 'Let my people go, so that they may celebrate a festival to me in the wilderness.'"

—Exodus 5:1

Ben was one of those wildly creative little boys who always approach life from left field. Unfortunately, he was born into a very rigid family. When he was in third grade, he asked for an appointment with me, his pastor, and brought his father along. The topic for discussion was how they could coexist in the same house when he needed freedom and his father insisted on keeping everything in perfect order. After a long discussion, we all agreed on creating a "freedom space" for Ben. An area (approximately 9' x 12') was taped off in the basement. Within these limits, Ben could be as messy as he needed to be in order to express his creativity.

Three weeks later, I got a call from Ben asking for a second meeting. When I inquired as to the problem, Ben told me that his father had ordered him to clean up his freedom space! It seemed to Ben that this was an infraction of the agreement. It took some strong negotiating but we finally reestablished the "freedom space."

As a result of our conversations, I learned to lighten up with my own children. But perhaps more important, I learned to allow myself some freedom spaces not only physically but also emotionally. Not everything in life can be tidy nor should it be. When I loosen up there is more opportunity for the Spirit to reach me. New ideas as well as solutions to life's problems flow more freely when I'm not so uptight about everything.

Spirit of God, move into my life and rearrange it as you see fit, so there will be room for surprise. I am open to your presence. Amen.

When they kept on questioning him, he straightened up and said to them, "Let anyone among you who is without sin be the first to throw a stone at her."   *—John 8:7*

On Kevin's first day of preschool, he kicked the teacher in the side as she was sitting in the story circle on the floor. She told him that kicking wasn't allowed at preschool. He stomped out into the hall to look for his mother.

I was waiting at the classroom door as he arrived the next day. When I invited him to talk about appropriate school behavior, he darted across the hall and into the empty crib room. I followed. As he crawled under the cribs, complaining about our "stupid rules," I crawled behind him echoing his frustrations and feeding back his feelings. "You really are angry, aren't you? You surely don't like the rules here, do you?"

Kevin's volume was getting lower and the pauses between his comments were getting longer. After about an hour of this little game, he crawled across the hall and sat defiantly in the doorway of his classroom. I did the same. In silence, we watched the other children playing together and having fun. When the class gathered in their story circle, Kevin eased his way into the circle. With a nod from the teacher, I returned to my office and never again heard of Kevin causing any trouble.

Sometimes I wish people were where I think they should be in their faith journey, spiritual development, or emotional maturity. But then I remember Kevin and adjust my thinking. When I meet people where they are, rather than being frustrated that they are not where I want them to be, the changes begin to happen.

Forgive me, Lord, for judging others rather than trying to understand them. Remind me of your love for me and strengthen my resolve to love others. Amen.

Week 22, Friday   My Agenda Is Not Always God's Agenda

> *The wolf shall live with the lamb,*
> *the leopard shall lie down with the kid,*
> *the calf and the lion and the fatling together,*
> *and a little child shall lead them.*
>   *—Isaiah 11:6*

One of my greatest joys as a minister has been the opportunity to do "children's moments" during the Sunday morning worship services. These are not "junior sermons" but rather a time when the pastor and the children can share insights on the text of the morning. The adults are permitted to listen in.

One Sunday morning, I was struggling to get a point across. Most of the children were "with me," but four-year-old Ryan was clearly someplace else. Yet, he kept trying to get my attention. Two things were obvious to me: he had something he wanted to say and it wasn't on the topic of the morning. When he persisted and it became obvious that he would not give up, I stopped and turned to him.

"What do you want to share, Ryan?" I asked.

He said, "Paul, I just wanted to tell you that I love you."

A hush fell over the entire congregation as the significance of the moment settled in. They had perceived my frustration at Ryan's attempt to distract me from my agenda—such a contrast to his innocent and tender expression of love that touched the congregation in a way my agenda never would have. Since then, I view interruptions both to my children's moments and to my highly scheduled days with more openness.

Eternal God, you can do whatever you want with the agenda I have set for today. My hours belong to you. Use them as you see fit. I will remain open to you. Amen.

Week 22, Saturday   Fearless Love Can Open Doors

For I am convinced that neither death, nor life, nor angels, nor rulers, nor things present, nor things to come, nor powers, nor height, nor depth, nor anything else in all creation, will be able to separate us from the love of God in Christ Jesus our Lord.
—Romans 8:38-39

The dentist's office is not my favorite place to visit, but I try to make the most of it, knowing that the pain won't last long. After signing in with the receptionist, I found my seat in the waiting room. The only other person waiting was an older gentleman. I greeted him but got no response. Shortly thereafter, a lady came in and joined us. She, too, said a friendly hello to the man but got only a frown in response.

A young woman and her three-year-old son were the next to arrive. She cheerfully greeted us and we all responded—except the man. He didn't even look up from his magazine, the frown still on his face. The little boy walked right over to him, put a hand on his knee, and said, "Hi, there." To our surprise, the man picked up the little fellow, sat him on his lap, and began talking with him. The tension left not only the man's face but the whole room as well.

Sometimes it takes a fearless love to open a closed door. When we adults got no response from the man, we retreated. Perhaps it was fear of rejection that kept us from saying anything more. But the little fellow knew no fear. His gesture of courage and friendliness made a difference. He was able to go where we were not welcomed.

Now, when I catch myself feeling fear in uncertain situations, I remember that little boy and focus on love instead of fear—and I find new possibilities where there didn't seem to be any.

God of never-ending love, give me the courage to go beyond fear and express my love for others without concern for the response I will get. Amen.

Week 23, Sunday   Truth Liberates

Then Jesus said to the Jews who had believed in him, "If you con-tinue in my word, you are truly my disciples; and you will know the truth, and the truth will make you free."   —John 8:31-32

As Suzy, our youngest daughter, ended her sixth-grade year, we noticed a pattern of illness beginning to develop. Every couple of weeks, she would complain of a sore throat or a stomach-ache and insist that she was too sick to go to school. Yet within an hour of the time that school would have started, she seemed to recover remarkably. Over the following summer, Suzy rarely ever complained of any health problems. When school began again in the fall, the pattern returned.

In a nonconfrontive way, I asked her to think about what was going on. After reflection, she admitted that it was her way of getting a break from the pressures of school. It wasn't academic pressure. She was an easy straight "A" student. The pressure was from boredom with the routine and a lack of challenge. Through negotiation with the principal of the school, we got permission for Suzy to take a day off once a month before she got "sick." We called them "mental health days." She hasn't missed a day due to illness since.

I, too, am better now at identifying when I need some time away from the job. To be able to admit that my energies are waning is not easy for me. It seems more socially acceptable to get time off because of illness. But staying healthy is a lot more fun. My "mental health days" are more enjoyable than sick days.

O Great Physician, lead me in paths that are healthy so that I may enjoy the fullness of life. Give me the wisdom to identify my true needs and the courage to meet them. Amen.

Week 23, Monday   Don't Be Inhibited by Others' Opinions

When his family heard it, they went out to restrain him, for people were saying, "He has gone out of his mind."   —Mark 3:21

Sometimes the children I had to watch out for at Children's Moments were my own! One Sunday, I wanted to get across that you cannot always tell what something is by the way it looks. I had a clear glass filled with 7-Up which had sat out long enough for the bubbles to disappear.

"What do you think is in the glass?" I asked. The children all agreed it was water. I assured them it wasn't and made my point that appearances are sometimes deceiving. Then I invited them to guess again.

"I know," said Angie, our older daughter. "It's wine!"

I quickly invited her to taste it. "Yep," she shouted, "it's wine all right!"

Angie has never been inhibited by the opinions of others. She expresses herself with utmost confidence. I have learned a lot from her lack of inhibition. Just being myself is all that God asks of me. Sometimes when I find myself holding back for fear that someone might not like my idea, I remember the "yep, it's wine" moment and find the courage to speak out.

Limitless God, re-create me in your image, so that I can freely express all that you have placed within me. Amen.

If we live, we live to the Lord, and if we die, we die to the Lord;
so then, whether we live or whether we die, we are the Lord's.
                                                  —Romans 14:8

When our girls were in elementary school, they found a kitten
that had been abandoned. It was weak and frightened. They gently
placed it in a box with some soft rags and fed it milk with an eye
dropper, sure that their tender loving care would save it. But the
next morning it was dead. The girls were devastated. This was their
first experience with the death of a pet.

I offered to bury the kitten in the backyard and promised to
mark the spot. This seemed to help but they insisted that bury-
ing the kitten without a proper funeral would never do. Carefully, the kitten was wrapped in silk cloths and placed in a pretty
box. Then the entire family was marched into the sanctuary of
the church. Appropriate words were shared and a prayer was
said. We were then led to a spot in the flower garden that would
be the kitty's final resting place.

At first, I thought it strange that we had to go through all this
ritual for a kitten they had just found the day before. But gradually I began to perceive the deeper level of what was happening.
The girls understood that all of life is precious and that the
length of familiarity with a creature doesn't determine its sacred-
ness. Even the stranger is my neighbor!

God of oneness, show me the wholeness of your creation and
my part in it, as well as what I owe to every person who
comes my way. Amen.

Week 23, Wednesday   **Love Overcomes Labels**

And I tell you, you are Peter, and on this rock I will build my
church, and the gates of Hades will not prevail against it.
                                                  —Matthew 16:18

Peter seemed like anything but a rock. He was more like shift-
ing sand. He often opened his mouth without thinking. He
stepped out in front of the others only to fall behind them. Yet

Jesus saw something in him that he didn't even see in himself. Jesus saw beyond the surface and into the future. Peter would indeed become the stable foundation for the church. Oh, to be able to see with the eyes of Jesus.

Our first foster child was an infant girl who had been badly battered by her father. She came to us from the hospital barely able to move. We were so excited to have a child in our family that we called all the relatives to share the good news. My mother wanted all the details and remained excited about Becky Sue until I mentioned that she was biracial.

"Oh, I don't believe in that," she said with disgust.

I was crushed and didn't know how to respond. I worried about how visits with Grandma would go. But I needn't have. On our first visit home, the minute Mom saw Becky Sue she fell in love with her. Suddenly she was a precious infant, not an abstract category. Prejudice was replaced by love.

Facing difficulties in the abstract is scary. But I am learning to confront what I fear, what I don't understand, or what I understand only in limited ways. Putting a face on a situation, meeting a real person, has meant that a lot of my prejudices have disappeared.

God of surprises, shake me up. Shatter my categories. Help me to see people and situations from your point of view. Amen.

Week 23, Thursday   Courage Overcomes Fear

Although Daniel knew that the document had been signed, he continued to go to his house, which had windows in its upper room open toward Jerusalem, and to get down on his knees three times a day to pray to his God and praise him, just as he had done previously. —Daniel 6:10

Daniel should have been afraid. The king was powerful and the promised punishment (the lions' den) for praying to anyone else but the king was severe. Yet Daniel did what he knew was right, trusting that everything would turn out okay. And it did, though he didn't escape the lions' den.

In seminary, my professional leadership class required me to focus on one age level. I chose preschool because that was the age-group about which I knew the least. I was assigned to work in a preschool program at a nearby church. During my first time in charge of the playground, I panicked. Three-year-olds were climbing to the top of the wooden jungle gym, which was at least seven feet tall. What if they fell? I quickly found the teacher in charge and shared my concern. She reassured me that they were safe. They did it every day.

Often, I am more fearful than the children with whom I work. They have an inner courage that permits them to go places and do things that I would hesitate to do. Perhaps I need to read again the story of Daniel and be reminded that if what I am doing is right, I do not need to fear.

God of courage, forgive my fears. Remove the barriers that hinder me from doing what you want me to do. I am ready to move forward unafraid. Amen.

Week 23, Friday   **Follow Your Passion**

And Jesus said to them, "Follow me and I will make you fish for people."   *—Mark 1:17*

"So, you love to fish. Follow me and fish in a new way."

Jesus understood the passion of the fishermen and invited them to follow that passion, but in a different way. When Jesus calls us he invites us to do what we love doing, but to do it in ways that make a difference. A carpenter can be a carpenter for Christ. An accountant can be an accountant for Christ. A lawyer can be a lawyer for Christ. A teacher can teach in such a way that it truly brings about a better world.

Eight-year-old James loved trains more than anything else in the world. He played with trains, read about trains, and talked about trains—endlessly. Every time I saw him at church he had something to tell me about his trains. Once he asked me if he could bring one of his toy trains and share it at Children's Moments. I told him he could if he could think of a way to relate the train to Jesus. He assured me that he could.

The next Sunday, as promised, James brought his train. He explained how it worked—how the engine pulled the rest of the cars and they followed wherever the engine led them. "It's like that with

Jesus and us," he said. "Jesus leads us and we follow him. And if we disconnect ourselves from Jesus, we really won't get anywhere."

I saw James last month. He is now a teenager. He still loves trains and he is still following Jesus.

Lead on, Jesus, I am following. I know that you will keep me on the right track. I am ready to use all my abilities and interests for you. Amen.

Week 23, Saturday   A Little Faith Changes Things

Then Jesus answered her, "Woman, great is your faith! Let it be done for you as you wish." And her daughter was healed instantly.   *—Matthew 15:28*

The daycare program in my church took the children to a nearby park as often as possible. It was a wonderful opportunity for them to play outdoors. Whenever I could break away from the office, I would go with them.

One beautiful summer afternoon, I joined them on the playground, where I noticed that Tommy wasn't participating. Soon he came running over to me holding his stomach and saying he was going to be sick. My intuition said it was more emotional than physical. So, I leaned down and asked him if he could feel the gentle breeze blowing. He paused and then slowly nodded his head. I suggested that he lean against a nearby tree for a moment and allow that breeze to blow right through him, taking his stomachache with it. I watched in amazement as he followed my instructions. Within minutes, the pain was gone and Tommy was playing with the other children.

It's harder, I know, to handle my own "aches" and "pains" with a positive attitude. But Jesus told his followers that if they had faith the size of a mustard seed they could move mountains (Matthew 17:20). Wouldn't a little bit of faith be able to chase my problems away? Tommy trusted my words and the wind (Spirit) eased his mind and cleared up the pain in his stomach. I will learn to trust God's words like Tommy trusted mine.

O God, I do believe. Help me when I doubt. Cause your Spirit to blow through my life renewing each part of it. Amen.

Neither is new wine put into old wineskins; otherwise, the skins burst, and the wine is spilled, and the skins are destroyed; but new wine is put into fresh wineskins, and so both are preserved.
—*Matthew 9:17*

In a church I was serving recently, I noticed that on frequent occasions there were children wandering through the building while their parents were at choir rehearsal or attending committee meetings. The kids were not getting into any trouble but seemed bored. Most of them, I knew, had computers at home.

"Would it be a good idea for the church to get computers for you to use while you're in the building?" I asked Chris and Daniel, two of the fourth-grade boys.

Chris replied, "Yes! I think it's about time the church gets into modern technology," and Daniel agreed.

Within a few months, we had established a children's learning center complete with Pentium computers and color printers. We loaded them with Bible study software and kept the door to the center open whenever there were children in the building. It was used constantly.

Sometimes we resist change. The old ways are too comfortable. I remember using flannelgraph boards and filmstrip projectors in my Sunday school classrooms. But today's children are used to TV, video recordings, and computers. When we insist on using the old ways, we are communicating that the good news is a thing of the past. Chris and Daniel reinforced for me the importance of utilizing modern technology to communicate the gospel.

God of tomorrow, help me to be open to the new ways you find to make yourself known to your people, and to perceive your presence in my everyday experience. Amen.

Week 24, Monday   **Trust Your Intuition**

He said to them, "Why were you searching for me? Did you not know that I must be in my Father's house?"
—*Luke 2:49*

Jesus was only twelve years old, but he sensed where he belonged, and it surprised him that his family did not understand.

Tracey was about twelve years old when she attended our annual Liturgical Arts Day for children. After learning about the seasons of the Christian year and the appropriate symbols for each, she chose to create an artistic expression for Easter. Before leaving the workshop, she began sketching her symbols.

Two months later Tracey and her mother came to my office about a week before the projects were to be turned in. When I glanced at her project I was surprised. What I saw was a lifeless drawing of traditional Easter lilies. Without saying a word, I glanced at Tracey's face and realized there was no excitement there either.

"Tracey did another picture," her mother offered, "but it was the wrong lily for Easter, so I had her do this one."

Gently, I asked to see the other drawing. When Tracey brought it in the following Sunday morning, her face matched the liveliness of the drawing. She had sketched three beautiful calla lilies. Each pencil stroke seemed to radiate new life. Clearly this drawing spoke of the resurrection.

I still catch myself second-guessing my intuitive sense. It usually happens when my superrational side takes over. But I am learning on a daily basis to trust what comes to me from my intuition.

God of Spirit, strengthen my trust in you, and I will follow your still, small voice that speaks to me from deep within my being. Amen.

Week 24, Tuesday   When You Need Love Most

So he set off and went to his father. But while he was still far off, his father saw him and was filled with compassion; he ran and put his arms around him and kissed him.   —Luke 15:20

One evening in our Personal Growth Group for teens, we were experiencing a guided meditation. At one point in the meditation, the youth were invited to visualize a picture on the wall and to enter that picture if they were comfortable doing so. As the guided meditation continued, Trevor, our most troubled youth, began to cry softly. Here is what he shared with the group later:

"I saw a picture of my father holding me when I was a baby. When I entered the picture, Dad was still holding me but I was the age that I am now. It felt wonderful to be held. I wish I could feel that closeness with my father today. I really miss it. Now all we do is fight."

We concluded our session by reading the story of the prodigal son and the forgiving father. Together, we remembered just how much we are loved, and we felt that love surrounding us for a moment. Over the next few months, I noticed a gradual growth in the relationship between Trevor and his father.

Trevor's experience not only reminded me that we need love the most when we seem to be the most unlovable, but also continues to help me in my ongoing relationships.

Heavenly Father, you love me without condition. Your love searches for me when I am lost and celebrates with me when I come home. I want to feel your love holding me all the time. Amen.

Week 24, Wednesday You Cannot Hide What Is Inside

Woe to you, scribes and Pharisees, hypocrites! For you are like whitewashed tombs, which on the outside look beautiful, but inside they are full of the bones of the dead and of all kinds of filth. —Matthew 23:27

Elizabeth is a twin. When she was born her sister weighed seven pounds, four ounces. Elizabeth weighed in at four pounds, seven ounces. The doctor said that her sister had been getting all the nourishment.

As she grew, Elizabeth never caught up with her twin. When they started to school, the children picked on her because she was so little. In first grade, Elizabeth asked her mother if she could take karate lessons. After a few lessons, an interesting thing began to happen at school. The kids stopped teasing Elizabeth. They no longer pushed her around. She had not told anyone that she was taking karate lessons. But somehow she was different and the other children perceived it.

What we have inside us makes a difference. When we fill ourselves up with the positive feelings of knowing who we are and
whose we are, we exude a confidence that can be perceived by
those around us. Some days I have to remind myself that God
made me and that God doesn't make junk. I am somebody not
because of what I do, or don't do, but because of whose I am. As
a child of God, I have a right to be here and to enjoy the goodness of life that God has created.

Creator God, shine through me. Melt me, mold me, fill me,
use me for your purposes. Amen.

Week 24, Thursday   Say Yes Whenever Possible

And a woman in the city, who was a sinner, having learned that
he was eating in the Pharisee's house, brought an alabaster jar
of ointment. She stood behind him at his feet, weeping, and
began to bathe his feet with her tears and to dry them with her
hair. Then she continued kissing his feet and anointing them with
the ointment.   *—Luke 7:37-38*

When the Sunday school superintendent asked if I would be
willing to teach the class of third- and fourth-graders, I readily
agreed. But no one told me the reason I was asked was because
Ben was in the class. Ben was one of those kids who always challenged the status quo. He was bright and creative and would not
sit still for things staying as they had always been. He was filled
with "why's" and would not settle for "Sunday school" answers.

One Sunday our lesson was on the Tower of Babel. In order to
get across the point of building to the sky, I brought in some card-
board building blocks from the nursery department and we
began to build a tower. After building as high as the children
could reach, I tried to pull the group together for a discussion
time. Ben exploded. "This is stupid! Our tower is only six feet tall.
The story says they built a tower to the sky."

"We have built as high as we can reach," I explained.

"I know where there's a ladder," Ben replied, "and if we get it,
we can build to the sky, too!"

At first, I wanted to say no, but somehow I knew better. We got
the ladder and we built that tower clear up to the ceiling of the

room. Ben proudly climbed the ladder and slid the last block into place. The smile on his face told me the point of the lesson would be remembered for a long time.

God of new possibilities, open me to the great Yes that you speak to me each day. Take away my limited ideas and replace them with your infinite wisdom. Amen.

Week 24, Friday　　　　**Rules Are to Help, Not to Hinder**

Then he said to them, "The sabbath was made for humankind, and not humankind for the sabbath; so the Son of Man is lord even of the sabbath."　　　　　　　　　*—Mark 2:27-28*

We knew Jim from the time he was in middle school. It was no surprise when he announced his intention to enter the ordained ministry. He was obviously gifted for it and called to it. Jim hung out at our house a lot and was practically part of the family. When we moved to a new parish, he would often come to visit us.

Once when the girls were in their elementary years, we sent them to the community pool for an afternoon of swimming. About suppertime, they returned bringing Jim along with them. The three of them had purple stains all over their hands from picking and eating mulberries. When they had eaten all the low hanging berries, they told us, Jim had driven his car under the tree. The three of them had climbed up on his car and kept picking and eating. Picture it: an out-of-town minister and the local pastor's two daughters standing on top of a car, picking and eating mulberries from a tree at the park.

I thought of a dozen reasons for the inappropriateness of their actions, and started to share them. But looking at the joy on their faces and the purple on their hands, I laughed and suggested they wash up for dinner.

Lord of the Sabbath, loosen me up so that I can enjoy all of your creation—and rejoice when others do so as well. Amen.

He said, "Truly I tell you, this poor widow has put in more than all of them; for all of them have contributed out of their abundance, but she out of her poverty has put in all she had to live on."   *—Luke 21:3-4*

A terrible fire destroyed the home of a family in our community. I announced it at worship the next morning and invited people to contribute toward a fund to help the family rebuild. That afternoon the doorbell rang. Standing on the porch of the parsonage was a little girl holding a piggy bank. She had gone home from church to get the money she had been saving for a bicycle. She wanted me to take it all for the family that had lost their home. I took it—and will always remember the look of joy on her face. She had given all that she had and felt wonderful about her gift. Surely this is what Jesus observed in the courtyard of the temple as the widow gave what she had.

Most of our giving, I suspect, is calculated carefully. We want to be sure that we will have enough left over for our own needs. Yet the most joyful giving I have experienced has been spontaneous and sacrificial. When I have given not from plenty but from the little that I have, I have reaped the greatest benefits. Giving seems to mean more when there is an element of risk involved. Giving at this level also invites a deeper level of trust that God will always provide.

Generous God, you give us so richly all things to enjoy. Teach me to give freely and joyfully, knowing that I will freely receive from your loving hands. Amen.

7
GETTING INTO GOD'S WORD

J. Ellsworth Kalas

From childhood you have known the sacred writings that are able to instruct you for salvation through faith in Christ Jesus.
—2 Timothy 3:15

If you ask me how I feel about the Bible, I will almost surely tell you more than you want to know. That's what happens when you inquire about an old friend—and the Bible is, indeed, my old friend. How old? Well, the oldest book in my personal library is a book of Bible stories that I received as a four-year-old, a gift from "Grandma Fallon," an old friend of the family.

I won my first Bible as a nine-year-old, for memorizing Bible verses. It is now in an honored place in my office, held together by a large rubber band. It was the first Bible I ever read from beginning to end. I made that trip through so often, beginning with my eleventh year, that it was pretty well worn out by the time I was in my early twenties.

I was fortunate, of course. We were economically deprived in my childhood, and the only college graduates I knew were my minister and my schoolteachers. But I had the Book, and that made all the difference. It gave me a foundation in literature, and provided the setting in which God's Spirit could speak to my soul. Today we are such good friends that each time I pick up my Bible, I smile, and feel stronger. You can't find a better friend than that.

Thank you, dear Lord, for the Bible and what it can mean in a person's life. Help me not only to cherish it, but to live in it and to share it. Amen.

Study to show thyself approved unto God, a workman that needeth not to be ashamed, rightly dividing the word of truth.
—2 Timothy 2:15 KJV

When I was eleven years old, and a new Christian, a Presbyterian evangelist came to our little Methodist church. During a Sunday dinner visit to our home, he learned that I had a call to the ministry. He pressed me with a demanding question: Had I read the Bible through yet? When he found out that I hadn't, he gave me a method. Read three chapters each weekday, he said, and five chapters each Sunday, and you'll finish the Bible in a year. And go straight through, beginning with Genesis 1.

The most important feature in his formula was *discipline*. I know of no worthwhile achievement that can be accomplished without putting ourselves under a discipline. His rule was very simple; even an eleven-year-old could master it. But the secret was the dailiness of it.

We often call the Bible the bread of life. If we take that term seriously, we will make it a daily part of our lives; one doesn't try to go long without bread, or its equivalent. Of course we don't have to discipline ourselves to eat! Hardly!

I'm happy to report that the Bible now has such a place in my life. After a while a good discipline becomes a blessed habit. Now I can't imagine starting a day without reading my Bible. And it all began with a three-by-five discipline.

And yes—I finished the whole Bible that first year.

Lead me, I pray, O Lord, into a blessed daily discipline with your Holy Word. Amen.

Oh, how I love your law!
It is my meditation all day long.
—Psalm 119:97

Somewhere, years ago, I heard of a great biblical scholar who began each day of study by laying his face on his open Bible, asking for understanding. He felt that the only proper attitude in approaching this book is reverence.

I recommend such a mood for Bible reading. Not superstition; the Bible deserves better than that, because it is not a book of magic. But if we are to get the full benefit of its words, we need a mood of reverence.

For me, that reverence springs from my conviction that the Bible is, in a unique sense, the Word of God. But suppose you don't think of the Bible that way; how can you feel something of the awe that brings deeper significance to your reading? Well, perhaps you could begin by remembering that it is an ancient document, with wisdom that somehow has transcended the usual barriers of time and culture. And you could remind yourself that it is the most translated and most widely distributed book in the world.

Still more, you will want to ponder that people love this book so much, and have found it so life-changing, that they have literally given their lives to translate and distribute it. And this has been going on for hundreds of years. Then marvel that you hold such a remarkable treasure in your hands. And bow in reverence as you begin to read.

Thank you, dear Lord, for the Bible. Amen.

Week 25, Wednesday **Holy Expectations**

> *With open mouth I pant,*
>   *because I long for your commandments.*
>   *—Psalm 119:131*

Whether it's a matter of reunion with my wife after a trip, a visit to my adult children, seeing a long-awaited play, or being able to sit down with a book by a favorite author, expectation adds to excitement. And that sense of excitement leads eventually to greater enjoyment of a given event.

I try to approach my Bible that way each day. I have read the Bible so many thousands of mornings that I suppose I could allow it to become a commonplace. Not so! I like to approach a new day's reading by thinking, *What do you have to say to me today?* I remember someone who said that he read the Bible each morning to get his "marching orders" for the day. And I think of a woman who reads her Bible each morning until she comes upon a verse that will be her theme verse of the day. In any event, these persons come to the Bible with a sense of holy expectancy. Their reading may be a habit, but it is not routine.

Those of us who have such an attitude have come to it by experience. My expectations are not idle hopes; they are based on an accumulation of personal research. And by now this research has taken on remarkable dimensions. What I read this morning I have read scores of times over the years. I've even preached on part of it. But this morning, it was fresh and new and uniquely true for this day. No wonder I'm looking forward to tomorrow's reading with such expectation!

Speak to me today through your Word, dear Savior, in a unique and special way. Amen.

Week 25, Thursday   **Find That It's True**

> *I rejoice in following your statutes*
> *as one rejoices in great riches.*
> *—Psalm 119:14 NIV*

The story is so wonderfully simple that I have sometimes thought it was made up, but I have a feeling it's true. The evangelist told us of seeing a Bible owned by an elderly woman. As he leafed its pages, again and again he came upon the carefully printed notation, "T & P." When he inquired about the symbols the woman answered, "That means, 'Tried and Proven.' These are verses I've proved true in my own experience."

I've never made such a notation in my Bible, but I could. Come to think of it, I could mark scores (perhaps hundreds) of verses that way. That's one of the reasons the Bible is such a special book for me, and for millions of people over the centuries. It isn't a collection of clever theories. It's a record of God's dealings with earlier generations of our human race. Each succeeding generation has proved its truths in their own time and in their personal lives.

I encourage you to read the Bible in a "scientific" way; that is, in an experimental way. As you read, ask yourself if any of what you're reading has proved true to your own experience. And when you come upon a passage that is significant to some current need, lay claim to it; seek the faith to apply it to your own life in such a way that you will be able, if you want, to mark it "T & P."

Grant me the faith, I pray, to make your Word a living, effective power in my life. In Jesus' name. Amen.

Week 25, Friday   Time Matters

> *My eyes stay open through the watches of the night,*
> *that I may meditate on your promises.*
> *—Psalm 119:148 NIV*

It is difficult, if not impossible, to build a great friendship on scattered minutes. Occasionally one has an airport conversation that makes a stranger seem like an old friend, but it's deceptive; friendships grow in the deep soil of time. Quantity doesn't guarantee quality, but it's hard to get quality without it.

The Bible, then, needs more than an occasional hurried glance. Let's take a hard test: How much time do I give to the sports page? Or to my professional publications? Or—perhaps especially—to television? Should I be surprised, then, if I know more about a team's current winning streak or an entertainment personality's taste in clothing than I do about the Sermon on the Mount? Which is ironic, when you consider that a person can read that entire wondrous document in less time than you might spend on the evening newscast.

Your health adviser will tell you that you can do wonders for your heart by jogging or walking vigorously for fifteen minutes a day. Let me offer a prescription, too. You can bring new vitality to your eternal soul by reading your Bible fifteen minutes a day. And if you start at Genesis, you will complete the whole Bible in a year. Still more important, you will find yourself establishing a friendship of real depth and permanence—with God, and with his Book.

I want, O Lord, to give time to that which matters most— including time in your holy Word. Help me with my resolve. Amen.

May my tongue sing of your word,
for all your commands are righteous.
—Psalm 119:172 NIV

I have a special advantage when I read the Bible. I know I will probably have an opportunity to use what I read, either in a sermon, a lesson, or a book. You probably can't count on such an immediate experience. Not unless you teach a class or perhaps lead a small group.

But this gain I enjoy is also a danger. The first purpose in reading the Bible is not to get a sermon or a lesson, but to meet with God and to be nourished on the bread of life. It's too easy for me as a preacher to use the Bible as a source of sermons for others while not allowing it to speak clearly and convertingly to my own soul. So when you and I read the Bible, we ought to read it for the nurturing transformation it can make in our lives.

Still, the Bible ought to be something we put to use. Not as an instrument with which we bludgeon those who disagree with us, but as a joy and a strength we share. Some of this will happen as the phrases and insights of the Scriptures become part of our very person. But something even more significant will happen to us, even though it may not be as easy to identify. As we feed daily on the Bible, it will become a constant, often unconscious, influence on our conversation, our thoughts, and our deeds. Because, in the spiritual realm as well as in the physical, we are what we eat.

O Lord, as I feed on your Word, help me to bless others from the new strength I have received. Amen.

Week 26, Sunday   **The Bible and the Sports Section**

If anyone competes as an athlete, he does not receive the victor's crown unless he competes according to the rules.
—2 Timothy 2:5 NIV

I confess that I'm a sports fan. My first reading each morning, after my Bible, is the sports section. I used to justify this on the ground that when I'm reading the sports section I can tell the Good Guys from the Bad Guys. But I'm no longer so sure. In this era of steroids and broken contracts, it's hard to know for whom to cheer.

In such a world Paul's words seem almost quaint. "Compete according to the rules"? Maybe they did so in the first-century Olympics, but now you can hardly hope for it in the Little Leagues, let alone professional or major college sports.

Except, of course, for the Game Paul is talking about. You're interested in the Big Leagues? Hey, man, this is *really* the Big Leagues! You're interested in a life-and-death match? This is *really* it. And in this game, you never fool the Umpire. Sometimes all of us get by when we should have been caught, and some people seem to get by most of their lives. But there's one Umpire who just doesn't miss a call.

What's more, this Umpire even knows the intentions behind our deeds. Sometimes our deeds are rather impressive, but our motives are less than noble. This Umpire knows the difference.

This is definitely a different ball game. It's no place to fudge on the rules.

Help me to play each day's game with integrity, O Lord; to your honor and to my own good benefit. Amen.

Week 26, Monday   The Bible and the Sports Section (II)

I press on toward that goal to win the prize for which God has called me heavenward in Christ Jesus.
—Philippians 3:14 NIV

The apostle Paul must have been a great sports fan. His favorite figures of speech seem to come from the world of sports. He makes references to boxing (1 Corinthians 9:26), racing (Galatians 2:2, 5:7), wrestling (Ephesians 6:12 KJV), and winning the Olympic wreath (2 Timothy 4:7-8), to name several.

But nowhere is Paul more emphatic in his sports lingo than when he writes to the Philippians. "But one thing I do: Forgetting what is behind and straining toward what is ahead, I press on toward the goal to win the prize for which God has called me heavenward in Christ Jesus" (Philippians 3:13-14 NIV). The word that our Bible translates "straining" is a word right out of the first-century sports world. It meant literally a racer going hard for the tape. Such was the intensity with which Paul lived the Christian life.

I'm troubled that so few Christian men seem to have this passion for Christian excellence. I know many men who want to achieve in business, scholarship, sports, or politics, but they don't have a comparable passion to achieve in the realm of faith. I admire their ambition for themselves and their families; I only wish they had the same ambition for what matters most. If it is true (as I believe it is) that Christ died to save us, how can we possibly be content with mediocrity in the lives we live for him?

Give me a holy passion, O God, for winning the eternal race. In Jesus' name. Amen.

Week 26, Tuesday   The Bible and the Headlines

> *The LORD is a warrior;*
> *the LORD is his name.*
> —*Exodus 15:3*

If the newspaper headlines tell us anything, it is that we live in a world of conflict. Whether the subject is political or international, business or human relations, we get a feeling that wars little and big are going on every day.

That doesn't surprise me, because I read the Bible. Several years ago, a book I wrote, *The Grand Sweep: From Genesis through Revelation in 365 Days,* caused me to go through the Bible again in a relatively short period. When I had finished the writing, a friend asked me what dominant impression I had received in this intensive study. "That we're in a battle," I said, "that life is a struggle."

We're introduced to the conflict between good and evil in the third chapter of Genesis. From that point on the struggle continues. Sometimes it is war between nations, sometimes between individuals, as in the Psalms, which are marked again and again by prayers for vengeance on evildoers. The prophets thunder repeatedly against evil. In the New Testament, Jesus is in conflict with the Pharisees and other religious leaders, which leads to his death. The story ends in Revelation with massive conflict and the final triumph of righteousness.

I find comfort in this, because it's good to know what we're in for. We're in a fight. I intend to stay with it, on the side of the right.

Grant me the strength, O Lord, to stay true to you, no matter what the pressures of the world around me. Amen.

Week 26, Wednesday   **The Bible and the Obituary Column**

Teach us to number our days aright,
that we may gain a heart of wisdom.
—Psalm 90:12 NIV

When I was a boy, no hour of the week was more riveting than the radio program from *Time* magazine, "The March of Time." It was punctuated at regular intervals by a stentorian voice that announced, "TIME . . . marches on!" At a particular point each week the announcer stated gravely, "Last week death came, as it must to every man, to . . ." and began a listing of names.

The writer of the fifth chapter of Genesis would have agreed with that phrase, "as it must to every man." Genesis 5 isn't exciting reading in its series of very brief biographies, but it is instructive, as it concludes each one with the inevitable line, "he died." The fact of our eventual death isn't news that we're anxious to hear, but it may help us to focus our lives to better purpose.

In my thirty-eight years as a parish pastor, I spent a good deal of time in cemeteries. I'm grateful for those experiences; they taught me that I do not have an unlimited supply of days, though it is easy to think otherwise. How is it that we can be so careful in budgeting our money, which is replaceable, and so lax in budgeting our days, which are not? Our days are the loveliest gift God bestows on us on this earth. Take this priceless one on which you are now embarking, claim it with thanksgiving, and use it as if there were never to be another.

Thank you, O Lord, for this wonderful day! I want to return it to you at day's end, well used. Amen.

All hard work brings a profit,
but mere talk leads only to poverty.
—*Proverbs 14:23 NIV*

If you enjoy *Forbes,* the *Wall Street Journal,* and the business section of your daily newspaper, you'll find plenty of reading material in the Bible. You're only a little ways into Genesis when you discover that Cain was a farmer and Abel a rancher. Farther along you'll discover that Abraham had an operation of such proportions that he had over three hundred male employees (Genesis 14:14). And Jacob might well be described as the original entrepreneur, a man who could turn unlikely prospects into a fortune.

The book of Proverbs contains all kinds of good counsel for doing business—down-to-earth counsel that, as the saying goes, you can put in the bank. The writers of the psalms often pray about the varying fortunes of life, and thank God for their prosperity. No doubt about it, the Bible has much to say about business.

Including warnings. When Jesus was confronted one day by a man who was unduly concerned about wealth, he told a story about a rich man whose crops were so plentiful that he had to tear down his barns and build bigger ones. "Eat, drink, and be merry," he told himself, "because you don't have to worry about your future." But God called the man a fool, because his soul was not right. That's the peril, Jesus said, with anyone who makes a fortune but who is not "rich toward God" (Luke 12:13-21). We need that wisdom to balance the business section.

Help me to realize, O Lord, that the bottom line is not in my checkbook but in my relationship with you. Amen.

Week 26, Friday   **The Bible and the Editorial Section**

A wise man will hear, and will increase learning; and a man of understanding shall attain unto wise counsels.

—*Proverbs 1:5 KJV*

I'm often disappointed when I turn to the editorial section of my newspaper. Perhaps I shouldn't be surprised. A veteran newspaper writer told me years ago that a daily paper struggles to come up with two or three meaningful editorials every day. No wonder, then, that the editorials often seem trivial or superficial, with biases that lead to predictable conclusions. And so often they're short on hope.

I'd like for the editorials to be as honest about life as the writer of Ecclesiastes is when he confesses that he has tried everything this world offers and has found that it's empty. I wish they were as hopeful as Jesus when, knowing that judgment and death are only hours away, he declares, "Take courage; I have conquered the world!" (John 16:33). And I'd like for the editors to say what Jesus said, that true greatness is found in serving others (John 13:12-17).

I wish they would see greatness as Jesus did, when he identified a very poor woman as being the most generous of the temple contributors, not because her gift was measurably large, but because it was so big in comparison to what she had (Luke 2:1-4). I wish our editorials would more often pay honor to such hidden heroes and heroines—people who quietly do magnificent things week after week, year after year. If the editorials would do so, they'd be better reading. And the world would be better, too.

Help me, O Lord, to serve you and others, whether or not I am cited in an honorable editorial. Amen.

Week 26, Saturday   The Bible and the Comic Pages

Read Luke 11:5-8.

Yes, I read the comic pages every day. Not indiscriminately; I choose my comics. But when I'm out of town, I'm disappointed if the local paper doesn't carry some of my favorites. I look to several strips not only for a daily dose of humor, but also for pungent insight on living.

But what do the comics have to do with the Bible? For one thing, the Bible believes in laughter. Unfortunately, we often miss that fact because we read the Bible with such painful seriousness. The Bible should by all means be taken seriously. But we'd get the message more clearly if we would see the setting of humor in which it is delivered.

The Bible tells us that people loved to be around Jesus. They were always inviting him to their dinner parties. They didn't invite him because he came with a long face; they knew his presence meant pleasure.

Take the story in Luke 11. Jesus is making a wonderfully serious point, that we ought to be persistent in prayer. But he does so by telling a funny story about a man who wakes his neighbor in the middle of the night and upsets his household in order to get some food for an unexpected visitor. The neighbor won't get up out of friendship, Jesus says, but only to avoid being bothered further. It's a fun story with a serious lesson. Just like a good comic strip.

Help me to see the humor in life and have a good laugh today, O Lord. And help me to share the laughter with somebody else. Amen.

Week 27, Sunday   The Bible in My Everyday: Walking

I therefore, the prisoner of the Lord, beseech you that ye walk worthy of the vocation wherewith ye are called.
—Ephesians 4:1 KJV

Walking is in fashion, but not as a means of getting somewhere. People still park their cars as close as possible to the grocery store or the entrance to their work. Walking is now a health feature, so that people who park next door to all of their engagements choose to walk for two or three miles in the morning or evening for their health. There may be some inconsistency in this pattern, but the walking is good, nevertheless.

Walking has an especially good name in the Bible, where it is a favorite figure of speech for *living*. Thus the contemporary translations of the verse I've chosen for today substitute "live" or "lead a life" where the King James Version more accurately and picturesquely says "walk."

I like "walk" better. It gives a more vivid picture of what life is like. Some people act as if life is a quick sprint, and still others hope it's a free ride. But life is mostly walking: doing the right thing day after day.

That's the way to live the Christian life. The secret is in the dailiness of it. Almost anyone can do a noble or heroic thing on occasion, but the good life is done step by step. There's a certain wonderful doggedness in that word *walking,* a certain consistency. And in the end, a certain beautiful achievement. Just walking.

Help me, O God, to live each day with consistent, faithful goodness; to the glory of your name. Amen.

Week 27, Monday   The Bible in My Everyday: Sleeping

Scripture: Read Genesis 28:10-17.

You never know what will happen while you're sleeping. I'm not talking about world events. I'm thinking of what happens in our own selves while we're sleeping. In the course of the night, you may travel to the other side of the world, visit with people—dead or alive—that you haven't seen in years, and bring together incongruously people, events, and times that never convened in real life. Dreams are like that.

And maybe, just maybe, God might visit you in your dreams, the way Jacob was visited so long ago. He was a day's journey from home, and he didn't know when he would return. He knew that his life would be in danger if he chose to return, because his estranged brother had already made his intentions known. He had no idea what the future would hold. He could hardly have been in a more perilous position.

But as he slept that night, Jacob dreamed of a ladder reaching from earth to heaven, with angels ascending and descending. Then the Lord God spoke to him, to reassure him. Suddenly the perilous journey was full of promise. No wonder Jacob said when he awakened, "Surely the Lord is in this place—and I did not know it."

When you go to sleep tonight, deposit your life in God's hand. Who knows what dreams you may have. In God's care.

O God, when I lie down to sleep, help me to give my cares and frettings to you. In Jesus' name. Amen.

Week 27, Tuesday   The Bible in My Everyday: Dreaming

Your old men shall dream dreams.
                    —Joel 2:28

There are two kinds of dreams, sleep-dreams and day-dreams. I know more about the latter than I do about the former, because I seem to forget my night dreams before I've finished getting out of bed. But daydreams have blessed me all of my life. They have occupied me when I didn't have some reading material in reach, and they have anesthetized me through some dreary banquet programs. But mostly, they have added to my enthusiasm regarding the possibilities of the future.

I'm not at all sure that the prophet Joel was talking about daydreaming when he promised that in a grand future time, the old men would dream dreams. Probably not. But it's a good idea nevertheless. And when I read the story of Joseph (Genesis 37–45), who had such wonderful dreams—all of which were fulfilled—I can't help feeling that he dreamed not only at night, but also in the daytime. Otherwise he probably wouldn't have told his brothers and his fathers about his dreams. And in those dark days when he was sold into slavery by his brothers, and then later put in prison unjustly, I'm certain he was buoyed up again and again by his daydreams—rehearsing, probably, the dreams he had received long ago at night.

Dreams can get out of hand, of course; and they always need to be backed up with thinking and working. But dreams are good. They're another of God's lovely gifts.

Dear Lord, give me an excitement for life that causes me to dream wondrous dreams—to your glory. Amen.

Week 27, Wednesday   The Bible in My Everyday: Eating

Then they told . . . how [Jesus] had been made known to them in the breaking of the bread.   —Luke 24:35

I like to eat. Before you chuckle and say you'd like to see my waistline, note that I said I like to eat, not overeat. I got past the overeating pattern many years ago, except for an occasional dessert beyond the necessary. But I love to eat, because its the best opportunity to communicate with other people. If no one's with me, I communicate with a book or a paper.

Meals are important in the Bible. Think, for example, of how many feast days the Jews had. There was some fasting but mostly feasting—celebrating the goodness and love of God with special meals. As you read your New Testament, notice how many of Jesus' miracles or special conversations took place during a meal. And the major sacrament for Christians is a meal.

No wonder, then, that believers through the ages have paused to thank God as they prepared to eat. Eating is one of God's loveliest gifts to us human beings, if we will allow it to be more than a simple filling of our stomachs. At its best, every meal can be a kind of sacrament, every glass of iced tea and every cup of coffee a symbol of praise. In the process of life's most necessary and most frequent act, the thankful ones are led into the presence of God.

Teach me, O God, to see every meal as a symbol of your love and to make it a joyful occasion. In Jesus' name. Amen.

Week 27, Thursday   The Bible in My Everyday: Working

Six days you shall labor and do all your work.
—Exodus 20:9

My father loved to tell an old Iowa story about a not-too-diligent farmer who one day announced at the general store that he had a call to the ministry. "I saw it the other day in the sky," he said. "There it was, as plain as could be, the letters *P.C.*—'Preach Christ.'" And one of his cronies slowly answered, "Bill, are you certain those letters didn't mean, "Plant Corn'?"

If Bill had read his Bible faithfully, he would have considered carefully what his neighbor said. Because virtually everyone in the Bible who was ever called to some special work for God received his call when he was working. Moses was tending sheep. Gideon was threshing grain. Amos was pruning sycamore trees. Peter, Andrew, James, and John were all taking care of their fishing business. Matthew was collecting taxes. It seems pretty clear that God believes in people who believe in work.

And of course it's worth nothing that the wonderful fourth commandment, which grants us a day of rest (and, indeed, commands us to take it), also seems to give a command to work. Six days, we're told, we should work, and then the sabbath is a day of rest unto God. After all, it doesn't make much sense to rest if you haven't first done some work.

God began the creation by working, and he calls for us to do the same. Even without the letters in the sky.

As I go to work today, O Lord, I am dedicating my labor to you and to your glory. Amen.

Week 27, Friday,   The Bible in My Everyday: Celebrating

I was glad when they said to me,
"Let us go to the house of the LORD!
—Psalm 122:1

If you think religion is a dreary business, perhaps you should look at the word *holiday* in the dictionary. You'll find that it began as two words, *holy* and *day*. The first idea for a holiday, its first recorded appearance for our human race, was as a holy day, a day to celebrate God. It's almost like saying that the Bible invented fun. To be honest with you, that's what I believe, but I won't go into the long business of proving it.

The Old Testament is full of holidays, some of them stretching over several days, and most marked by special foods—all celebrating God's goodness in both past and present.

And *celebrate* is the word I want to use. *Fun* is really too trivial a word; it doesn't go deep enough, last long enough, or reach high enough. When I hear the ancient poet saying, "I was glad when they said to me, / 'Let us go to the house of the LORD,' " I get the feeling of celebration. Because that's the way I feel when I contemplate Sunday morning, and the opportunity to go to church. It is the weekly occasion for putting life in perspective, for joining friends (and strangers) in worshiping God, and for being reassured of my eternal worth. It is a particular, beautiful time to celebrate.

Help me, O Lord, by faith to make every day a holiday, a holy day to celebrate your love. Amen.

Week 27, Saturday   The Bible in My Everyday: Cleaning

The LORD said to Moses: "Go to the people and consecrate them today and tomorrow. Have them wash their clothes."
—Exodus 19:10

Contrary to what many people think, you won't find "Cleanliness is next to godliness" in your Bible. (We get it, actually, from John Wesley.) But you will discover, especially as you read the Old Testament, that cleanliness is a factor in godliness. The nation of Israel had codes of personal sanitation unlike any of their neighboring nations. Some students of medicine say that it was not until well into the nineteenth century that medical practices of sanitation caught up with the procedures outlined in the books of Exodus and Leviticus.

The reason behind Israel's conduct was practical, but it was even more profoundly spiritual. Or perhaps I should say that the results were practical, but the reason was spiritual. The Israelites did what they did because they believed God wanted them to—and as it turned out, they were healthier because of what they did. They were motivated by their belief that cleanliness was commanded by God and that it pleased God. After all, God had made a beautiful and orderly universe; oughtn't we to maintain it in a fashion worthy of such a God and such a gift?

So I wash my hands to the glory of God, and I say a prayer when I pick up trash someone has left behind. Cleanliness may not be next to godliness, but it can be a holy deed, dedicated to the God who has given us a beautiful life.

Help me to honor you today, dear Lord, by acts of order and cleanliness. In Jesus' name; amen.

Week 28, Sunday   **The Bible and Human Experience: Sickness**

Before I was afflicted I went astray: but now have I kept thy word.
—Psalm 119:67 KJV

The so-called man in the street sees sickness as unmitigated bad news. The Bible sees it as potentially purposeful. I don't believe that God sends sickness, but I'm very sure that God can use it. The ancient poet who gave us our text of the day discovered by experience that affliction worked a beneficial change in his life. Previously he had gone "astray," but after encountering a setback, he kept God's Word.

Sickness has a way of focusing our attention, but only if we will let it. A person with no faith-base in life will only ask, "Why should this happen to me? What have I done to deserve this?" Or perhaps he will say, "Life is just one fool thing after another." But faith—and the Scriptures—will cause us to ask, "What can I learn from this experience, and how can I put it to good use in my life?"

One thing for sure: any experience of sickness makes us realize how wonderful good health is, and what gratitude we ought to feel for each day of health and strength. I thank God every day for my health, because it seems to me that I have been especially favored in this regard. But on those occasions when I have had to undergo surgery, I have taken a fresh look at my health, and my sense of gratitude has moved to a deeper level. And perhaps that is partly what the psalmist meant.

When I am well, O Lord, make me thankful; and when I am sick, help me to learn. Amen.

Week 28, Monday   **The Bible and Human Experience: Success**

Read Ecclesiastes 2:1-11.

Probably nothing on earth is so earnestly pursued as success—and nothing is so disappointing in comparison to the effort expended. That surely is the conclusion of the writer of Ecclesiastes. He sounds like the original Yuppie, or Generation X, someone who staked his life on getting it all, only to discover that he was working with a wrong definition of *all*. He was so disillusioned, in fact, that for a while he felt as though the whole business of living was nothing but vanity, empty air.

The Bible honors success. The Old Testament teaches that advancement comes from the Lord. When you read the extraordinary story of Joseph in the book of Genesis, as he moves from slavery and even prison to the second highest place in government, you realize that the writer intends us to see not simply Joseph's virtue but more especially, God's blessing. Joseph acknowledged as much by giving his second son a name that meant, "God has made me fruitful in the land of my misfortunes" (Genesis 41:52).

But the Bible also recognizes that what appears to be success can be gotten by unworthy means. Not even the whole world is worth the losing of our souls, Jesus warned (Luke 9:23-25). And that means that everything our culture considers success isn't necessarily worthy of the name. Not if it is bought at the hurt of others, and not if in getting it we forsake God.

Whatever success I may gain, O Lord, may it be in a fashion that pleases you. Amen.

Week 28, Tuesday   The Bible and Human Experience: Fear

I will not be afraid of ten thousands of people, that have set themselves against me round about.   —*Psalm 3:6 KJV*

The Bible knows a great deal about fear, because the people who wrote it lived in a world where fear was so often a justified emotion. War was a constant factor—not somewhere over the ocean, but perhaps tomorrow from the city-state only a day's march away. Today a crop failure means only that some food item will cost more because it will have to be shipped in from a farther destination, but for people in biblical times, a crop failure meant starvation. Literally. We worry about illness, but we have hospitals, skilled medical specialists, and wonder drugs. The average person in the ancient world lived always on a razor's edge between sickness and health, between life and death. Fear? They had reasons to know it firsthand.

The Bible readily acknowledges the existence of fear, but its writers constantly respond with declarations of victory and inner peace. Take David, to whom Psalm 3 is attributed. As you read the psalm, you can see that he is in big trouble. His enemies are so numerous he can't count them. It sounds as if he is writing from a battlefield. Death may be imminent. But he tells us that he has been able to lie down, and sleep, and wake up again—because the Lord has seen him through. So he's not afraid, not even if his enemies number in the ten thousands. His confidence is in God.

You can't do better than that.

When I am afraid, O Lord, help me to put my trust in you. Thank you! Amen.

A merry heart doeth good like a medicine.
—Proverbs 17:22 KJV

I don't know how Christianity has gotten the image of dour-
ness and discomfort when one of its key attributes is joy. Next to
singing, the most characteristic sound in worship ought to be
laughter. Not just the laughter that comes from the telling of a
joke. I mean the kind of laughter that is the product of a merry
heart.

And who has better reason for a merry heart than the person
who is at peace with God and in love with life and humanity? If
we're at peace with God, we've taken care of the biggest business
of all—the state of our souls—and we're ready for whatever
comes in this world or in the next. Having peace with God goes a
long way toward helping us to love life and humanity. Of course
some circumstances and some people will put this peace to the
test, but they can't destroy it. Not if we keep the basic relationship, the tie with God, in good order.

A merry heart, the ancient wise person said, does good like
medicine. Think of it as a time capsule, but a really long-term
one. Instead of releasing portions of a medicine at stated intervals over part of a day, the merry heart releases spurts of gladness as needed, day and night, as long as we live. Talk about
good medicine! And you can get it without a prescription.

*I offer you my life today, O Lord, so I will be ready to receive
your gladness. In Jesus' name. Amen.*

A friend loveth at all times, and a brother is born for adversity.
—Proverbs 17:17 KJV

I wish I could bequeath to my children in my will the friends
who have blessed my life. If I could, I know they would always be
rich. The greatest friendship, of course, is my relationship with

God. I say without hesitancy that this is the friendship without which I cannot survive. But next in line in the order of life's blessings is human friendship, and in that I have been blessed far beyond my deserving.

Everyone should have some friends who prove their friendship by telling us when we're wrong; that kind of friend is absolutely essential. But we also need a friend who is simply always on our side. I have a friend like that. He has always stood by me. Whatever turn my life might take, I know he will be cheering for me. I may be wrong and know it, but still this man will be on my side.

There's a danger in this kind of friendship, of course, because such a person may confirm us in error when we ought to be redirected. But because he is such a good person, his favor hasn't affected me that way; rather, knowing that he is for me, I've become more self-critical, just to be sure I deserve his support.

I wish such a friend for you.

Make me worthy of good friends, O Lord. And please, be my special, eternal Friend. Amen.

Week 28, Friday   **The Bible and Human Experience: Betrayal**

> *Even my bosom friend in whom I trusted,*
>   *who ate of my bread, has lifted the heel against me.*
>   *—Psalm 41:9*

The greatest pain I have seen in people I have pastored has been the pain of betrayal by someone they trusted. Sometimes it was a business associate, sometimes a cherished friend, and sometimes, of course, a spouse. Few human experiences can be worse. A betrayal is a two-edged sword: it hurts our opinion of the perpetrator, and it diminishes our opinion of ourself.

Psalm 41 is credited to David, and the words of verse 9 might have come from any number of experiences in his life. I suppose that persons in positions of power are especially likely to be betrayed; their role invites it. The New Testament applies this verse to Jesus' experience when Judas betrayed him (John 13:18).

It's possible that when we feel betrayed, it is because we're in a mood of self-pity, which causes us to turn a molehill into a mountain. But even when the betrayal *is* a mountain, we have to climb it and not be intimidated by it. It's all too easy to let the fallout from betrayal be more destructive than the betrayal itself. And especially, it's important not to lose self-confidence. You must know who you are, no matter what the other person may have done to you—someone whom God loves and will never forsake.

May I never be guilty, O Lord, of betraying another; and if I am betrayed, help me to draw strength from Jesus Christ, my Savior and example. Amen.

Week 28, Saturday   **The Bible and Human Experience: Forgiveness**

Happy are those whose transgression is forgiven, whose sin is covered.
                                                            —Psalm 32:1

Our contemporary culture is trying hard to make forgiveness unnecessary by eliminating any sense of sin. We keep seeking ways to excuse our conduct without confessing that we have done wrong; it's our glands, we say, or our upbringing, our environment, our genes, the times in which we're living—or, of course, the stars, or fate. But rationalize as we will, something instinctive in us knows that we've done wrong. Pop culture may tell us that we ought to be satisfied with ourselves because we can't help ourselves, but we know better. We know we ought to do better than we've done.

That's why we need to be forgiven. By people, when it is people we have hurt, and by God. It's also why we need to forgive others. By forgiving others, we make our own experience of forgiveness more accessible. It's no wonder that in the Lord's Prayer we ask to be forgiven even as we forgive (Matthew 6:9-13). We have no ultimate capacity to receive forgiveness except as we extend it to those we think have done us wrong.

But especially we need to be forgiven by God. That person is happy, the psalmist said, whose transgression is forgiven, whose sin and guilt are gone. The result is the gladness of being given a clean sheet of paper or an unsoiled napkin, of facing a new and unspoiled day. And it is God's gift for those who will receive it.

I ask you, O Lord, in Jesus' name and because of his cross, to forgive me my sins this day, and to help me forgive my debtors. Amen.

8

LEARNING TO SEE
MORE DEEPLY

John Killinger

Do you have eyes, and fail to see? Do you have ears, and fail to hear?
                                                                —Mark 8:18

Jesus was in a boat with his disciples. They were worried because they had forgotten to bring any bread. Knowing their concern, Jesus reminded them that he had recently fed five thousand people in the wilderness and they had afterward picked up twelve baskets full of broken pieces of bread. He had also fed four thousand people on another occasion, and they had recovered seven baskets full of pieces. "Do you have eyes," he asked them, "and fail to see?"

In other words, they were in the boat with the Master of all bread-making, yet they were worried about not having any bread.

It is easy for us to see the spiritual blindness of the disciples. But what about our own? Jesus is with us as well, every day of our lives. Yet we fret and fuss about the shortages in our own existence—not having enough money, enough time, enough friends, enough love.

Suppose we made it our project over the next four weeks to learn to see more deeply into the nature of life in Christ Jesus. Maybe then we would stop worrying about the lack of things in our lives and marvel at the abundance. Maybe we would begin to see and hear with the sharpness of real disciples. Maybe our lives would become filled with wonder and mystery, and we would live with true excitement.

It's worth a try, isn't it?

Help me, O Lord, to peer more deeply into the meaning of discipleship, and to see what a joyous thing it is to be your follower. Amen.

Week 29, Monday   Being Touched Again by Christ

Read Mark 8:22-26.

This is one of the most remarkable stories in the Bible because it is the story of the only miracle Jesus had to perform twice. Why is that? Why didn't the miracle work fully the first time?

Is it possible that the Gospel writer wanted us to put ourselves in the blind man's place? Perhaps he wanted us to realize that we don't always see perfectly the first time we encounter Jesus, that we don't yet know all that this new life requires. We don't, do we? Human nature being what it is, we learn to see a little at a time. We actually *grow* in understanding and perception. It is a gradual process, not a sudden achievement.

Maybe at our first meeting with Jesus, our sight is much improved, as this blind man's sight was. But we may still have certain doubts, prejudices, and misunderstandings that have to be dealt with. So we keep returning to Jesus and asking to see better, to be more sensitive to life and its meanings, to have a clearer sight of the things that really matter, that give honest perspective to our existence. And Jesus continues to give us better vision.

Abraham Lincoln wrote once that he did not have much use for a man who is not wiser today than he was yesterday. Maybe that is why we are given a whole lifetime to learn and grow. And perhaps that is why, as followers of Jesus, it is so important for us never to assume that we have perfect vision and so stop praying for improvement.

Being given the ability to see well is truly a miracle. And it is a miracle we ought to ask for every day of our lives, until, by the time we die, we will be able to see well God and Christ in everything around us.

Touch my eyes again and again, O Christ, that I may see ever more clearly, until I see you face-to-face in this life or the one to come. Amen.

> *When shall I come and behold*
> *the face of God?*
> *—Psalm 42:2*

Psalm 42 paints a beautiful picture of a deer in arid country looking for water. The psalmist had probably seen such a sight, for he lived where summers were hot and dry, droughts could be long and hard, and the land often became parched and dusty. Then, in a great leap, he turns the picture around. "That is what my soul is like," he says in effect, "as thirsty as a deer seeking everywhere for water, for flowing streams to slake its thirst."

Sometimes our lives are like that. We go through times of drought and starvation, longing for spiritual depths we have been unable to find. We can understand the psalmist's cry, "When shall I come and behold / the face of God?" For we too have thirsted as he did. We too have felt wrung out and bone dry from our experiences. We want to see the face of God, but he seems far away or completely absent. For me, those times have come when I have been too busy with my work and have allowed my spiritual life to deteriorate into mere perfunctory gestures. I have felt lonely, worthless, and deserted.

The psalm ends, however, not in despair, but in exaltation. "Hope in God," the psalmist writes, "for I shall again praise him, / my help and my God" (v. 11). In other words, sometimes we don't see deeply enough into the nature of life and events to realize that God is there in the desert. But that is where faith comes in. Faith teaches us to wait and hope, to realize that God hasn't deserted us. Eventually we will see God, and when we do, our joy will be full again.

Learning to wait, in the knowledge that God is never far from the longing heart, is an important part of seeing.

Like the deer, O God, I too am thirsty for the living streams. Give me patience, and help me to know that I shall indeed see your face. Through Christ my Lord, Amen.

Week 29, Wednesday   **Hoping for What We Can't See**

I consider that the sufferings of this present time are not worth comparing with the glory about to be revealed to us. . . . Now hope that is seen is not hope.   *—Romans 8:18, 24*

Some of the greatest songs of hope and expectation have been composed by people who appeared to have the least to hope for in this world. Think about the wonderful Negro spirituals created and sung by enslaved people living in desperate circumstances, or the psalms and hymns written by those in prison or in exile. The faith of those people shames us for our small complaints about life—our minor illnesses, our setbacks at work, our failure to secure a promotion, our inability to afford something we really want, such as a new car or a larger house.

One of the great things about the Christian faith is the way it sets all things in perspective. Through Scripture it reminds us that nothing in this life—no suffering or hardship or lack of anything—is worth thinking about in comparison with the fullness of God's glory that is always on the verge of being revealed to us.

There are times when we lose sight of God's glory, even though there are signs of it all around us all the time. Then we are truly impoverished, because we become imprisoned by earthly things. We have not learned to see truly and deeply. That is why it is important to continue to be touched by Christ, so that, in hope, we can see what is invisible to the merely human eye but has been revealed to us by the grace of God.

Keep touching my eyes, O Christ, until I see the glory of God both in this present world and in the world yet to be born. For, having heard of such glory, I am not content with anything less. Amen.

Week 29, Thursday   Seeing the World as God Sees It

God saw everything that he had made, and indeed, it was very good.   *—Genesis 1:31*

This remarkable statement occurs at the conclusion of the account of creation. After God had made the world, the sun, the moon, the stars, the animals, the fish, the birds, the plants, and man and woman, like a master craftsman God simply looked at the results of his efforts and admired them.

The Hebrew language, in which the Old Testament was written, did not have the adverb *very* that we use. When it wanted to intensify a verb or an adjective, it merely repeated the word. The word for "good" in Hebrew is *tuv*. So what the writer of Genesis really wrote was that God looked at what he had made and saw that it was *"tuv tuv."* It was double good, "very good."

There is nothing more wonderful than to be able to see the world as God saw it, to look at it and see how beautiful it is. "Lord, I do fear / Thou'st made the world too beautiful this year," wrote Edna St. Vincent Millay in her poem "God's World." If she sees one more burnished autumn leaf or hears one more bird calling in the sky, she will not be able to bear it.

Let us spend time every day looking at God's world until we see beyond the surface appearance. Then the world will indeed become as beautiful for us as it was for Millay, for we shall see the creative hand of God in all of it. Every day will be more filled with love and worship than the day before.

Teach me to see everything as you see it, O God, so that I may rejoice with you, both in the creation and in the new creation. Through Jesus my Lord, Amen.

Week 29, Friday   Seeing Our Sin

In the year that King Uzziah died, I saw the Lord sitting on a throne, high and lofty. . . . And I said: "Woe is me! I am lost, for I am a man of unclean lips, and I live among a people of unclean lips."   —Isaiah 6:1, 5

One of the results of seeing more deeply into the nature of things is the realization that we ourselves are very imperfect and unworthy. When the prophet Isaiah had his vision of God in the temple, he was suddenly struck by feelings of humility and unworthiness.

Such feelings are good for us as human beings, reminding us of our place in the economy of existence. It is when we become proud and self-reliant that we offend against the laws of nature.

"What does the Lord require of you," asked the prophet Micah, "but to do justice, and to love kindness, and to walk humbly with your God?" (6:8).

The story is told that a group of tourists were being shown through the home of Paganini, the great violinist, when a young girl impetuously snatched up his Stradivarius violin and began to play on it. When she had put it down, the guide resumed his talk by saying that Fritz Kreisler, another famous violinist, had recently visited the house.

"Oh," said the girl, "I'll bet he did just what I did and played on Paganini's violin!"

"No, miss," said the guide. "Everyone begged him to, but he said he was not worthy to play it."

Seeing who we really are in the eyes of God and the world is necessary part of our living truly and well.

Let me see your face, O God, in order that I may know who I am in relation to you. Then let me walk humbly and modestly in the world, for Jesus' sake. Amen

Week 29, Saturday   **Seeing and Purity**

Blessed are the pure in heart, for they will see God.
—Matthew 5:8

Sometimes we think the innocent are blind and don't see very much. They are often pictured as stumbling into problems because they simply aren't wise enough to avoid them.

But biblical faith says otherwise. It is those whose hearts and minds are pure, who are guileless and childlike, who will really see the face of God.

What can we do to be pure of heart? Is that something we can work to achieve, or is it something natural that cannot be won or forced? The Bible speaks of purity as a quality that comes from constant association with God and living in the Spirit. We can see this kind of change in ordinary life. It is remarkable how different a worldly, cynical person becomes through prolonged experience in a spiritual situation, such as living in a monastery or being around good, simple folk on a farm. Everything about the person changes over time—attitude, language, expectations from life.

I have a musician friend who lived and worked most of his life in an ethos that was cruel, bitter, and earthy. A few years ago he married a woman who was sweet and pure and who adored him for the marvelous music he was able to make. Gradually the man's attitude and behavior have changed. Now he speaks softly and gently, and has begun to see the hand of God in his life, guiding him into better things. He has joined a church and is learning the joys of servanthood.

Spending time in the presence of God makes us pure. And the purity, as Jesus' words in our text say, enables us to see God. We don't have to be scholars, understanding everything in the Scriptures. We don't have to be preachers or teachers or anything else. All we have to do is associate with purity by living prayerfully and spiritually; then we can begin to see God everywhere.

Teach me, O Lord, to long for purity of heart, in order that I may see the one thing I would most like to see—your face in the midst of the world where I live. Amen.

Week 30, Sunday   Learning to See the Logs

Why do you see the speck in your neighbor's eye, but do not notice the log in your own eye?   —Matthew 7:3

As we learn to see more deeply into the nature of life and godliness, we look at our neighbors with more charity and ourselves with more suspicion. That is, seeing how wonderful God's world is and how God is present in his world makes us more loving and forgiving to our neighbors, while making us more aware of our own shortcomings and failures.

Jesus was addressing a large group of disciples when he talked about judging others. It is best, he said, not to judge others at all, for we are sure to be judged by the same standards we apply to them. And he fully understood our human tendency to see the tiny faults of others while ignoring the major faults in ourselves. So he asked this comical question about how we can see the speck in our neighbor's eye while missing the log in our own.

If you will take the log out of your own eye, he said, you can see more clearly to remove the speck from your neighbor's eye.

It may seem unrealistic to overlook the faults of others, especially in the world of business, where competition is often fierce. But how happy is the person who regards others as the children of God and as a result minimizes any mistakes or malformations of character seen in them. Such a person is bound to be close to the heart of God!

Forgive me, O God, for finding fault with others when I have so many faults of my own. Teach me to work at freeing myself from such faults so that I may see more clearly the beauty and goodness in my neighbor. Amen.

Week 30, Monday   Seeing the Lamb

The next day he saw Jesus coming toward him and declared, "Here is the Lamb of God who takes away the sin of the world!"
—John 1:29

"If I could close my eyes and then open them to see whatever I wanted, what would I most like to see?" That's a game I have sometimes played. Some people would like to see a beautiful lake nestled among the trees, or snow-covered mountains. Others would like to see a lovely young woman or a handsome young man. Still other might wish to see a magical scene at the bottom of the ocean. I would like to see my mother and father, who are both dead, or my sister, who died when I was still a child.

But what more wonderful sight could any eyes behold than the one seen by John the Baptist, who looked up from the riverbank where he was baptizing people and beheld Jesus coming toward him. "Here is the Lamb of God!" he exclaimed, anticipating the day when Jesus would die on the cross even as the sacrificial lambs for the Passover were being slaughtered by the priests.

Think how it would change your life to be able to see what John saw that day. Would anything ever be the same? E. Stanley Jones, the great missionary, wrote in his autobiography about a man he had met in Africa whose name was "After." He named himself that because he was a vastly different person after he had met Jesus than he had been before.

The wonderful thing about spiritual vision is that you *can* see Jesus coming toward you. And you *can* be changed by what you see. It is all a matter of learning how to see.

Lord, give me the spiritual vision to see you coming toward me now. Let me dwell on your presence until I can actually dwell in your presence forever. Amen.

Lift up your eyes on high and see:
Who created these?
—*Isaiah 40:26*

This question, asked of human beings by God, sounds very much like the questions God asked Job about the creation (Job 38–40), beginning with, "Where were you when I laid the foundation of the earth?" (Job 38:4).

Through Isaiah, God tells us to raise our eyes. The command isn't merely rhetorical. We are to lift our eyes on high—beyond the scale of usual seeing, beyond ordinary lines of vision, to behold what is extraordinary about God's creative powers.

Think about some of the great things you have seen in your lifetime: an ocean whipped to ten-foot waves by a powerful storm; majestic mountains rising above the plains, craggy and forbidding; a raging forest fire, blazing and crackling as it devours hundreds of acres of timber every minute; a herd of elephants stampeding through a small native village; a pod of dolphins leaping and falling and leaping again in the ocean; a tornado grinding and chewing its way through the helpless countryside, tossing houses and cars in the air as if they were made of plastic.

Don't these visions direct your thoughts to God, whose power is greater than the sum of all of them? Don't they make you want to sing the "Hallelujah Chorus" and kneel in worship of the Almighty?

I remember standing once in an ice cave deep inside a glacier in Switzerland. The sunlight coming through the thick walls of ice appeared blue and I felt as if I were in a gigantic freezer. As the ice moved and shifted, I could hear great cracking sounds. I felt very insignificant before such a mighty part of the creation, and was filled with a deep sense of wonder and adoration.

Seeing what God has made or done does determine who we are and how we live, doesn't it?

O God, I fall down before you in praise and worship, for you are greater than all the wonders of your creation. Through Jesus Christ my Lord. Amen.

There is an evil that I have seen under the sun, and it lies heavy upon human kind: those to whom God gives wealth, possessions, and honor, so that they lack nothing of all that they desire, yet God does not enable them to enjoy these things, but a stranger enjoys them.   —*Ecclesiastes 6:1-2*

If we learn to see life truly, we are able to learn lessons from the evil and misfortune our eyes behold.

Qohelet, the preacher of Ecclesiastes, was saddened to see how many people who are greatly blessed with material possessions don't really enjoy them at all. Sometimes other persons enjoy their possessions more than they do—maybe the people who work for them or the families who live with them. And sometimes it is even the people who come after them—their heirs and descendants—who really enjoy the fortunes amassed by the hardworking progenitors.

What should we learn from such a sight? That the getting and holding of wealth does not make people happy. Sometimes the poorest people in the world are the happiest, for their minds are unburdened by the care and management of great estates. There is a story about a Zen master whose little home was burgled while he was away. Nothing remained when he came back. But looking out the window and seeing the moon, he commented, "At least they didn't take that." Accustomed to little, he cared more about the natural world he could still enjoy than about his few possessions.

Is it possible that there is a correlation between seeing and having? That the more we have, the less we see? What would that say about developing a spiritual life?

You have blessed me with so much, dear God, that I am embarrassed when I come into your presence. For, in your presence, I must admit that none of it means half as much as being with you. Amen.

And let us consider how to provoke one another to love and good deeds, not neglecting to meet together, as is the habit of some,

*but encouraging one another, and all the more as you see the Day
approaching.*   *—Hebrews 10:24-25*

Here is another aspect of spiritual seeing. It has to do with seeing the great Day of the Lord as it approaches, the day when
earth's structures will melt and give way to great anti-structures
of God, when Christ will come and reign over the entire world,
and justice will roll down like waters.

Most of us, from the stance of our polite, civilized religion, do
not speak or even think very much about the Day of the Lord. It
is considered an extravagant idea, one belonging only to the
apocalyptic expectations of primitive peoples and not to a sophis-
ticated culture like ours.

But perhaps we are missing something in our seeing by
neglecting the idea. Jesus believed in the Day of the Lord. So did
Peter and John and all the others founders of the church. It was
a central tenet of their faith and understanding. Can we accept
them as spiritual guides if we so easily dismiss this important
aspect of their teaching?

We don't have to join a fanatical band living in the mountains
and waiting for the Day of the Lord to come at any time. Jesus
said it will come as a thief in the night, without fanfare or warning. But meditating on it as a habitual part of our eschatology can
be very helpful in setting life and its priorities in order.

It might even lead us to want to "provoke one another to love
and good deeds," as the scripture says.

*Lord, help me not to be snobbish about this great idea from
the Bible, but to see it as a reminder of the fragility and tem-
poral nature of the world I live in. Then I shall walk more
humbly and circumspectly, knowing that any day could
become the Great Day. Amen.*

Week 30, Friday   **Looking Up to the Hills**

*I lift up my eyes to the hills—
    from where will my help come?
My help comes from the LORD,
    who made heaven and earth.*
                                        —Psalm 121:1-2

Part of learning to see deeply into the nature of life is acquiring the ability to look to the hills—to look up to God, who made heaven and earth. It does not mean that God will always answer our prayers the way we expect or hope. Sometimes the loved one with cancer dies, or the one out of a job never finds suitable work. But there is something steadying, anchoring, about looking toward God. It reminds us that we are not the center of the universe: God is. And knowing that God is there, that we worship the Creator of everything, has a way of diminishing our problems, of setting them in their proper order in the universe. We feel better, just knowing that God is God.

Some years ago when I was overseas, I received word from my father that my mother was dying. For two days I couldn't get plane reservations. Feeling very powerless, I sat down with my Bible and began reading the book of Acts, which is filled with stories of God's power and the miracles that occurred in the lives of those first Christians. At last a sense of God's presence overcame me, I became calm and my heart was relieved. I prayed for Mother and commited her to God. I had lifted up my eyes and seen the Source of all our help.

Mother did recover and lived several more years. But even if she hadn't, I would have been comforted. I had seen what we all need to see in times of great distress or trouble, that despite everything, God is always in charge of the world.

Remind me, O God, to lift up my eyes daily to the hills. For if I truly have faith in you, I will be able to lose or to profit, to suffer or to abound, with equal joy and satisfaction. Amen.

Week 30, Saturday   **Seeing God's Power to Save**

See, the LORD's hand is not too short to save,
nor his ear too dull to hear.
                                        —Isaiah 59:1

Seeing is not an option according to Isaiah, but a command. "Look!" says the prophet. "See! Stare at this thing! Notice it!" It is as if he took us by the shoulder, shook us, and ordered us to look at the ability of God to save us when we are in trouble.

His message was for the Israelites. He had been upbraiding

them for the falsity of their worship and the way they had been neglecting the ways of God by desecrating the sabbath and failing to care for the poor and needy. Then he simply stopped and said, "See this: God can still save you."

But the message applies to us as well, doesn't it? We too have a way of forgetting that God can save us, can extricate us and set our feet in the right direction again. Our problem is that we try to go on in our own power and wisdom, making things worse instead of better. We compound failures in business, problems in marriage, difficulties in interpersonal relationships, without stopping to realize that God can help.

Sometimes it takes a complete breakdown, a crash of some kind, to bring us to our senses and make us turn to God.

But a person who is learning to see life better every day will start factoring in the power of God to save. He will say to himself, "I must always remember, before my troubles start to pile up, to call on God, because God's arm is never too short to reach down and help me. He will hear my prayer and answer at any stage."

Forgive me, O God, for the many times I have tried to make it on my own in spite of problems. Teach me to call on you at all times, in order to prevent the problems from ever getting a foothold in my life. Through Jesus my Lord. Amen.

Week 31, Sunday   **The Light in the Darkness**

For it is the God who said, "Let light shine out of darkness," who has shone in our hearts to give the light of the knowledge of the glory of God in the face of Jesus Christ.
—2 Corinthians 4:6

Unlike cats and bats and other nocturnal creatures, we human beings require light in order to see. It is no wonder, then, that the gospel of Jesus Christ often talks about the Light that came into the world at his birth. "The light shines in the darkness," says the Gospel of John, "and the darkness did not overcome it" (John 1:5). Light and darkness became figures of speech to signify our inability to find life and direction for ourselves without intervention from beyond; we needed—absolutely required—the coming of light in order to find our way.

Writing to the Christians at Corinth, the apostle Paul made a connection between the God who first made light for the world by creating the sun and the moon and the God who showed us his heavenly glory by sending Jesus into our spiritual darkness. Jesus himself, standing in the temple during the festival of the Jews that featured the use of mirrored candlelight at night, announced, "I am the light of the world. Whoever follows me will never walk in darkness but will have the light of life" (John 8:12).

As we grow in our ability to see everything more clearly, it is good to acknowledge our indebtedness to this Light, to realize that we would have no true vision if it were not for this Light that came shining into our mortal darkness. However wise we become, however acutely we learn to see, we will never grow beyond the brilliance of Paul's observation that God has shown us his glory in the face of Jesus.

I will set my face toward this Light forever, O God, so that I will never walk in darkness; for he illumines my path as no one else is able to do. Amen.

Week 31, Monday   Seeing Angels

And I saw another mighty angel coming down from heaven, wrapped in a cloud, with a rainbow over his head; his face was like the sun, and his legs like pillars of fire.

—Revelation 10:1

Have you ever seen an angel? Chances are, you haven't. There have been a lot of books and articles written in recent years about the sighting of angels, but the percentage of those who have reported such sights is still only a fraction of 1 percent. The rest of us are left to debate whether they have witnessed real messengers from heaven or mere illusions of the mind and heart, and to ask what the significance is anyway of seeing angels in this world.

In the Bible, angels always serve a single purpose: they are emissaries of God to carry messages or to remind people of God's presence. They are intermediaries, representatives of the Holy One of Israel.

That there are so many reports of angels today probably

speaks well of the religious fervor of our time. It means that many hearts are tuned to receiving the messages of God. And it may well be, if you are learning to see with more and more spiritual discernment, that you will one day receive an angelic message.

But don't hold your breath. The sighting of angels isn't necessarily a reward for spiritual devotion. Many great saints have never spoken of being visited by an angel. They have simply gone on from day to day trying to learn to live more completely in the divine presence, whether they saw anything special or not. And that is what we all have to do. There is plenty of time, in the world to come, for seeing angels.

I have already seen all I need to see, dear God, by beholding you in the face of the Lord Jesus Christ. Help me to be faithful to that vision, and to celebrate the reports of angels in the lives of others. Amen.

Week 31, Tuesday   Rejoicing in the Human Things We See

See what large letters I make when I am writing in my own hand!
—Galatians 6:11

This intriguing sentence comes near the end of Paul's letter to the Christians in Galatia. Apparently he had used an amanuensis, or professional writer, to pen the letter for him up to this point. Then, in a desire to become more personal, more intimate, he seized the stylus from the writer's hand and scribbled some words himself. But when he looked at his marks on the papyrus, he saw how large and awkward they seemed in comparison with the writer's.

The Galatians doubtless saw many things as they read Paul's letter, for it was one of his masterpieces. He showed them the folly of continuing to be entangled in legalism after discovering the grace of God in Jesus Christ. He talked extensively of the difference between living by the flesh—human nature—and living in the Spirit of God. But they were probably greatly intrigued by the sight, at the end of the letter, of Paul's own handwriting, which made the letter all the more personal and meaningful.

In today's mail I received a packet from a woman in another

state containing a small booklet of her minister husband's writings. I had known him years ago. The writings are not outstanding but they were dear to my friend's wife and she wanted to honor him after his death by having them published. I read them quite reverently, because I know how important they were to her. My face still feels a little crusty from the tears I shed as my friend's writings brought him and his personality vividly to mind.

One of the things about learning to see in the Spirit of God is how much more meaningful it makes the little things of life—the handwriting of a loved one, a letter from a friend, the sight of calluses on an old person's hand, the beauty of a teacup, the taste of a loaf of bread, the smell of a rose. For then we see that it is all part of the interrelatedness with which God has made the world, and the richness of the lives we are permitted to lead. And the little things then bring us back to God—sometimes with tears in our eyes!

Thank you, dear God, for the sometimes overwhelming beauty of the world in which I live. Grant that I may never see anything at all without being reminded of you, through Jesus Christ my Lord. Amen.

Week 31, Wednesday   Seeing Is Believing

Unless I see the mark of the nails in his hands, and put my finger in the mark of the nails and my hand in his side, I will not believe.   *—John 20:25*

These are the famous words of the apostle Thomas, speaking to his fellow disciples after they said they had seen the risen Christ. They pinpoint a problem we all have: it is very hard to believe fully in what we have not actually seen or handled with our own hands.

But one of the advantages of spiritual seeing is that one comes more and more to understand and rely on things that are unseen in this world. We begin to realize that reality is something that transcends mere physical existence. In fact, the very greatest things often don't have a physical embodiment—things such as faith, love, joy, peace, heaven, and God. Part of what it means to achieve a mature spiritual nature is to arrive at the point where one trusts the unseen world as much as the world that is seen.

Jesus of course showed himself to Thomas a few days after Thomas made his statement, and invited him to put his hands in the wounds to verify that it was indeed his Master. But the beautiful thing was that Thomas was so overwhelmed by the presence of his Lord that he didn't need to touch him anymore. He merely fell down and cried, "My Lord and my God!"

With Thomas, we too are trying to move from seeing to not-seeing, or from seeing with our physical eyes to seeing with an inner vision—a vision that cannot be confused by mere physical appearances.

Lord, help me to see your love and power in my life at all times, and not be swayed by doubts or earthly problems. Amen.

Week 31, Thursday   Seeing the Past

The people worshiped the Lord all the days of Joshua, and all the days of the elders who outlived Joshua, who had seen all the great work that the Lord had done for Israel.   —Judges 2:7

Part of our learning to see deeply involves a constant reviewing of all that God has done for us in the past. Whenever the people of Israel remembered what God had done, they remained faithful and walked in the paths of righteousness. When they forgot, they began to go astray. It is the same with us: remembering helps us to walk in the presence of God.

Life goes so fast today that most of us don't spend as much time recalling the past as people once did. We don't go out onto the front porch after dinner and while away the hours until bedtime talking about our fathers and mothers, aunts and uncles, siblings and cousins, and what we all did in previous years. Our orientation is toward the present and the future, and we run breathlessly onward, seldom realizing why life seems to be out of control.

It is important, if we truly desire to see with inner vision, to review the past and learn from it. Someone has said, "He who does not know history is doomed to repeat it." That is, if we don't understand the past and what has occurred in it, we will make the same mistakes as before and remain helpless in the flow of events.

It is especially important to remember what God has done for us—the food we've eaten, the jobs we've held, the homes we've had, the people who've befriended us, the illnesses and problems we've survived—the whole panorama of blessing and growth that has been our lives. When we remember, we will praise God and life will seem good.

Forgive me, dear Lord, if I have failed to remember all the good things you've done in my life. Teach me to rehearse them daily, that I may walk in your presence forever. Amen.

Week 31, Friday   Seeing an Inspiration

He looked up and saw rich people putting their gifts into the treasury; he also saw a poor widow put in two small copper coins. He said, "Truly I tell you, this poor widow has put in more than all of them; for all of them have contributed out of their abundance, but she out of her poverty has put in all she had to live on."
—Luke 21:1-4

They were tiny, almost worthless coins. *Lepta,* they were called in Greek. So small and valueless that nobody bothered to put an inscription on them. Just little hammered-out disks of copper.

But they were all the widow had. And she said a prayer and dropped them into the box at the temple.

It touched Jesus' heart. It was the kind of true devotion he so often missed in Israel, where wealthy people usually made a great show of putting in large amounts of money they could well afford to give. And he immortalized the woman's gift.

The world is full of beautiful sights like this. If we only have eyes to see them, they can become constant inspirations to us, and help us to live at deeper and deeper levels of commitment. People caring for aged parents. Parents pushing a wheelchair with a crippled child. Children sharing toys with each other. Neighbors running next door to carry a loaf of freshly baked bread. One homeless person giving another half a sandwich he has just purchased.

But we have to *see*. And real seeing begins where it did for Jesus—in the hours and days he spent alone with God. He saw everything in the world more clearly because he was a man of deep prayer. So will we see everything more clearly, when we become persons of prayer.

I want to see the world through Jesus' eyes, dear Lord. Help me to walk and live as he did, in order that I may begin to see as he did. For his name's sake. Amen.

Week 31, Saturday   Seeing When We Can't See

Saul got up from the ground, and though his eyes were open, he could see nothing; so they led him by the hand and brought him into Damascus.   —Acts 9:8

There wasn't anybody in the Bible more full of certainty about what he believed and how he should behave than the ardent Pharisee known as Saul of Tarsus—who later became the apostle Paul. He was so sure of his way that he went everywhere persecuting the Jews who had succumbed to belief in a Messiah named Jesus. He was on his way to Damascus, a city where there was a large contingent of Christians, when he was suddenly struck down by a great light and heard the voice of the Lord addressing him.

Perhaps as a reminder of his erroneous way of seeing things, he was struck blind and had to be led into the city, where he remained in darkness until God sent a man named Ananias to restore his sight. What a humbling experience it must have been for Saul, being led about by another person.

But in his blindness he learned something: he learned who the Lord of his life really was, and what he must now do to serve him. Saul's lack of sightedness became a blessing, and helped to produce in him a way of seeing that would be his soul's salvation.

Sometimes, if we are proud and self-centered, we too have to be struck down before we see the real light and our lives are greatly changed. Pray that it may not be so with you, but that you will live each day eagerly trying to see the truth God has for you and determined to live by that truth as you find it.

It is true, dear Lord, that we can sometimes see more with our eyes shut than with them open, especially if they are closed in prayer. Help me to see what you want me to see, so that I will never need the drastic treatment Paul received in order to do your will. Amen.

Week 32, Sunday   The Blessedness of Seeing God's Works

Then turning to the disciples, Jesus said to them privately, "Blessed are the eyes that see what you see! For I tell you that many prophets and kings desired to see what you see, but did not see it, and to hear what you hear, but did not hear it."
—Luke 10:23-24

How privileged the disciples were, Jesus told them, to behold God's kingdom coming in their time. They had just returned from their first mission to preach the gospel and were telling Jesus what had happened on that trip. They were excited to speak of the response of the people and the power with which the kingdom had come upon them.

But if the disciples were privileged, how much more are we, to have seen the mighty acts of God throughout history, as well as in our own time. We live in the age of electronics, when more people have heard the good news than at any time before us. Billy Graham alone has preached to more people than all the evangelists in the nineteen centuries before ours.

Perhaps we don't stop to think of the importance of this, of how many lives are daily being changed for God around the world. Part of learning to see deeply means discovering where God's Spirit is at work in the world and how it is touching millions of people. What the Spirit is doing in our own lives is important too, of course. But what is happening to us is enhanced when we realize that it is only a small part of what God is accomplishing at any one moment. The sheer *bigness* of the divine work is enough to produce a sense of ecstasy in our hearts!

Help me, O Lord, to see beyond my own life and realize that you are affecting the lives of millions at this moment; and let this be a cause of celebration and joy to me, through Jesus Christ. Amen.

Jesus answered him, "Very truly, I tell you, no one can see the kingdom of God without being born from above."

—John 3:3

Jesus was talking with the Jewish leader Nicodemus about how we become fulfilled in God's eyes. The only way to do it, Jesus said, is to be born from above. Not just born again, as the older translations of the Bible put it, but from above. We see the kingdom, he said, when we are given the gift of sight from above.

No one can force this sight. It isn't something we get for going to Sunday school without fail for forty-two years or for memorizing scripture verses. It is a gift we only hope to receive before we die. And the only thing we can do to put ourselves in the way of receiving such a gift is to live receptively, ready to recognize the gift when it comes upon us.

This is what the life of prayer and meditation is all about. It is about putting ourselves so often in the way of the presence of God that there is a better-than-average chance that the presence will come to us, and we will feel caught up in it and will be changed, transformed, born from above.

Jesus went on to explain to Nicodemus that it all has to do with the Spirit. This experience is not of the flesh or the world, but of the Spirit. When the Spirit takes over, there are no limitations to what can happen. But the Spirit only takes over when we stop trying to control everything and give the reins to God. And that only happens when we become people of prayer and devotion.

It frightens me, dear God, to think of losing control and being lost in the Spirit. Teach me the joy of abandoning myself, that I may be found in you. Through Christ my Lord. Amen.

Week 32, Tuesday   **Seeing More Than Meets the Eye**

As he came out of the temple, one of his disciples said to him, "Look, Teacher, what large stones and what large buildings!" Then Jesus asked him, "Do you see these great buildings? Not one stone will be left here upon another; all will be thrown down."   *—Mark 13:1-2*

One of the true marks of spiritual discernment is the ability to look at impressive things and see their real nature, not their mere appearance.

The disciples, country men and strangers to the city, were overwhelmed by the size of the stones in the Jerusalem temple and by the sheer magnificence of the temple buildings themselves. But Jesus saw beyond the grandeur of the temple. With a prophetic understanding of God's displeasure with Israel, he knew God would allow the Romans to destroy the city of Jerusalem, and that not a single stone would be left standing on the site.

The sensitive Christian, trained to see into the nature of things, is not misled by the beauty or size of anything into supposing it is more important than it really is. He knows that the love of a small child is better than the insincere flattery of a business associate or an official in the government. He sees that a job he can do with a whole heart is preferable to one that might pay much more but give less inner satisfaction. He understands that a faithful, loving wife, however plain in appearance, is far better than a beautiful woman with a selfish nature.

The Bible says that God judges by the heart, not the outer appearance of people. That is the way we learn to see things when we spend time in the presence of God and acquire the ability to penetrate to the inner worth of everything.

I want to see as you see, O Lord, and judge things as you judge them. Teach me to look through your eyes, that I may truly understand the world. Through Jesus Christ. Amen.

Week 32, Wednesday   Seeing the Way Back

Create in me a clean heart, O God,
and put a new and right spirit within me.
—Psalm 51:10

Sir Francis Chichester, the famed British explorer, was the first man to fly across the Tasmanian Sea. It was a long, difficult trip requiring him to stop and refuel at a tiny island en route. Soon after he left the ground, clouds filled the sky and turbulence began blowing him off course. He knew that if he missed his island, he would perish in the sea.

Watching for a break in the clouds, Chichester abandoned his course, and began to fly toward the opening, where he used his sextant to work out new bearings and chart another course to the island. He had to do this several times in the journey, and feared he might miss the island by miles. But eventually he flew under the clouds at the spot where he thought the island would be, and almost as if by a miracle, there it was.

Life is like that for most of us. We are constantly being blown off course by this or that. The important thing, whenever we see the sun breaking through, is to head for the light as fast as we can and take new bearings to get ourselves back on course.

Even those who see deeply into life don't always live in God's presence. But they learn to return to that presence and chart a new course whenever they can. This is what David, the psalmist, was doing in this psalm. He had sinned against God, but he courageously returned and asked God to give him a fresh start.

I understand these words, O God, for I am often blown off course in my own life. Help me to keep my attention fixed on you, and, whenever that attention is broken for any reason, to hurry back to you as quickly as possible. In Jesus' name. Amen.

Week 32, Thursday   **Seeing the Lord in Others**

Then the righteous will answer him, "Lord, when was it that we saw you hungry and gave you food, or thirsty and gave you something to drink? And when was it that we saw you a stranger and welcomed you, or naked and gave you clothing?"
                                                            —Matthew 25:37-38

I was in the Detroit airport the day after Mother Teresa died. The newspaper headline read: "Mother Teresa says, 'I see God in every human face.'" I thought about it as I walked along and discovered she was right. When I looked for him, God was there in the face of a crippled man in a wheelchair, in the face of an elderly woman being led by a child, in the face of the child. I only needed eyes to see.

But Jesus' parable requires action on our part as well as seeing. And that may cost us more than a mere gesture or a cup of water. After I had said in a sermon that we ought to see Jesus in the faces of those who come to us in need, a man in my congregation in Los Angeles wrote me a letter. The suggestion had been an expensive one, he said. He had answered an ad from someone who wanted to give away a wolfhound, and had agreed to meet the owner on the beach.

"As the man approached with the dog, I could see why he wanted to give the dog away. It was in terrible shape, and so was he. It was obvious he had AIDS and hadn't long to live. My first instinct was to keep on walking and not even acknowledge that I was the person who called him. Then I remembered that sermon. So help me, when I looked in the fellow's face, I couldn't help imagining I was seeing Jesus. I took the dog, so he wouldn't worry about it. The dog is going to be fine but it has cost me a lot of money in vet's fees!"

Even though the man was fussing, he felt good about what he had done. Learning to see Jesus in the faces of people in need—and taking appropriate action—is a good step toward personal spirituality, and brings a promised blessing.

While I could never deny you, dear Christ, I could easily deny others. Teach me to know when you are present in others, awaiting my love and care. For my very soul's sake. Amen.

Week 32, Friday   Seeing the New Heaven and New Earth

Then I saw a new heaven and a new earth; for the first heaven and the first earth had passed away, and the sea was no more. And I saw the holy city, the new Jersualem, coming down out of heaven from God, prepared as a bride adorned for her husband.
—Revelation 21:1-2

These words help describe one of the most beautiful visions ever seen by a human being, the vision of John in Revelation showing what heaven is like.

One of the great rewards of a spiritually intense life is the sense that one can almost pass from this life into the next and stand in the middle of heaven. Paul spoke on one occasion of having passed into the "third heaven" (2 Corinthians 12:2). Various mystics through history have felt that they were carried into heaven and stood in the presence of God and Christ and the holy angels. When I was a very young man I had an experience of an angel that has proved comforting and encouraging to me through the many years since.

The importance of such an experience is the way it influences our lives in this world. The more powerfully we are able to envision heaven as our goal, the more we think and behave in ways conducive to our spiritual growth and understanding.

This is essentially what we are requesting every time we pray the Lord's Prayer: "Thy kingdom come, thy will be done, on earth as it is in heaven." It means we are eager for the two spheres to become one.

Try letting yourself dream more and more about heaven. It may do wonders for your spirituality, the way daydreaming about a trip to the seashore actually prepares us for the adventure of being there. But remember, the reality will be even more glorious.

It is hard for me to imagine what it will be like, dear Lord, to be in heaven with you and not have to struggle with evil every day. But grant that I may begin to understand what it is like, and to experience heaven even before I get there. Amen.

Week 32, Saturday   **On Really Seeing God**

> *I had heard of you by the hearing of the ear,*
> *but now my eye sees you.*
> —*Job 42:5*

The final goal of all seeing is to see God. It is to God that the path of deep inner seeing eventually leads us. Along the way, we see and learn many things about life, the world, and ourselves. But the ultimate goal is God.

In the end, it is important to know God intimately on our own, and not merely to depend on what we have heard about God from other sources.

In his book *The Province Beyond the River,* W. Paul Jones tells about his experience in finally knowing God for himself. He had been a professor of theology for years but had never had an actual knowledge of God he could call his own. So one summer he went to a monastery in the Rocky Mountains. He prayed, went to chapel, worked in the refectory and the garden, read his Bible, and waited for the experience of God. Eventually it came, and illuminated everything Jones had been teaching.

That is what finally happens to us, when we have sought the way of inner prayer and meditation. At first, the way seems hard and fruitless. We are often tempted to give it up. Then the way becomes easier, and yields the reward of understanding more about life and ourselves. At this point, we are encouraged to continue. And then at last, sometimes when we least expect it, there is a sudden breakthrough, and the light floods everything. The world is bathed in it. And we want to fall down and worship, for we know we are in the presence of the Holiest of the Holy.

I want to know you, O God, beyond everything else in life. Help me to stay on pilgrimage till I find you—or realize I have been found by you, which is the same thing. Through Jesus Christ. Amen.

9
BEING GOD'S FAMILY MAN

Walter Kimbrough

Read Ephesians 5:15-20; 6:4.

As a young boy, I longed with all my heart for a meaningful relationship with my father. Though I couldn't have put it in those words, I wanted a relationship that would provide a lasting presence. I wanted words of encouragement to help me become a mature and responsible man. I wanted and needed a strong, positive role model. None of that ever materialized. In fact, my parents' marriage ended when I was six. So, I grew up in a single-parent family with the mother as the head of the household. I had two older sisters and no brothers.

Yet the desire and the need for a constructive relationship with my father did not vanish with his departure from the family. In elementary school, we used to sing a song that put my feelings and longings into words: "I'd walk a million miles for one of his smiles, my daddy." The song made my heart cry because my daddy was not present and would never be present at any major event in my life. As a result, I determined to be different as a father. I resolved that when I married, I would be in a loving relationship with my wife, chosen by God, and I would maintain a vital presence and loving relationship with my children.

The words of Daniel Iverson continue to echo my desire and are my prayer request:

> Spirit of the living God, fall afresh on me.
> Spirit of the living God, fall afresh on me.

Melt me, mold me, fill me, use me.
Spirit of the living God, fall afresh on me.

O God, may your Spirit be upon my life and empower me to be the kind of father that will bring pleasure to your heart. Amen.

Read Genesis 2:18, 21-24.

A common question I receive from people when they learn that Marjorie and I have two adult sons is, "How many grandchildren do you have?" So far we have none.

I wanted grandchildren, I told our sons as they matured, but I insisted on having daughters-in-law first. Perhaps some would call me old-fashioned and out of step with the times, but I strongly believe that children ought to be conceived as the result of a loving relationship and be born into a home where they are wanted and can be cared for. Wayne is happily married, and we are still praying that God will bless Walter with a wife.

Fathers must be a loving, positive role model for their children. Each of us is called to be in a loving relationship with our wife. Remember the words of God, "It is not good that the man should be alone; I will make him a helper as his partner" (Genesis 2:18). We must love the partners God made for us. Our children learn from what we do more readily than from what we say, so our words must always come alive in our activities. Some little boy is looking at you, observing the activities of your life and is declaring, "When I grow up I want to be like that man." So, I ask you, what will that boy be like as a man if he succeeds in being like you?

Are you a man after the heart of God? Are you in a loving relationship with your wife? Have you resolved to be the best that you can be with God's help?

O God, empower me to accept your wisdom in the choice of my life's mate, and enable me to commit to a loving relationship with her. Amen.

Read Proverbs 22:6.

After I graduated from seminary, Marjorie and I left Atlanta for Chicago where I was being appointed as pastor of the Calvary Methodist Church. During that summer of 1966, while she was preparing breakfast, Marjorie fainted. We later learned that she was pregnant. Joy filled our house at 7801 South Aberdeen.

The nine months that followed were exciting, as we looked forward to the birth of our son. Actually, no test was administered to determine the baby's sex. I simply claimed the son and announced to the congregation the date of his birth! We began to worry, however, during the winter of 1967, especially when the big snow came in January and women had to be airlifted to area hospitals to deliver their babies. Thankfully, we were spared the snow ordeal, and on April 22, 1967, Walter Mark was born— exactly as I had announced to my congregation the Sunday before. *Then* it snowed!

It was a nurse at Wesley Memorial Hospital who helped me understand the responsibility of fatherhood. Marjorie was being discharged from the hospital, and when the nurse brought Walter into the room, I reached for him. After all, I was the father and therefore had every right to take possession of him. The nurse, however, sternly informed me that hospital rules dictated that she carry the child to the front door of the hospital. She would not release him to me or anybody else until that time. "Furthermore," she said, "you don't need to be so anxious to hold him, for you will have the rest of his life to care for him."

Wow! The rest of his life! Or at least the rest of my life.

Fatherhood is a lifelong experience. Once you get into it, you can never get out of it. So I join with John Greenleaf Whittier in praying:

> Dear Lord and Father of mankind,
>   Forgive our foolish ways!
> Reclothe us in our rightful mind,
> In purer lives Thy service find,
>   In deeper reverence, praise.

God, help me to be a faithful father to my children through-out my whole life. Amen.

Read Isaiah 40:31; 41:10.

The time comes when even our adult children need a word of encouragement. Are we willing to take time out of our busy schedule, amid the hustle and bustle of everyday living, and spend quality time with our children? Are they worth a few precious moments of our time?

Recently Wayne, our youngest son, phoned to say that he wanted to talk with me. That would be fine, I told him, all the time wondering what he wanted. You see, this is the child who has caused us to *earn* the title of parent. My wife has said that if the second child had been born first, then we would have had only one child. But God knows best. I am so glad that we have two sons. They are very different—and they both belong to us.

Do you have that child who succeeds in testing your grace and stretching your patience? Fatherhood is not over when the child reaches age eighteen.

Wayne came by and we talked about the concerns of his heart. I sensed his relief and gratitude that I would stop my activities to focus on his perceived needs. Perception becomes real when it is imbedded in your heart. I was blessed that he wanted to talk with me and that I was able to share with him.

I tried to offer words of encouragement to him and reminded him of God's words through Isaiah (41:10 NIV):

> So do not fear, for I am with you;
>   do not be dismayed, for I am your God.
> I will strengthen you and help you;
>   I will uphold you with my righteous right hand.

Lord, strengthen me so that I may be able to encourage my children through the challenges of their lives. Amen.

Week 33, Thursday   **Offer Strength**

Read Luke 22:31-32.

I have always wanted the story of my life to reflect the words of the song, "If I can help somebody as I pass along, / Then my living shall not be in vain." Often our world becomes so busy that we miss out on opportunities to know others and share love with them.

As a part of my ministry, I do volunteer work in the Atlanta public schools. One of them is Leslie J. Steele Elementary School. From time to time there are students in the waiting area of the administrative office. I know that either they are not feeling well and are waiting for someone to pick them up or they are in trouble for some reason.

One day I began to talk with four boys who were sitting there. Not only had they been misbehaving but they were also having academic problems. One of them, Andrea, was failing and was about to be put out of school.

I believed in Andrea and began to meet regularly with him. I consistently gave him words of encouragement that came from my heart. He did not fail me or himself. This young lad went forward and started making straight A's. The next year he was elected president of the student body.

All things are possible if only somebody believes. I believed in Andrea and I still do.

I also believe that every man needs to assume the responsibility for giving something back out of gratitude for God's hand on his life by helping someone else in his growth process. There are thousands of individuals needing encouragement, crying for someone to help. Jesus said to Simon, "Strengthen your brothers" (Luke 22:31).

O God, make me a source of strength for someone who needs an encouraging word. Amen.

Week 33, Friday   **Reach Out**

Read Acts 15:32.

Human life is the creation of God who declared it good. Life is to be lived in community, to be shared with others rather than left in isolation. In Acts we read that "Judas and Silas . . . said much to encourage and strengthen the believers." If we belong to each other, then we ought to emulate them by being servants to one another.

Recently, I received a telephone call from a woman who asked if she could come by my house. I told her she could, even though it was Saturday night, which I usually reserve for sharing time with family and spending time in meditation with the Lord as part of the preparation for Sunday worship. When I informed Marjorie of the call and my response, I was pleased that she was in agreement with me.

In less than a half hour, the caller was at my door. In the house she slammed her daughter's report card on the table, saying angrily, "You take her because I can't do anything with her."

I suppose that my response could be misconstrued as cold and indifferent. I simply said, "No problem. I can handle it"! The issue was a high school senior whose first-quarter grades reflected a posture of failure. I was the student's pastor but, more important, I was her friend and servant.

The joy of this story is the fact that Shannon and I had an excellent relationship. As a result of her mother's visit, she would spend selected Saturdays with me. That meant attending confirmation classes, funerals, weddings—and of course lunch was always on the agenda. Because of the positive affirmation, her grades turned around to honor roll status, because studying was no longer a chore but a delight. Learning became essential and central for her. She graduated on time, improved her SAT score by hundreds of points and is now enrolled in a state university.

A man who knows that in Christ we belong to each other sometimes becomes a father to one who biologically is not his.

Thank you, God, for the man who reaches beyond self to embrace others. Make me one of them. Amen.

Week 33, Saturday   Sharing Wealth

Mark 12:41-44.

To be an effective servant of God does not require any academic certification, nor any ecclesiastical ordination, only the desire to be of service to someone else. I shall never forget a lesson I learned early on from a man in the community where I grew up. He was not even a high school graduate, nor was he considered a strong man in the faith community. I remember him, however, as a devoted husband and father who always carried himself in a respectable manner in the community.

One day four or five of us boys were out playing when he came walking by. He stopped and engaged us in dialogue and then asked us to let him borrow a quarter. Of course, we replied that we did not have a quarter even between us. A quarter was a lot of money when I was a boy. When we did not have a quarter, he asked for a dime, then a nickel, and finally a penny. To each request we expressed deep regret that we could not help. Each of us were totally broke, not a cent to our name.

This wonderful man went into his pocket and gave each boy one penny with the admonition that we must never be broke again.

I cannot forget that day and experience. I may not have much, but I am not broke. Praise the Lord!

Mark tells us of a beautiful story where a widow woman gave two copper coins that added up to one penny, but in doing so she gave more. She gave her all. Her sacrifice was total.

Jesus challenges each of us, every man, to be sacrificial in his giving to others. Then the world will be a better place to live.

O God, create in me the generosity to give whatever I have, even if it's as small as a penny, to help transform human life. Amen.

Week 34, Sunday   Manhood

Read 1 Corinthians 13:11.

As a black male I grew up in a home with a strong mother figure. My oldest sister got married and moved out, the sister next to me finished college and moved to New York. I was left alone with Momma. She was strong, focused, and autocratic. I lived by the rules of the house she set, and I danced by the music she played, even when I did not like the rules or the music or did not want to dance. She was the head of the house, not me.

I married during my second year of graduate school, and I moved out of Momma's house to live for the rest of my life with Marjorie. I was twenty-four, legally married, and felt like a mature adult. My mother, however, still wanted to make decisions for me by informing me of what I needed to do and how I was to do it.

Now, I was indeed a married man. So I thanked my mother lovingly for all that she had done for me and my two older sisters. But, I said, her mission had been accomplished. I was ready for life beyond her controlling dictates. If there was anything she had not done, it was now too late. If I made mistakes, then I would have to suffer the consequences. The message came through to her crystal clear, and her relationship to me became one of affirmation.

We either claim our manhood or it is denied and taken away by someone else or by some system. If you are facing this issue, then read the scripture for today, "When I was a child, I spoke like a child, I thought like a child, I reasoned like a child; when I became a man, I gave up childish ways" (RSV). You are now a man, so put an end to the ways of a child.

Thank you, O God, that you have helped me grow into manhood chronologically. Help me to claim my manhood by acting like one. Amen.

Week 34, Monday   Challenged to Excel

Read 2 Corinthians 8:7.

On the Sunday before the students in my congregation were to return to school, I always made it a custom to have them come to the altar so I could pray for them and offer words of encouragement. I would also challenge them to strive academically to make either the Pastor's Honor Roll, with all A's for the school year, or the Church's Honor Roll, with a B average and with no grade less than B. I insisted that C's were unacceptable if they were not brain damaged and did not have to work a full-time job outside of school to support the family. If they were full-time students they should always do well academically.

Each student was required to fill out a 3 x 5 index card to be turned in to me, indicating their goal of either the Pastor's or the Church's Honor Roll.

One year, before they left the altar, I happened to see Ricky's card. His goal was to make the Church's Honor Roll. I had taught

Ricky in confirmation class and knew that he was a bright young man but had never made all A's in school. I also knew that he would not tell a lie in church. So I challenged him right there. I told him that he *could* make all A's. With the encouragement of his mother, he drew a line through "Church" and inserted "Pastor." He would go for all A's.

History will declare that Ricky made all A's the first semester, and the second semester, and the next year, and the one after that. He graduated from high school as the valedictorian of his class. He went to Duke University and continued to distinguish himself academically. He is now out of school, married, and gainfully employed. All because someone dared to challenge him to excel.

O God, I accept your challenge to excel. Give me the vision and the wisdom to pass the challenge on. Amen.

Week 34, Tuesday   **It Is Well**

Read John 11:20-26.

Death affects all of us at some time. Even when we know that people are dying every day, death always seems to come as a stranger, with surprise and shock. The question is, How should we respond in the face of death?

The Bible teaches us that Jesus cried over the reality of death, but he didn't stay in his grief. He acted, and demonstrated his power over death.

As a pastor, I am often brought into contact with the reality of death as I spend time with families during their grief. Sometimes the shock and grief become personal. One Wednesday night at church I was with a grief support ministry group that my sister and I co-lead. A staff member interrupted the group to tell me I was needed immediately in Fellowship Hall. A computer seminar was just starting, and a man who had registered had suffered a massive heart attack.

I went to his side not as a medical technician, but as a pastor who was able to administer mouth-to-mouth resuscitation. The emergency medical team arrived some minutes later and eventually transported the man to the hospital. I knew, however, that he had already died. Died in spite of my attempt to revive him. I watched him die.

The words that give me consolation as a pastor and as a man are by Horatio G. Spafford:

> When peace, like a river, attendeth my way,
> When sorrows like sea billows roll;
> Whatever my lot thou hast taught me to say,
> It is well, it is well with my soul.

I believe that it was well with Robert's soul.

Thank you, God, that when I am confronted by death you are with me. Amen.

Week 34, Wednesday   Marriage

Read Genesis 2:24.

I am always excited when I hear the words, "Therefore a man leaves his father and his mother and clings to his wife, and they become one flesh." The union of a man and a woman forms a new family. A marriage is more than a ceremony, it is a commitment for life.

Marjorie and I are still newlyweds even though we have been married for thirty-three years. Have these years been full of trials and tribulations, hardships and disappointments? In some ways yes, but in other ways the answer is obviously no. Because we made a commitment to love each other for better or for worse, we seek to find a common ground when we have problems. We are free to disagree without being disagreeable.

The family is the most fundamental organism in all of society. But its success most often is dependent upon the quality of the marriage. Therefore we must constantly strive for intimacy in our marriage. Maintaining communication will help move you in the right direction. When you are intentional in sharing your thoughts and concerns with your wife, then she will not be an outsider in your life. After all, she is the person with whom you share a oneness.

Pray without ceasing—constantly, in your work and at home. This will keep you focused on things that are spiritual and are of

God. Pray about your problems. Spend time in prayer with your wife. Be intentional and specific in asking God to bless your marriage and family.

Dear God, you made me in your image and you declared that it was not good for a man to be alone. I pray that you will help me to be effective and fruitful in carrying out your will for my life. Amen.

Week 34, Thursday   Servanthood

Read Matthew 20:26.

This is election time in my city. People who want to get into public office spend thousands of dollars in an attempt to accomplish their goal. The campaign trail is not only costly but can be vicious as well. Character assassinations become the order of the day. Sometimes the damage done in the campaign is beyond repair. These are people seeking positions of leadership in the city. Actually they are seeking to become public servants, just like the police, the fire fighters, and the garbage collectors.

I am a pastor of a United Methodist congregation. With the other pastors, I am a servant of both God and the people. I was neither elected by the people nor chosen by the congregation, but I was called by God for this ministry of servanthood. I did not volunteer but was drafted into service. Yet to be a servant is a great work. The scripture teaches us that "whoever wishes to be great among you must be your servant"—not mayor, not governor, not pastor, but *servant.*

Every man should major in being a servant—a servant to his God, family, and community. Being a servant does not belittle the man but rather elevates him to new heights previously unknown. The man who never does anything for anybody else cannot really appreciate nor understand what it means to receive. It is the giver who is really blessed.

What is your goal in life? Do you want to be the leader? Or will you be a faithful servant? God bless the servants.

O Lord God, I want to answer your call to serve others. Help me to serve with joy. Amen.

Read Matthew 25:31-40.

One of my favorite places to visit is the prison. I have been given the opportunity to preach at Sunday evening worship services in a maximum security prison for women. We also share with boys in a youth detention center. Our congregation believes in this ministry. Matthew's Gospel records the words of Jesus, "I was in prison and you visited me."

Several years ago we were privileged to have Nelson Mandela speak to our congregation. He spoke from the heart and without notes. I was in awe at his softness of touch and the intensity and power of his personality as he told how the church had made a significant difference in his life. He was educated by the church and was thus prepared for service to humankind. Soon after his visit with us, he was elected president of South Africa.

Here is a man who was incarcerated for more than twenty-seven years and yet never lost his vision or his mission. He committed himself to proper diet, and the exercise of mind and body. Neither time nor circumstance destroyed his will to achieve release and be the servant of the people. I am still being inspired by him.

Each man must choose his course in life. Plan now to make a difference in somebody's life; then your living will not be in vain.

Dear Father, help me to become sensitive to the needs of my brothers and sisters in the world and covenant to work with your community to bring healing and wholeness to the world. Amen.

Week 34, Saturday   **Seniors**

Read Psalm 37:25.

The fastest growing segment of the American population is the elderly. We are living longer. Someone must assume the responsibility of caring for our senior citizens. They are our parents and grandparents. Special provisions are necessary for them when physical and mental limitations prevail. If everyone continues to live long enough, we all will be where they are for we will be one of them.

One of the fascinating components of my work occurs at senior citizens housing units. Most of the residents are women—an indication that they live longer than men. Each Wednesday morning they gather for a worship service. The praise of God goes forth even though their physical limitations prevent them from getting up and down to sing. In fact, their coming and going is in slow motion. Time does indeed take its toll.

A real transformation takes place among them when young men come to share. They really liven up! Though I am by no means young, I do reflect a youthfulness to them. Each week that I am privileged to speak to them, I see a gleam in their eyes that brings a joy to my soul. We worship God together and fellowship with one another.

When did you last spend time with a senior citizen, perhaps your parent, or someone in your church or community? You'll find it a rewarding experience. We must care for our elderly in a loving way that is pleasing to God. We are their keepers and must never renege on that moral obligation. William Merrill's hymn challenges us:

> Rise up, O men of God!
> Have done with lesser things.
> Give heart and mind and soul and strength
> To serve the King of kings.

May we rise up to the task before us now so that the elderly will be blessed and the Lord praised.

Dear God, open my eyes to see the needs of the elderly in my community, and grant me the strength and courage to do my part in caring for them. Amen.

Week 35, Sunday   **The Power of Prayer**

Read Acts 4:4-31.

I often tell church people that if I could start my ministry over I would do it differently. I would put prayer at the top of my priority list.

221

A church growth specialist described the reasons given by pastors of my denomination for the rapid growth their congregations were experiencing. They were preaching, teaching, music, friendly people, program, location, facilities, staff, and the like. None, however, gave prayer as a cause. The specialist didn't negate these reasons or contradict these pastors and congregations. He did ask the question, though, of whether there would have been greater growth had prayer been a priority.

Many pastors pray Psalm 19:14 before they preach: "Let the words of my mouth and the meditation of my heart / be acceptable to you, / O LORD, my rock and my redeemer." We are acknowledging that it would be sin to stand before the people of God in our own strength, and we are seeking God's intervention to get us out of the center of the event so that the people will see Jesus.

Not just pastors but all of us must be men of prayer. Children in the home need to encounter a praying father. Our wives need to experience the strength and vitality of God-fearing husbands who know how to pray. Our congregations need praying men who will help keep the church of Jesus Christ on the right road and with a strong foundation.

Our scripture in Acts tells us that the believers in the church in Jerusalem were active in fervent prayer. So today, men must be praying believers. Then broken families will be restored and cities will come alive with new vitality. Praying men will revolutionize the world.

May our prayers be summed up in the letters of ACTS: Adoration - Confession - Thanksgiving - Supplication. Please pray every day.

O God, today I pray for my church and its members, and especially for the members of my extended family, that we will make a difference in our cities. Amen.

Week 35, Monday   **Time Out**

Read Genesis 1:1–2:3.

Time out! With this phrase, teams can pause to regroup and refocus on the task before them. Sometimes the time-out serves as the pause that refreshes, allowing a few moments to rest.

Highly paid and well-conditioned athletes look forward to the time out.

Just like the athlete, every one needs a time-out. I call my time-out vacation. Every man needs a vacation, and we ought to be ashamed if we fail to take at least one a year. You need not go far away, stay long, or even stay in expensive hotel accommodations, but you ought to go somewhere and take your family with you. Be intentional in taking your time-out. If you don't, you will wear yourself down, and eventually out, resulting in work that is not only less than your best but is also ineffective. God wants your best. Call time out.

God himself called a time-out. Our scripture tells us that God was busy creating all of the beauty of the universe over a six-day period of time, that he established a system of quality control after each creation and certified that it was good. But, after the sixth day, God called time out and rested. God rested from all of the labor required in creation and did not offer an apology.

What are your vacation plans? When did you last take one? Is your body telling you it's time for a vacation? If so, then call time out. Even if it's just for two or three days, take it. Get out of town away from the worries of work. Discover that you can breathe again. Remember, it is all right to call time out.

O Lord, thank you for letting me know that it is all right to call time out. Help me to be wise in caring for my body. Amen.

Week 35, Tuesday   P.T.A.

Read Ephesians 6:1-4.

For many years I felt as if the P.T.A.—the Parent Teachers Association—had been misnamed. It was really an association of mothers, it seemed; teachers attended only by mandate, and fathers were basically absent, with a very few exceptions.

Fathers are as much parents as are mothers. A father should be involved in the total life of the child. The years of a child's education are critically important for the whole family. That is when the foundation is laid for the child to build on forever. The presence of the father in the school environment ensures that educators know two parents are involved in their child's education.

It has been my privilege to be involved in the life of the P.T.A. My mother was involved during my years in the public schools, so I felt it was my duty to offer to my sons what I had received and appreciated from my mother in my schooldays.

My mother was a domestic worker with a very low income. She received little to no child support from my absentee father, and spent 20 percent of her weekly salary on school lunches. She also visited each of our schools once each semester. We were not in trouble, yet she religiously came to our schools because she cared about us and wanted the officials of the school to know it. Her efforts and sacrifice will always be a treasured part of my memory.

When was the last time you visited your child's school? How often do you volunteer? Do you know the teachers, principal, and some of the students? Are you an active member of the P.T.A.? Men are needed to make a creative difference in the world and the community. The school is an essential part of the community and we can ill afford to be found absent.

O God, I pray for the youth of my community and the schools where they learn. Show me the part I must play in the education of our children. Amen.

Week 35, Wednesday   The Challenge of a Blessing

Read Genesis 9:1.

There are some things we need to unlearn. For instance, there are sayings and phrases that sound good, have a good beat, are popular, and yet are theologically bad. One such phrase is "When praises go up, blessings come down." It implies that we can flatter God into doing things for us, that all we have to do is feed God's ego by sending up praises and God will be moved to send us blessings in return. I don't think God works that way.

Our Sovereign God is always positive. We can never get ahead of God. We are always the reactors, responding to the leading and the moving of God in the course of human history. God's blessings have consistently been made manifest in our lives in spite of ourselves or our actions and even when we have not asked or expected anything from him. God is categorically looking beyond our faults and seeing our needs. Blessings are the results of our needs and sometimes the fulfillment of our wants.

The gift of a blessing, however, does carry with it an expected response. The scripture lesson today says it well: "God blessed Noah and his sons, and said to them, 'Be fruitful and multiply, and fill the earth.'"

Noah and his three sons received a blessing with a challenge to do three things that ought to speak to the consciousness of every man:

- Be fruitful. Give to life and the world more than you found—not just in reproduction but in every area.
- Multiply. Do more than is expected. Find ways to be creative so that productivity is accelerated.
- Fill the earth. Go all the way in getting the job done.

Men are the keys to the success of the nation. We have been blessed and challenged to be productive by God.

O God, I want to be productive and creative in doing your will in all areas of my life. Amen.

Week 35, Thursday   Medically Concerned

Read Mark 5:22-23.

When our sons were small I was usually the one who took them for their doctor's appointment. The doctor was a wonderful man, an excellent pediatrician, and I always enjoyed our visits with the chance to talk and share ideas. On those rare occasions when Marjorie took the boys to the doctor, he would always ask where I was. At the time I don't think it registered with me that I was missed because the doctor saw so few fathers. It must have been a joy for him every time a man came into his office with a child.

I was reminded of my experience in the doctor's office when the lay leader of my congregation, a young man with a young daughter, called me from the doctor's office where he was waiting with his daughter. He is in a loving marriage, but he enjoys the responsibility of showing concern for the medical well-being of his daughter. So he is the parent who takes off from work, demonstrating the fact that he is medically concerned.

Now, read our scripture lesson for today. "Then one of the leaders of the synagogue named Jairus came and, when he saw him [Jesus], fell at his feet and begged him repeatedly, 'My little daughter is at the point of death. Come and lay your hands on her, so that she may be made well, and live.'" A Jewish leader comes to Jesus medically concerned about the well-being of his daughter. The implication is, when all else fails seek Jesus.

So, the message to every man who is a father has to be:

- Show consistent concern for the medical wellbeing of your child or children.
- Seek the intervention of Jesus in times of need as well as times of joy.
- Be intentional in asking for the touch of his hands that will activate healing.

Your gentle and sensitive caring as a father means much in the life of your child. Never lose sight of being medically concerned.

O God, help me to be sensitive to my children's illnesses and pains so that I can play an active part in seeking their healing. Amen.

Week 35, Friday   **When Faced with Death**

Read John 11:21-27.

"Old men must die, but young men may die," said Benjamin E. Mays.

The length of our days is not known to us. The challenge, however, is to live a quality life; one that brings pleasure to God, that is productive and is shared meaningfully with others. We must live life to the fullest each day because we have not been promised tomorrow. There is an urgency in the now.

A father of five found himself having to make funeral arrangements for his first-born son who had just turned twenty-nine.

Grief filled the father's heart in having to face the reality and finality of death. Certainly, he would have preferred to be the first to die. Yet, the choice is not ours to make.

Consolation came to the father and others in the family at the point of acknowledging that their loved one had enjoyed life to the fullest, even though it was for a short while. They had wondered why he was always in a hurry. The answer came in his death, for then they recognized his destiny with eternity.

The words of Jesus offer hope in the time of death. Listen to them: "I am the resurrection and the life. Those who believe in me, even though they die, will live, and everyone who lives and believes in me will never die." We can hold on to these words of assurance. Despair must not be on the agenda of the believer, for we know that even in death we have the victory in Jesus.

Lord Jesus, give me strength and grace to face death when it comes within our family circle, whether to take away from us a child or one who has lived a full life. Thank you that you are the resurrection and the life. Amen.

Week 35, Saturday   **Something to Shout About**

Read Psalm 100.

A father exuberantly announced, "My daughter is now a real doctor." She had completed all of the required course work for the M.D. degree and had graduated from medical school some months before. Yet, to this father, the real accomplishment, the proof of the pudding, came when his daughter successfully passed all of the exams required for certification as a practicing physician. He knew that a degree without certification does not bring completion to the mission.

His little girl has grown to be a responsible adult, a physician by training and practice. All of the prayers, the countless hours of study and the thousands of dollars spent on her education have proved to be a wise investment. There is great rejoicing when a child perseveres and finishes a significant accomplishment like becoming a certified practicing physician.

Lest any one of us proudly tries to take the credit for any accomplishment, it is good to read again Psalm 100:

Make a joyful noise to the L ORD, all the earth.
   Worship the L ORD with gladness;
   come into his presence with singing.
Know that the L ORD is God.
   It is he that made us, and we are his;
   we are his people, and the sheep of his pasture.
Enter his gates with thanksgiving,
   and his courts with praise.
   Give thanks to him, bless his name.
For the L ORD is good;
   his steadfast love endures forever,
   and his faithfulness to all generations.

God, I thank you for my children, for their accomplishments, and that we are all your children. Amen.

Week 36, Sunday   Facing Temporary Failure

Read James 1:22-25.

I know of a single young man who recently committed his life to a study of God's Word. While he was growing up, the church had been a part of his life, but the commitment to grow in the Word was absent. He was in the church, but not really part of the church. So the challenge to serve others had little or no meaning for him.

Now, however, with a new lease on the Christian life and a revitalized understanding of what it means to be a disciple of Jesus Christ, he is actively seeking to be a servant for others. He offered to become a mentor to a teenager, a good boy but very vulnerable to mistakes in judgment. The initial result of his mentoring has been temporary failure. What should the mentor do?

Every Christian is under obligation to be present in the world making a positive difference in the quality of people's lives. In this classic case of a troubled boy needing somebody to keep on caring, the old saying is still true, that if at first you don't succeed, try, try again.

The words of James are applicable here: "Be doers of the word, and not merely hearers." Failure to continue working with someone means that we have forgotten or ignored what the Word says.

Life is tough, but it is possible. You can make a big difference in somebody's life, especially if you are willing to risk being uncomfortable in the interest of helping to build a better humanity. I pray for your faithfulness—especially in the face of temporary failure.

O God, even though my efforts to do good may sometimes fail, help me never to give up trying to do my best to help someone else. Amen.

Week 36, Monday   **Father of the Bride**

Read Genesis 2:18-24.

In more than thirty years as a pastor, I have had the opportunity to participate in hundreds of weddings. Even now I find much joy in celebrating the sacrament of marriage.

Fathers of the bride are interesting people to watch. When the question is asked, "Who gives this woman to be married to this man?" it is usually the father who answers, "I do" and then is seated. There was one father, however, who answered the question "I do" and did not sit down or shut up. He continued to speak, saying to the groom, "Now I deliver her to you in good health. I expect you to keep her doing as well as she is now or better. If you can't, then bring her back where you got her. I can take care of her." She was, indeed, daddy's girl!

Fathers need to teach their daughters by example what to look for in a man as husband. The way we treat our wives speaks volumes, as we spend our entire lifetime working to bring intimacy into our marriage. A good father must also be a good husband.

God recognized that it was not good for the first man to be alone and decided to make a partner for him. The first surgery was performed by God with the removal of a rib from man to make woman. Man and woman in marriage give up their separateness with the commitment to become one flesh.

I believe the presentation of your daughter into Christian marriage fulfills the intent of God for humankind. It is my prayer that you will have the grace to release her from your home and continue to love her as your daughter. And for those of us who have no daughters, our love for our wives will be a living example for our sons.

O God, help me to be a living example of love, caring, and nurture to all the young people in my life. Amen.

Week 36, Tuesday   A Lesson to Be Taught

Read Ecclesiastes 3:1-8.

We had spent the night in Valdosta, Georgia, on our way to Atlanta. It was foggy that morning. Less than a half hour after we got on the interstate, the highway patrol directed us to the state road. I-75 North had been closed due to the heavy fog and a multi-car accident. The drive on the two-lane road was very slow as a result of the increased traffic from I-75. When we finally were able to get back onto the interstate, our youngest son advised me to make up the time we had lost.

Opportunities to teach occur in the strangest ways and places. I took that moment to teach Marty that time was so valuable, once it was lost it was gone forever. There was no way I could make up the lost time. Even if I drove far beyond the speed limit, we still wouldn't make it up. Some things we have no control over, but we ought to be very careful as to never waste time. Time is one of the most valuable assets we will ever possess.

I agree with the preacher, "For everything there is a season, and a time for every matter under heaven." May you be a faithful guardian of the time given to you.

Dear God, help me to value the time you have leased to me and to be a responsible steward of it. Amen.

Week 36, Wednesday   When Marriages Don't Work

Read Matthew 19:4-6.

Weddings are expensive. The wedding ceremony with all of the trimmings can go from the very modest to the ultra elaborate, often costing thousands of dollars for what is meant to be a once-in-a-lifetime experience. Friends from far and near share in the beauty of the ceremony. Toasts are offered wishing the couple a long and happy life together, echoing the words of Jesus that are often quoted at church weddings: "Therefore what God has joined together, let no one separate."

Jesus' words point us to the ideal. When you marry, the commitment you make is meant to last for the rest of your life. Sometimes, though, a marriage just does not work. The couple discovers that marriage was not like they thought it would be. "What do I do," you ask, "when both of us experience each day filled with misery and resentment?"

Seek help in a hurry! In prayer, ask God for guidance. Call upon the pastor who shared in your wedding or the person who conducted your premarital counseling. Locate a Christian counseling center in your community and make an appointment to see a counselor. Husband and wife must both commit to participate in the sessions. Any marriage worth having is worth the investment of time and money. Pray for God to give you understanding, help you change, and restore your love.

But what if it still does not work?

I now remind you again of what our Lord Jesus said, that we must not separate or divorce or destroy that which God has joined together. As a couple you covenanted to enhance, embrace, and cultivate the marriage. Keep working at it, with God's help.

Yet, in spite of all of your efforts, what if the marriage just doesn't survive?

When all has failed, agree to go your way in love and friendship. Just maybe your marriage was the result of your desire and not the will of God.

I ask you, dear God, for wisdom, honesty, and love in my marriage and my relationships. Thank you that you love me in spite of my mistakes and failures.

Week 36, Thursday   **A Single-Parent Father**

Read Matthew 19:13-15.

Children are very special and precious. They did not ask to be born into the world, yet here they are. Because they are here with us, they must be adequately provided for. Jesus said, "Let the little children come to me, and do not stop them; for it is to such as these that the kingdom of heaven belongs."

What do those words mean when we face the reality of divorce? Who has custody of the children? It is usually assumed that the children will live with the mother. The inference is that she is the only capable and acceptable person for this task. We shouldn't forget, though, that the father is just as much a parent as is the mother.

Can a single father successfully handle the care of the children? I am proud to answer the question with a resounding yes. The inability to maintain a successful marriage cannot and must not be equated with the inability of either the father or the mother to successfully raise the children. Some fathers are doing an outstanding job of parenting, while many others desire to do more but have been restrained by the judicial system.

Many success stories can be told about single-parent fathers. I think of a young man who was not the biological father of the little boy and girl for whom he accepted the responsibility of parenting. He was their older brother. Yet, he raised them as his children and they both grew up to become responsible and mature adults. Where there is a will, there is a way.

Are you a divorced father with children? Do you have custody of them? If not, are you faithful in observing your visitation rights? Commit to be the kind of father who will make a significant difference for the better in your children's lives. And then live out that commitment. Mothers do not successfully replace fathers in their children's lives. Only the man can authentically be the father for his children.

O God, I ask for strength to be a committed, faithful father to the children you have put in my life. Thank you for being my faithful, loving Father. Amen.

Week 36, Friday   **Save the Boys**

Read Exodus 1:16, 22.

The order was given to kill the boys. They must not be allowed to grow up into manhood and become productive as fighters of war, producers of children, and providers for families. Destroy the people by killing the boy babies. That was the directive of the pharaoh of Egypt in a time when Joseph had been forgotten and

Moses had just been born. With God's help, Moses was preserved to become his people's savior.

The close of the twentieth century is a critical time for our boys. In many ways, orders have been given to kill them—by neglect, violence, drugs, disease. Or we lose them through mediocrity—that lack of the desire to excel. Someone must make a passionate plea to let the boys live, and then train them well so that they will become productive citizens and help in building the nation. The time is now for the elders in the community to covenant with God and each other to intentionally work together to save our boys from themselves and from all others who would do them harm.

Do you have a boy that you call your own? Or is there a boy somewhere in your wider life, your community, whose life could be made better if you chose to share with him? As God has blessed you in your adult life, bringing you to manhood and a reasonable level of success and productivity, will you now give something back to help a boy grow into manhood? I pray that you will. Our boys still must be saved from lostness and misdirection.

When our boys are saved and grow into responsible manhood, then our daughters are glad because they have a variety of choices for a life's mate. We are never alone in the world. We need each other. So, help save the boys.

O God, thank you for your hand on my life. I offer it to you for the boys you have given me to care for, so that they may experience love, and live long, productive lives. Amen.

Week 36, Saturday   "I've Got It in Me"

Read 1 Samuel 16:7.

The story is told of the cat who wanted to sing like the bird. Even though he tried and tried, he never could sing. Then one day the bird flew down onto the ground and the cat caught and ate him. "I still can't make music," the cat exclaimed, "but at least I've got it in me!"

What is in you? What is the stuff that you are made of?

Our scripture highlights for us the directive given to Samuel by

God to select a king for Israel. The people had asked for and had received Saul as their king. This was not God's desire for them. So now God is making the selection from among the sons of Jesse.

Samuel is impressed by the stature of all the handsome young men Jesse presents to him. But God rejected them all. Remember these powerful and transforming words of God: "For the LORD does not see as man sees; for man looks at the outward appearance, but the LORD looks at the heart" (NKJV). So, it was the youngest son, David, who had been relegated to herding the sheep, who was chosen as king of Israel instead of the older brothers in the army.

If God is looking on the heart, is your heart in right order? It is sad to be clean externally but dirty on the inside, to be color coordinated on the outside but messed up on the inside. God wants a clean heart. Let us join with David in petitioning God to create within us a clean heart and renew a right spirit within us (Psalm 51:10).

As men of God we must reflect his will in our living. God sees everything we do and hears everything we say. Nothing is hid from God. Is God pleased with you, man?

Cleanse my heart, O God, and fill me with your Spirit, so that I might serve you fully and joyfully all my days. Amen.

10
THE MAN IN THE GYROSCOPE

Martin L. Camp

In the beginning was the Word, and the Word was with God, and the Word was God.   —*John 1:1*

Our God is a God of and in community: Father, Son, and Holy Spirit. We are made in his image, and when we live according to his plan, we will live not in isolation but in community—in a circle of relationships.

What does it mean to live in community? An image that helps me understand this dynamic is that of a man in a gyroscope. The gyroscope is in constant motion, as the man is influenced by and is influencing the people who come in and out of his life. To the north are the relationships of his origin: his parents, grandparents, and the countless generations who came before. To the east are other relationships chosen for him: his brothers, sisters, cousins, uncles, aunts, and others in his family. To the south are his own children, grandchildren, nieces, and nephews in the next generation. To his west are the relationships of his own choosing: his wife, his friends, his coworkers, and others in his community.

For the next four weeks we will look at the man in the gyroscope and these four sets of relationships. Using the insights of Scripture, we will try to understand what our faith teaches us about living in community—with our parents, our children, our wives, our friends, our neighbors, and the world around us. For each of us truly is the man in the gyroscope.

Heavenly Father, you have put so many people in my life. I pray for your guidance as I strive to understand your will for me in each of these relationships. Amen.

Week 37, Monday   In His Image

And God said, Let us make man in our image, after our likeness.
—Genesis 1:26 KJV

"He is the spitting image of his father."
"The apple didn't fall too far from the tree."
"Cut from the same cloth."
"Chip off the old block."
We have heard these expressions over and over again to describe fathers and sons. My own children love to tell me how much I look like my dad. "You have the same wrinkles around your eyes when you smile," my oldest son exclaimed one Christmas when the family was together. The two little ones chimed in with peals of laughter, "You both walk funny—your feet stick out!" completing their caricature of me—created in the image of their granddad.

The funny thing is, I see it too, and much more so as I grow older. Sure there are the physical similarities, the same **V** shape to my receding hairline, and my struggles with an unruly waistline. But there is more. As I grow older, live longer, experience more, make more mistakes, I am beginning to understand my father better. I had to have a wife and kids of my own, a job and its attendant struggles, in order to understand what his life was like. I had to live enough of my own life, to have enough of my own failures and successes, to begin to appreciate him for his own talents and sacrifices, his successes and failures.

As I think about being created in the "image" of my heavenly Father, I feel an awesome honor and responsibility. Just as I do not want to disappoint this earthly dad, I want to live up to my heavenly Father's expectations of me. And to do this, to understand how I, a mere human, can even hope to live such a life, where can I look? I thank God we have the example in the life of his Son, Jesus Christ. You can bet he is cut from the same cloth as his Father.

Heavenly Father, how amazing that you have created me in your image. Give me the wisdom and the strength to live the life this responsibility requires. Amen.

Week 37, Tuesday   **"I Had To Grow Up Fast"**

Read Luke 2:41-52.

"Your grandpa was a brilliant man. He was a great salesman. He was a great manager. He was a good butcher. He lost the battle with the bottle. I was about fifteen. He left. I was the oldest of three. I took over. I knew I had to grow up fast."

I had asked my dad about his dad. I had not known Grandpa well and remembered seeing him only a few times when I was young. When he died Dad went to the funeral alone—I was off at college. When I came home, my stepmother asked me to speak to Dad because he had not spoken since the funeral the day before. "Maybe he will talk to you," she confided.

And so I went into Dad's room and sat down beside him on the bed. We did talk, of many things. That day I saw my dad in a different light. I saw him not as the imposing figure he had always been in my life: the lawgiver, the dealer of punishment if I had done wrong, or the provider of wisdom and jokes and lessons, like how to bait a hook or play chess. No, at that moment I saw the fifteen-year-old dropping out of school, getting a job, growing up fast.

I was proud of Dad, prouder even than I had been before. He was a man.

As I have thought about that moment, I have come to see that this business of becoming a man really is a life's work. Each of us must take responsibility for our lives. In today's pop culture, too often people blame their parents for all kinds of personal problems. I agree that parents influence their children. But at some time we, as adults, have to stop looking for excuses and start acting like responsible men.

Jesus sets an example in the scripture reading. At twelve he had grown up fast and yet he also went back with his parents and "was obedient to them" (Luke 2:51). Responsibility is the hallmark of a true man.

Heavenly Father, help me to accept responsibility for who I am, and not blame family or circumstances for my failures. I want to seek you and your guidance and to move forward with my life. Amen.

Week 37, Wednesday   Honor Your Father and Your Mother

Honor your father and your mother so that your days may be long in the land that the LORD your God is giving you.

—Exodus 20:12

"Your children can surely disappoint you."

My friend uttered these words as she was talking about one of her children, a college sophomore who had not done well in his freshman year—hadn't achieved his potential. "We told him he would have to borrow the money for this year because we were so disappointed in him and we were not going to pay for his college if he didn't take time to apply himself."

My friend's pain was real. She was torn, as we so often are, between great love for this child—wanting to smooth the way and make life easier than it had been for her—and great disappointment that her son wasn't applying himself, wasn't taking full advantage of the opportunity her sacrifices had made possible.

What does it mean to honor one's parents? Can we honor someone and not love them? Can we honor a parent and not obey them once we are adults?

I think we can. This fifth commandment is a specific one, a call to honor our parents. Even if we do not love them, even if we refuse to do as they tell us, we must honor them. But how?

My friend's story gives us some insight. This son was not honoring his parents when he messed up at school. Honoring a parent is more than just giving lip service to the relationship or being nice. It includes, in addition to respect, striving to be one's best. If we do this, we will truly be a blessing to our parents. As Solomon said:

> A wise son makes a glad father,
> but a foolish son is a sorrow to his mother.
> —Proverbs 10:1 RSV

Lord, help me understand that being the man you have
called me to be honors not only you but also my parents.
Give me the strength to do your will, ever mindful of my duty
to my parents. Amen.

Week 37, Thursday   Big Daddy

Grandchildren are the crown of the aged,
and the glory of sons is their fathers.
—*Proverbs 17:6 RSV*

"Big Daddy took me fishing. Big Daddy took me to play golf. Big Daddy took me to the baseball game." My sixteen-year-old son was talking so fast it was hard to understand him as he tried to tell us all about his week at his grandparents. "Big Daddy" is the name Eric, our oldest child, bestowed on my wife's father from the moment he could talk.

Big Daddy—so simple yet so profound, for that is what grandfathers are, the Big Daddies, the patriarchs, leading by their lives, setting the standard, providing the example of how to live a full life.

My son calls my father Granddad. My father was not around as much when my son was little. A traveling salesman, he lived farther away in a different town. But as my son has grown and life has slowed down for my dad, they too have formed a lasting friendship.

My children are lucky to have two grandfathers alive. Men of a different generation. Men who have the wisdom gained in the crucible of experience. Eric attributes his athletic ability to Big Daddy—the high school and college athlete. He thinks some of his sense of humor and gift of liking people comes from my dad. He loves these two men and they love him.

What is the lesson in these scenes of a sixteen-year-old boy and his two grandfathers? Just this: if you are a grandfather yourself, be there for those grandchildren. Impart your wisdom to them and show them the love that comes from a special relationship between distant generations. And if you are a grandson, remember what you can mean to your grandfather. Honor him and show him that you love him.

239

Lord, I pray for all the grandfathers and grandmothers of this world. Bless them with grandchildren who love and honor them. Amen.

Week 37, Friday   Sins of the Father

As he passed by, he saw a man blind from his birth. And his disciples asked him, "Rabbi, who sinned, this man or his parents, that he was born blind?"   —John 9:1-2 RSV

"I've quit blaming my father and I've taken responsibility for my life. My mistakes are my own, but so are my accomplishments." The speaker was in his early twenties with a year left of college. He looked like an all-American boy, handsome and self-assured. We could have been father and son—me in my lawyer suit and briefcase and he in his jeans, college sweatshirt, and baseball cap sitting side by side at the airport.

I asked him what he was studying, what he wanted to be. He replied that it had taken him a while to decide. "I bounced around—to be truthful, I messed up a lot my first couple of years of college. Mom and Dad divorced. Dad, well, he had abused my sister and he was really emotionally tough on me and I guess I just got angry and rebellious and those two years—wasted. But then, one day, it hit me. This is my life! Do I really want to screw it up because I'm angry at this guy, my father? Then I started to get my act together, switched my major to business, started focusing and—in one year, I'll have my degree."

I'm not sure why he had to tell me these things. "Business" would have been an easy answer to my question of his career. But maybe he just needed to remind himself as much as me.

As the scripture passage shows us, the Jews felt that many problems were caused by the sins of the fathers being visited on their sons. There is some truth to this as shown in this young man's story. Parental influence, positive or negative, is great. But this young man had discovered the secret of breaking the cycle. He was taking charge of his life. He was going to be all right.

Heavenly Father, teach me to reject blame and excuses when I make mistakes and to take responsibility for my actions. Amen.

Read John 19:25-27.

My mother died when I was fifteen. She lost a long battle with depression and took her life. It hurt—still does. There is no one in our lives like our mother, no other human for whom we can have such a feeling. Whenever or however we lose a mother, it hurts. Some of us have lost mothers to death. Others have seen the relationship die. That, I think, would be worse—to have a mother alive but estranged.

When I was in my early thirties, I attended a church retreat where the topic was intergenerational communication and healing. The leaders talked about how the relationship of each of us with our parents affects us. Then they asked us how much we knew about our parents' relationships with their parents. I had never really thought about that. My mother was the youngest to survive to adulthood in her family and I was her youngest. Grandpa died when I was about six. I saw the stepmother who had raised my mom only occasionally, and she died when I was in high school.

Having to think of my mom as a child suddenly broke through a barrier of anger and frustration inside. Instead of seeing an adult who had abandoned me, I was able to see a little girl so afraid and in so much pain that all she knew to do in her confused state to stop the pain was to take her life.

It was during a church service on the last day of the retreat that this picture hit me. While the congregation sang, I began to cry—big, warm tears; tears of sadness and happiness, for I knew I had forgiven her and I knew she loved me.

If you are estranged from a parent, whatever the reason, pray for reconciliation.

Don't lose hope. Don't stop trying. They will not always be here to reconcile with.

Heavenly Father, I thank you for caring people who show us the way. I ask for insight and the power of healing and forgiveness. Heal all the broken family relationships, including my own. Bring sons and daughters and fathers and mothers together. Amen.

Read Genesis 45:1-15.

"My prayers have been answered!" my six-year-old son exclaimed as we told him that he was going to have a baby brother or sister. He had been the only child for a long time. Secretly, he had been praying for a brother or sister. He did not want to be alone.

Joseph did not want to be alone either, even with all his power and prestige as the pharaoh's right-hand man. He wanted his family and was willing to forgive his brothers the injustice they had done him.

This week we shift our focus from the generations before us to our siblings, cousins, aunts, and uncles. These are the people who were chosen to be part of our families and our lives. We come to know them while we are children, still developing, still coming into our own.

In this country, where mobility is the norm and smaller families are in vogue, we have lost the sense of the extended family. Many of us no longer grow up in the same town where we were born or live all our lives near our parents and siblings. We go off to college or to work, and never come back, except for holiday visits.

Recently our family spent three years in Kuwait. There I was struck by how strong the extended family is. Not only are families generally large, but often several of the married sons live in the same house as their parents and the cousins grow up together. Kuwait is basically one city, and so all the generations are there. Gathering at the family patriarch's house for Friday lunch is mandatory.

But here in America, I do not think we can go back to a simpler, more rural time where we live and die on the same farm, or in the same locale. And having a large family is not what most of us will choose, given the expense and pressures of today's world. I do believe, though, that we need to hold on to what ties we do have. We need to create opportunities for our children to interact with their extended families. We need to be a positive influence on our extended families.

Heavenly Father, you created me and placed me in my family. Bless and strengthen the relationships among these ones chosen by you to be in my family. Amen.

Read Genesis 4:1-7.

"He teases me too much."
"She started it."
"You're ugly."
"You're stupid."
Two bored kids less than two years apart in age, a lazy week-end afternoon too hot to go outside—and so the fighting begins. From time to time one or the other will run to me in my bedroom sitting area where I have attempted to escape to a good book and my comfortable recliner. They want to tell me their version of the story and sometimes to seek my intervention on their behalf. Dad, Solomon, the judge, jury, lawgiver, and dispenser of justice.

Depending upon the nature of the dispute, the other child may burst into the room in hot pursuit, blurting out his or her side of the story, of what "really happened." But sometimes, especially if someone is hurt physically, the offender has to be called in to explain, apologize, and if necessary, accept punishment.

Siblings fighting, jealous. It is as old as Cain and Abel; as Joseph and his coat of many colors that his brothers so resented. My kids even have their own special insult. It is called a "private stick-out" and involves sticking out one's tongue at the other but hiding it with your hand so that only the recipient (theoretically) can see. I cannot count how many times I have heard, "He/she gave me a private stick-out!"

I was struck by this picture of brothers and sisters quarreling the other night when I heard a minister on TV criticizing another denomination. Such fighting among or within denominations over whose "truth" is "the truth" wastes as much energy and seems as childish to me as a private stick-out. And I suspect God probably feels the same exasperation as I do with my kids.

After separating my kids and making them apologize, I usually tell them to go and find something constructive to do with their time. Maybe if we listen, we can hear God our Father saying the same thing to us.

Heavenly Father, help me to work together with my brothers and sisters for your kingdom and not waste energy on petty

differences when there is a world waiting to hear about you.
Amen.

Week 38, Tuesday   **A Taxi for My Brother**

Then the LORD said to Cain, "Where is your brother Abel?" He said, "I do not know; am I my brother's keeper?"
—Genesis 4:9-10

He was twenty-five and worked as a butler on the concierge floor of a five-star hotel on the island country of Bahrain in the Persian Gulf. An Indian, a Sikh, he had lived in Bahrain since his family had moved there when he was eleven. He did not finish high school although he loved school, he told me, because his father said he needed to work. So when he turned fifteen he began working in construction: hard, back-breaking, physical labor.

As he got older, he looked for work that would not leave him so exhausted that he couldn't do anything at the end of the day but collapse. He wanted to study, to learn English, to go to school again someday. He got a job in housekeeping at a run-down hotel. He did good work, was promoted to head of housekeeping, moved to a better hotel and a better job, took courses in English, and finally got this good job in the best hotel in the city.

He had been extremely helpful to me and we started to talk. I asked him why he worked so hard. What was he striving for? "First," he replied, "I must buy a taxi." I did not understand. He explained. "My older brother in India, he wants to get married. He is a taxi driver. We are poor. He drives for someone. He needs his own taxi. With his own taxi, he can marry. I must help him. Once he is married, I can marry. I also need to be able to take care of my mother. This is my duty."

I felt humbled. This was a true commitment to family. I wondered how many brothers in this country would make such sacrifices.

A few months ago I received a letter from him. He described the wedding. He had bought that taxi!

Father, remind me again what family really means and what a privilege it is to take care of each other. I am my brother's keeper. Amen.

Then God said to Noah and to his sons with him, "Behold, I estab-
lish my covenant with you and your descendants after you."
                                                    —Genesis 9:8 RSV

"When are we going to see our cousins again?"

We were looking at the pictures from the recent Camp family
reunion. We three siblings with spouses and all the eleven grandchildren and three great-grandchildren had convened in Okla-
homa at my sister's house to see Dad and his wife, Paula. We took
the mandatory family portrait to memorialize the event, and one
of my nephews video-taped us, trying to catch each of us with a
weird or funny look on our faces to preserve for posterity.

Looking at my then seventy-one-year-old father and Paula in
the center of the picture, my sister Joyce and her husband and
five children and three grandchildren, my brother Cameron and
his wife and their three children, I am struck that all this arose
from the love of two people so many years ago. Here is the true
image of a family tree vividly portrayed in the faces of the generations with their common physical characteristics and personality types.

But what my kids remember the most is seeing their cousins.
There is an instant bond with cousins. You are family. Not siblings with daily interaction and rivalries. Not strangers with
whom friendship is a choice. And for those three days, the
cousins played. My daughter, always sandwiched between her
older and younger brothers, shone as she joined up with my
brother's youngest daughter to play board games. My youngest
son got to be a "big brother" to younger cousins. My oldest
enjoyed being with my brother's oldest son, who is the same age.

Reliving this scene makes me wish we could treat all who
come to our churches as if they were cousins, people in the same
family, whether we have met them before or spent time with
them. How wonderful church would be for newcomers if they
truly felt welcomed by their "cousins"—their family in Christ.

Father, we are all your family. Your promise was made to
Noah and all his descendants. Help me to remember that
and to cherish my wider family. Amen.

Now Jesus loved Martha and her sister and Lazarus.
—John 11:5 RSV

"Uncle Mike! Uncle Mike! Uncle Mike is here!"

My children are screaming with glee as Mike walks into the villa in Kuwait where we are living during my three-year assignment. Mike had been an Arab-language expert in the marines. He had participated in the liberation of Kuwait in Desert Storm and had returned to work with American companies doing business in Kuwait.

I met Mike at a business club luncheon on my first visit to Kuwait. "When you return, look me up," he had said. I had taken his card and put it away. Then life became crazy with selling our home in Texas and moving halfway across the world to this strange place, Kuwait. Once there, things were a lot more difficult than I had imagined. Not speaking Arabic was a problem sometimes, especially as we tried to get all the permits and licenses and governmental approvals we needed. In the midst of my frustration, I remembered Mike. I called, begging for help.

Then the marines landed! Mike took over. To my wife he became a guardian angel, taking her everywhere and arguing for her in the markets as she tried to set up house. To the kids he was Uncle Mike, tossing them up in the air, teasing, roughhousing. To me, he became my best friend and confidant. He was family and we were his family.

A funny thing happened with Uncle Mike. We introduced him to my wife's sister who had come to Kuwait with us to be a schoolteacher. One thing led to another and they married. So now Uncle Mike really is Uncle Mike. And we all love him and are grateful for what he meant to us at such a crucial time in our lives.

Lord, you loved Lazarus and his sisters as if they were your own. Whether by blood or marriage or just circumstances, you have put people in my life who give me so much. I am grateful for these "uncles" and "angels." Amen.

Read Leviticus 25:25-28, 35-42; Deuteronomy 25:5-6.

We were poor. We had just moved to a new town, to start over, and the three-room duplex that was now our home seemed cramped. I was eleven and sad. I missed my friends, our old house, my school, my life. Sometimes I would close my eyes and pray that when I opened them it would all have been a bad dream and I would be back in the old days, the old place. But each eye-opening revealed the same scene in the same reality.

My uncle, Mother's brother, was a big man. He always had a cowboy hat, a face full of a big smile, sparkling eyes, and an easy laugh. He lived in this new town with his wife and son in a big brick house. My cousin, four years older than I, had it all—his own room, his own radio, even his own television. My eyes would bug out when we would visit. I tried to imagine what living in that house would be like.

One day my uncle came by in his truck. "Where's Martin?" he yelled out. I came running out of the house. There in the back of the truck was a most beautiful sight—a bike! My cousin's bike that he had outgrown—a three-speeder.

"Thought you might find some use for this," my uncle said. I hugged him and then helped him get the bike out of the truck. I rode that bike to school for several years.

The Old Testament law was very clear about an uncle's responsibilities to his brother's family, his nieces and nephews. If his brother died, he had to step in, take over responsibility. They were family.

I'll always remember that day and that uncle. Sometimes it takes so little to mean so much to a child. Thank you, Uncle Ford!

Lord, help me find ways to share your love with all my family members, to make a difference. Amen.

Week 38, Saturday   **The Matriarch**

The command of Queen Esther fixed these practices of Purim, and it was recorded in writing.
—Esther 9:32

Aunt Nedra is the matriarch, the Queen Esther of this clan. The oldest of my mother's nine siblings, tall, strong, a survivor, she stands out in my mind as the family head. Wonderful laughter

---

always rang out from her lips when we would visit. She set tables full of home-grown vegetables, wonderful meats, and scrumptious desserts. And always there were the jokes and the laughter with aunts, uncles, and cousins gathered around the big table on the screened-in car port. Such wonderful memories.

Nedra and her husband grew the largest watermelons in the world for three years running in the 1960s. A native of Hope, Arkansas, she went to the inauguration of President Clinton. On her living room wall is a plaque reading "We raise watermelons and Presidents in Hope."

Nedra is a survivor—and an inspiration. In her fifties she went back to school, got her nursing degree, and worked for many years. She raised all her children well. She took care of one of her sons who had Down's syndrome until he died in his thirties. When a daughter needed a new liver, she raised the money somehow.

Nedra believes in a risen Lord. She knows the difference between right and wrong and isn't afraid to tell you about it. And whenever she sees me, the grown child of her youngest sister, she reminds me that my mother loved me very much. I thank God for aunts like Nedra. Everyone should be so lucky.

Father, thank you for all the Nedras of this world who come into our lives, love us, and show us the way to live a good life. Help me to follow their example. Amen.

Week 39, Sunday   **The Right Path**

Train up a child in the way he should go,
and when he is old he will not depart from it.
—Proverbs 22:6 RSV

We had just finished a wonderful meal at my son Eric's favorite restaurant. On the way out, as he reached for a toothpick from the metal dispenser, he accidently knocked it down, and it hit the hard tile floor with a loud crash. Every eye in the restaurant was on us, it seemed, as Eric tried to pick up the toothpicks, which had scattered to kingdom come.

The manager ran out and told us not to worry. "Please, we will take care of it."

"Boy, that was embarrassing wasn't it?" I said to Eric as we walked out.

"It sure was," he replied.

"Did you die?"

"What?"

"Did you die of embarrassment?"

"No, of course not," Eric stated, still puzzled.

No one really ever dies of embarrassment, I explained, and we should never let the opinions of others or the fear of embarrassment keep us from doing something we really wanted to do and knew we should do.

"Is that a moral, Dad?" Eric asked as we drove away.

"Yeah, son, that's a moral."

In this third week we move to the area of our relationships with the generations that follow us—our children, grandchildren, nieces, and nephews. We are charged to teach by what we say, but more important, by example, by who we are. We are privileged to be able to be a part of the next generation's lives. We also have a duty to honor that privilege.

Father, it is a wonderful privilege to be parents, grand-parents, uncles, and aunts. Help us to remember the duties that come with this privilege so that we can train up the next generation in your ways. Amen.

Week 39, Monday   Immortality

Behold, my covenant is with you, and you shall be the father of a multitude of nations. No longer shall your name be Abram, but your name shall be Abraham; for I have made you the father of a multitude of nations.   —Genesis 17:4-5 RSV

"How's it going, Dad?" My teenage son had just called me. These were his first words, the introduction to his phone connection with me while I was working in a different city, miles away. There were no big problems, no important issues. He just wanted, needed to talk to his dad. And I felt, as I always do when he calls, like a very lucky man. This is one of the greatest privileges of parenthood—knowing you are connected to tomorrow in the lives of your children.

A Chinese proverb goes something like this: "There are three ways a man can become immortal: write a book, plant a tree or father a child." Listening to my son talk about the day's events and the rest of his week's plans, I remembered this proverb. And I also remembered a conversation I had had the night before, with my dad. "How's it going, Dad?" I had asked, and we had proceeded to laugh about the things that were going on in our lives and in the world. No big problems, no important issues. I had just wanted, needed to talk to Dad. And I know how much those talks mean to both of us.

Very often we turn to our heavenly Father in times of crisis. We pray fervent prayers for urgent needs. And there is nothing wrong with this—we are encouraged to come to the Father, to ask, seek, knock. But when I think about how I feel when my son calls and when I talk to my earthly father, I begin to see how my daily calls to my heavenly Father might bring joy to both God and me. We can stop at any time and talk to him as well as form the habit of regular, daily communication with him. He is always home and we'll never get a busy signal. He is waiting now.

Heavenly Father, please give me the wisdom to be a good father and a good son. Help me never to forget the importance of keeping my relationships strong—with people and with you—by regular communication. Amen.

Week 39, Tuesday   Life Isn't Fair

If you see in a province the poor oppressed and justice and right violently taken away, do not be amazed at the matter; for the high official is watched by a higher, and there are yet higher ones over them.   —Ecclesiastes 5:8 RSV

"It's not fair!" I can't count the number of times my children have said these words when they couldn't do what they wanted, or didn't get something they wanted, or didn't win at some game we were playing.

Fairness, justice, this sense that things ought to go according to some universally accepted way all the time—we all have it. And, like the author of Ecclesiastes, we all see unfairness and injustice in the world.

The other day my ten-year-old daughter called me all upset. A couple of weeks before, her dog had been hit by a truck and died. In her grief, she wanted a new dog as soon as possible, a black lab. She had saved up her money and would buy the puppy herself.

But this was the end of the summer, just a couple of days before school would start. Her mother had told her she would have to wait until next summer to get the puppy, so she would be able to play with and train the puppy. We have three other dogs and my wife was not up to taking care of another puppy while I was working out of town and Leigh was away all day in school, sports, Girl Scouts, and all the other activities that fill her fall and winter months.

But Leigh wanted the dog. She had called, not to try to get me to change her mother's mind, but just because she was upset and wanted to talk. My normal response to the "It's not fair" statement is to say, "Life is not fair." We then discuss various options like what can be done or the need to learn acceptance.

I fully expected Leigh to say, "But it's not fair!" She didn't. Instead, after one of my long monologues about how her mother's ideas made so much sense and she would have more time next summer for a puppy, she stopped me in my tracks and said, "I know, I know, I just wish life was fair." End of discussion, sentiments expressed, the bottom line.

"I do too sometimes, sweetheart," I replied.

Heavenly Father, thank you for the wisdom of children. Grant me the ability to accept whatever life dishes out, secure in the knowledge that you will see me through. Amen.

Week 39, Wednesday   **Being One's Own Man**

Read Luke 9:59-62.

"My father wants me to work in the family business." As my friend spoke these words, he rolled his eyes. Working in the family business would mean leaving the big city, its excitement, his circle of friends, the life he had come to love, and moving back to small-town America, which he had fled as soon as college offered an escape.

"I'm the oldest son," he continued. "Dad has dreamed of the day when he would hand over the reins to me. How can I disappoint him? And yet, how can I go? I can't imagine life back there."

I did not have an easy answer. I had never faced that dilemma. My father, a salesman, had retired. There was no "family business" to inherit. Sometimes, in my heart of hearts, I had envied my friends whose fathers did have businesses—a safety net, a place of refuge. "I can always go to work for my dad," I had heard them say.

But now I was seeing the other side of the equation, the dilemma. How can one be his own man, pursue his own dreams and life, if his father dreams different dreams for him?

I remembered Jesus' words to a reluctant follower to let the dead bury the dead. A Bible commentary I read one time shed some light on this difficult passage. In the culture of the time, a man was not free to "be his own man" until his father died. So this would-be follower was telling Jesus that when he was free, when his father died, he would follow Jesus.

Jesus tells him to seize the moment, to follow now. As I talked with my friend, I was suddenly happy that I did not have his dilemma. But I also know that I have a different struggle in my life and in my relationship with my father. And, for my children, I am determined to let them dream their own dreams, make their own choices.

Heavenly Father, give me the wisdom to be a good guide but to let my children dream their own dreams. Amen.

Week 39, Thursday   **The Spark**

Read Luke 18:15-17.

"She's the pretty one."
"He's the athletic one."
"She's the bookworm."

Isn't it funny how as children, especially in large families, kids often get labeled. And the labels stick like some self-fulfilling prophecy. Not all the labels are good. "The lazy one." "The fat one." "The plain one." "The dumb one." Sometimes the labels come from the kids. But too often adults originate them and, when coupled with the unbelievable habit adults have of talking about their kids in front of their kids as if their kids weren't there or were somehow not human, the label can hurt.

"Sally is our little ballerina." "Jim doesn't finish anything he starts." "Johnny is always getting into trouble." Innocent as this may sound, it affects our kids.

Jesus loved the little children. He warned his hearers not to hurt them. He gathered them to himself. He told us to be like them. It is a command we must not take lightly.

One of my father's gifts to me, which I am trying to pass on to my kids, is a belief in oneself. Dad always told us we had "the spark," that we could do what we set out to do, be what we determined to be. This kind of labeling, this kind of encouragement, building up, sustains and strengthens. And I tell my kids they have the spark, that they should be proud to be Camps and to pursue their dreams. And I believe that they will.

Father, keep me ever mindful of the difference between teasing and hurting. Help me to build up the young people in my life, not tear them down. Amen.

Week 39, Friday   **Fools Rush In**

Read Matthew 20:20-23.

"Can you believe she tried to have the other cheerleader candidate killed just so her daughter could be cheerleader?" My friend was appalled. So was I. A mother, so zealous for her daughter's career, was in jail on attempted murder charges. How could this be?

This case is the extreme, but it does seem to me that we are seeing much more negative parental involvement in our schools and our communities these days. A high school athletic director was recently sued by the parents of a graduating senior because he had benched the boy after the boy made disparaging remarks about him in the school yearbook. The suit alleged that the student was unfairly discriminated against in this benching. I found it hard to believe and hope the judge will throw out the case.

Even if the athletic director's action was harsh, or showed

poor judgment, whatever happened to respect for authority in the first place? What kind of message are these parents sending to their kids when they take the radical step of suing the man rather than explaining to their son that sometimes life is not fair and if you say bad things about someone in authority, there may be consequences. I wonder if they plan to sue every boss this young man ever works for if he does not learn some respect and diplomacy.

Like the overzealous mother of James and John, if we are not careful, we can do more harm than good. Jesus told her she did not know what she was talking about and that only God the Father could grant her wish. Sometimes we need to stand back and let our kids learn about life firsthand. We will not always be there. They need to be strong.

Father, help me know when to step in and when to stand aside as my children navigate the dangerous waters on the way to adulthood. Amen.

Week 39, Saturday   **All in the Family**

Read Luke 1:26-27, 36-41, 56-57.

The years had been hard on her. Life had delivered some tough blows. For a variety of reasons, she had never married. Relationships had come and gone, none had been permanent. It was past the time when she could have children of her own.

One day, in response to a question from her about my family, I found myself gushing forth about how important my relationship was with both my dad and my children. Receiving a call from my eldest son on the same day I had called my father had made me feel the circle was complete, I told her, and I hadn't really understood my parents until I had had children of my own.

Suddenly I heard myself and my words. Here was my friend with no children who would most likely never have children. What was she thinking as I blithely prattled on about what my kids meant to me? How insensitive of me. I stopped talking as soon as a natural break in my thoughts arrived.

There was silence for a moment. "I think I can understand some of what you are saying," my friend said. "I just took my twenty-year-old niece in for a while to help her get on her feet after a difficult time. My brother thought maybe in another city, away from the crowd she's been running with, she could get a fresh start. We've been close, this niece and I, over the years. She is the next best thing to having a child of my own and now, if I can give her the chance, see this through, I will feel I've been given the privilege of sharing parenthood with my brother."

Like my friend, and like Mary running to help her kinswoman at the end of Elizabeth's pregnancy, each of us needs to be committed to our extended family. Each of us has the ability to mean something to someone of the next generation. Whether family or friend, our generation needs to mentor those coming after us and to pass the mantle on.

I know my friend is a great aunt. What a lucky niece!

Heavenly Father, show me how to give myself to my family and to the next generation of young people. Amen.

Week 40, Sunday   The Good Life

Enjoy life with the wife whom you love.

—Ecclesiastes 9:9

"Have you been to a marriage encounter weekend?" my new friends asked me over lunch. They proceeded to talk about what it had meant to their marriage, how much closer they had become. The weekend had obviously been a wonderful experience for them.

This last week we are moving into the area of our relationships of choice. We choose whom to marry. We choose when to marry. We choose if we will marry. We choose to divorce. We have greater freedom in these matters than any earlier generation. Often it seems we are exercising this freedom in ways that do not promote strong family structures. We have moved from a family-oriented society to an individual-oriented society.

This freedom of choice is not bad. I do not think we want to return to a time of arranged marriages or a ban on divorce. But that is just the problem. Freedom always carries with it responsibility. Sometimes in our defense of freedom we do not give enough attention to the duties that flow from the decisions we have made. We may be free to divorce, but should we divorce if there is a chance of reconciliation?

My friends had the right response, it seemed to me, to a time of struggle in their marriage. They rolled up their sleeves and went to work to save it. Maybe we all could use more "marriage encounters."

Lord, your families are suffering even as we experience more freedom. I need your guidance to make the right decisions in my family life and your strength to keep it all together. Amen.

Week 40, Monday   The Perfect Couple

Husbands, love your wives, and do not be harsh with them.
                                            —*Colossians 3:19 RSV*

"My wife and I were a perfect match." My good friend spoke these words as he discussed some struggles he was experiencing in his own life and with his wife of many years. He continued explaining that in individual therapy and marriage counseling over the years, they had discovered that each had sought a mate that would allow certain character flaws to be played out and emotional needs to be met. "It wasn't healthy. I wanted someone more helpless, less accomplished than myself so I could always shine, be the hero. She needed someone who would allow her to be weak and with whom she could reaffirm her own poor self-image, and retreat into the shadows of depression.

"You know what is the most difficult thing in this process?" my friend asked. "Once the revelation is there, the understanding both of why we married each other and the unhealthy aspects of the relationship, we have to start all over again, trying to be a healthy couple. We are committed to the relationship, for the long haul, for the kids, in our faith, in our struggles. But it isn't easy and sometimes it can be hell."

I admired my friend's honesty and his commitment. Anyone who reads the papers can see articles reciting the divorce statistics. What is it now—50 percent, 60 percent or more of marriages end in divorce?

It is an unsettling trend and should concern all of us. Even those with success stories, intact marriages and children who grow to adulthood, must wonder if their children will marry someone from a broken home and how that will affect them. There is no easy solution.

I felt certain that my friend's strong faith, his relationship with God, played a pivotal role in his choosing to stick it out, to face the difficulties and save his marriage.

Father, I pray for all the marriages in the world. Give us, give me, the wisdom and the strength to keep struggling even when times get their hardest, knowing the rewards will be more than worth the effort. Amen.

Week 40, Tuesday   **Starting Over**

And the LORD restored the fortunes of Job, when he had prayed for his friends; and the LORD gave Job twice as much as he had before.   *—Job 42:10 RSV*

"Starting over is really hard." My friend of many years was filling me in on his new life—post divorce. We had not seen each other in many years. John had been married when I met him, and as is often the case with people we meet as a "couple," I had always thought of him as part of that unit. Now there was a new spouse to meet.

"When I divorced, suddenly there I was, in my early forties, no house, lots of debt, and my world shattered. The last three years of marriage had been hell, but I just never thought it would happen to me—divorce. But it did."

I could hear the pain in his voice, but I also saw his eyes light up when he talked about his new wife. "I guess I just believe in marriage. Can't see living alone and, Joan, well, she's a great person, a good wife. I'm lucky to have found her. The dating scene—I'm just not cut out for it."

For my friend there was a happy ending. I was glad that he had remarried and that it was working. But I also knew that his pain had been real, and part of him would always feel the ache of the failed marriage. He would continue to be reminded of it, especially at times like his daughter's graduation or marriage. The pain is part of the reality of life.

Life as a Christian is not pain-free. There are times when, despite our best efforts, things go wrong. But there is also hope in the Christian expectation that "all things work together for good for those who love God" (Romans 8:28). My friend had made the best choice when faced with the failed marriage. He found someone and tried again—started over.

Pray you never have to face this tragedy, either because of the death of a spouse or divorce. But if, despite your best efforts and your prayers, you find yourself a widower or divorced, pray for the courage to try again, to share your life with someone.

Father, I pray for the shattered lives of people who have seen a marriage end, and for the healing and hope that faith in you and your everlasting love can give. Amen.

Week 40, Wednesday   The Luckiest Man Alive

A good wife who can find?
She is far more precious than jewels.
—Proverbs 31:10 RSV

"I told my wife just the other day that I thought I was the luckiest man alive." My white-haired mentor friend blurted this sentence out over lunch as we discussed his recent wedding anniversary. Fifty years they had been married. They had raised a family, moved cities several times, had their ups and downs, good times and not so good times, but now in the evening of their lives they were together. Theirs was a success story. My friend explained that that morning he and his wife had spent a few moments thinking back about their life together. Now with both in retirement, with enough money to live comfortably, and with good health, good friends, and grandchildren, they felt richly blessed, lucky.

My friend and his wife were pillars of the church. He had served in just about every position possible for a layperson, not just once, but several times. He remained intensely committed to the church, not just our local congregation, but the worldwide Body of Christ. I could not help but believe that his commitment to his faith had to have played a major part in his successful marriage.

"What is your secret?" I asked him. "How did you make it for fifty years?"

"It was not always easy. At one time in midcareer I took a job in another city for a while. My wife didn't like it and it felt like we were drifting apart. But we held on, day by day. We weathered the storm and came out stronger.

"Pray and pray some more—that is part of the story. But the other part is just hanging in there; believing it will get better, trusting God to give you the strength to overcome the challenges. It worked for me. It will work for you."

As he spoke these words I saw the sparkle in his eyes and heard the contentment in his voice. I was listening to a victor. Maybe he *was* the luckiest man alive.

Father, help me to weather the storms in my life through prayer and trusting you, so that I, too, may come to feel I'm "the luckiest man alive." Amen.

Week 40, Thursday   Who Is My Neighbor?

Better is a neighbor who is near
than a brother who is far away.
—Proverbs 27:10 RSV

We started out as mere acquaintances who met at a Bible study. Raymond had been brought by a mutual friend and did not look comfortable at the meeting. I could tell he was scoping this out, trying to understand why ten otherwise "normal" business-men would get together at the ungodly hour of 7:00 A.M. at a greasy spoon restaurant to study events that happened thousands of years ago. He did not speak at that first Bible study, but he came back.

One day we decided to have breakfast together on a different workday. I wanted to know who he was, why he kept coming back when he didn't seem to enjoy the study and certainly did not participate. Before I could ask him about himself, though, he began a series of personal questions about me, about my child-hood and school, my motivations and hardships and accomplish-ments. I found myself telling him my life story as if I were being interviewed for an autobiography.

Then he started talking about his life, and the amazing parallels in our stories became more and more apparent. There were differences though. He was estranged from his brothers and sisters and family, and I was not. He had basically grown up without much formal church, and I had had twelve years of Catholic school. Faith had not played a part in his life, but he was searching, and so he had agreed to go to the Bible study.

We became close friends and continued with the Bible study. As he began to develop a faith, I found in sharing with him that I was forced to deepen my own understanding. Then I had to move from that city. At our last meeting Raymond thanked me for my friendship. "I thought I had lost my brothers," he said. "But I found a new brother in Christ in you."

Father, remind me each day that I am your hands and voice in this world. Let your light shine in me. Make us all brothers and sisters in you. Amen.

Week 40, Friday   The "Christian" Lawyer

Live your life in a manner worthy of the gospel of Christ.
—Philippians 1:27

"I've heard of you. You're that Christian lawyer in your firm." The young lawyer at the reception was staring at my name tag before he blurted out these words. I was embarrassed. What was I supposed to say? "Yes, I'm the Christian." It sounded so proud, so arrogant, so like the Pharisee who wanted everyone to know how holy he was.

The young man had heard about a Bible study I lead, he told me, and I had spoken at a Christian Legal Society meeting at his law school. Therefore I was the Christian lawyer. My "Christian credentials" were based upon these public actions.

So what was bothering me as I listened to him? It should have made me happy to be recognized as a follower of Christ. The words of the song, "They will know we are Christians by our love," kept going through my mind. Today, in our secular, politicized world we hear about the "Christian" this and the "Christian" that, too often in areas of controversy like abortion, school prayer, same sex marriages, or domestic partner health plans, boycotts, and marches. To many, this is how they know we are "Christians."

While I cannot help being labeled by some of my activities, what I really want is to be known as a Christian by my love, by Christ's love in me. And if more Christians were known by their love for their fellows, maybe I would not cringe when someone labels me as the Christian Lawyer.

Father, I want others to come to know you through me. Give me the strength to live as your son, following the example of Jesus Christ who loved me and gave himself for me. Amen.

Week 40, Saturday   What Do You Believe About Jesus?

Put on the whole armor of God. . . . And take the helmet of salvation, and the sword of the Spirit, which is the word of God.
                                                    —Ephesians 6:11, 17 RSV

I was working in Kuwait as the only American lawyer in a group of Kuwaiti and Egyptian lawyers. They were Muslim and I was Christian. I knew very little about their religion when I arrived. They knew some things about mine, but misunderstood others. We would talk sometimes, share stories from the Bible or the Koran, and could see the parallels, the similarities of the faiths.

One morning as I was preparing for work, a pamphlet fell out of a book I had picked up off a shelf in my study. It was one of those Christian texts that people sometimes pass out on the street or in parks. It had simple questions about Jesus, his life, what Christians believe, and about salvation by grace. I do not know when I had received this or why it was in that book. Probably someone had handed it to me one time and it just got caught in the pages of the book I was carrying. I did not remember having seen it before.

As I held it in my hand I found myself reading it, page by page, at the same time wondering why I was reading it. It seemed silly. *I know this stuff,* I thought. *I don't need this tract.*

Later that morning at work, the Sheikh, who was the Kuwaiti head of the local law firm, called me into his office. We were friends and I held him in great respect. A member of the royal family, he was a wise man with three law degrees, and had been minister of justice at one time.

After an exchange of pleasantries, he asked me, "What do you believe about Jesus?" I was shocked. We had not spoken of this before. I heard the questions I had read just that morning coming from his mouth and heard my answers as if I were reading that pamphlet. It made the hair on my neck stand on end, and I knew why I had read that pamphlet. I needed to be prepared for that one moment.

Lord, keep me ever mindful of the need to be a witness for you, because I do not know the time or the hour you will call on me to speak. Amen.

11

Men of God

James R. King Jr.

. . . while a wind from God swept over the face of the waters.
—Genesis 1:2

Some time ago I heard a man tell a story about teaching a Bible class to young adults. When he asked the students to turn to the book of Genesis, a young man quickly raised his hand. "I know where to find Matthew, Mark, and Luke," he said, "but where is Genesis?"

Like that young man, many men are confused both about the Bible and about how to live a meaningful life. They do not know where to begin. For a man who seeks to understand his purpose on earth, Genesis makes a good place to start to find God's intent for the world. The book of Genesis deals with the origins of the human race, and the word *genesis* itself means beginning. The Bible tells us that creation did not begin until the wind of God moved over the face of the waters. The wind of God is the Spirit of God. In other words, there is no life until the Spirit of God moves. To put it plainly, the essence of all life is spiritual.

It is easier for us human beings to focus on the material things of the world than it is to be led by that which can be experienced only by faith. It is great for us to build our physical muscles for work, play, and physical health, but unless we develop our spiritual muscles, we cannot know the truth about God and how God would have us live. When we men acknowledge that we are first and foremost spiritual creatures, then we have opened ourselves to the only way to know peace and fulfillment. A man who does not begin with God will at some point in his life have to turn around and go back to his origins, if he is to find himself.

O God of life, fill me this day with your Holy Spirit. Give me a keen awareness of who you are, and guide me to the way that you want me to live. Amen.

Week 41, Monday   You Are Very Special

Then God said, "Let us make humankind in our image, according to our likeness.   —Genesis 1:26

At the core of every person is the presence of God. For those who believe this, all life becomes sacred and valuable.

Some men are driven by belief systems that make them feel secure only when they consider themselves superior to others. To be part of the dominant race, to be male, is reason for pride. To have the fastest car, the largest muscles, or the prettiest girl becomes the only way some men can feel their worth. Other men feel unworthy because they have been ostracized by their fellows. They feel inadequate because of teasing and rejection.

There is good news for all of us. Jesus, the Son of the Living God, understands that beneath our pretense and our posturing is where you find the presence of the Holy Spirit. Jesus knows that the worth of a man comes from his relationship with God, not from his gender or his race, the type of car he drives or the kind of clothes he wears, or from his achievements. "Blessed are you," he tells all of us who know our hidden unworthiness, who are misunderstood, different, persecuted. We don't have to achieve status to inherit God's kingdom (Matthew 5:1-9).

It is great to see movements like Promise Keepers helping men to discover how special they are in God. But you can discover that right now. Say to yourself, "I am special, I am somebody in Jesus Christ. I have been made in the image of God. Glory hallelujah, all praise be to God."

Thank you, God, for sending Jesus Christ into the world and into my life to remind me that I have been made in your image. Amen.

God blessed them, and God said to them, "Be fruitful and multiply, and fill the earth and subdue it; and have dominion . . . over every living that moves upon the earth."

—*Genesis 1:28*

One of the gifts of the Holy Spirit is power (2 Timothy 1:7). Human beings have been blessed with the power to assist God in creating. They can help God by adding to what God has done. Here in Genesis 1 is the first job description of every man: to replenish the earth and manage (be a good steward of) what God has created. Wow! What an honor! What a responsibility! The key to how well the earth does lies in how we use the power that is given us, whether we use it to serve God's purpose or not. When we remember God's blessings and all the good gifts he has given us, we will take our responsibilities seriously, in order to preserve as well as multiply God's goodness.

Take, for instance, the command to multiply. How does a man show responsibility to God and to the children themselves if he thoughtlessly brings children into the world? In these days too many children are reared on too many hours of television, in too many fatherless homes, with too few relationships with Christ in congregational care. That is because too many young men have not been taught that the power of God in us is to be used to glorify God.

Our responsibility under God extends to every area of life. For instance, when we hear of issues like global warming, do we consider how the power given to us to multiply God's goodness has moved us in a deadly direction because we are producing things for material gain rather than for God? How will we change our ways? If we remembered our first divine job description, would we allow animal species to become extinct because we are misusing the power God has given us?

Today we are living in the center of a revival where men are being called to remember their first job description—to have dominion over the earth. How are you using your power?

Almighty and Eternal God, Creator and Sustainer of all life, guide me back to your wonderful plan for all creation. Help me to fulfill my responsibilities to care both for the earth and for the children. Amen.

God said, ". . . and every tree with seed in its fruit; you shall have them for food."   *—Genesis 1:29*

After God instructs the first humans to be fruitful and multiply, he tells them that the provisions necessary to keep them strong have also been provided, so that they can do the job God has given them. That is still true today. When God calls us and gives us a task, God equips us and provides for all our needs. Faith, believing God's promises, enables us to take action on God's Word.

Faith also connects us to another important process for action, and that is trust—a state of living connected to God, depending on him. In our human dilemmas and because of our pride, we don't want to trust God. So we need to be changed, to be born again, so that all of our activity flows out of a spiritual perspective.

When we trust God, God will honor our faith and our faithfulness. When we enter into covenant with God and remain obedient, God, who cannot fail, will make witnesses of us by pouring out more blessings than we could ever have imagined.

Take your health, for example. It is amazing to hear continuous medical reports that link what we eat to poor or good health. Daniel, whose behavior was directed by the Spirit of God, refused to eat food that was unhealthy for him, even though he was told by unbelievers he would be made stronger (Daniel 1:8-16). Daniel knew that his true strength and wisdom came from following God's laws, and he was proved right. How about your eating habits?

Our society encourages men to be competitive in order to survive. Imagine how men would treat each other if we truly believed in God's promise for us. Would not our behavior be modified immensely if we truly believed that God will provide for all our needs? The psalmist said it well in Psalm 23:1 (KJV): "The LORD is my Shepherd; I shall not want."

Thank you, God, for providing for all my needs. Help me to realize that my strength comes from you. In Jesus Christ's name, Amen.

God saw everything that he had made, and indeed, it was very good. —*Genesis 1:31*

Here, at the beginning of God's word, we find one of the most validating and inclusive statements in the Bible. God said of *everything* he had made, "It is good."

Every man needs to hear that word: that he is okay, that, made in the image of God, he is good. This does not mean that behavior that ostracizes, alienates, demeans, kills, destroys, or pollutes is okay. In fact, this word from God affirms that all creation, every part of it, is good and valuable, and therefore not to be mistreated.

If you are confused about your purpose, direction, or relationships, hear this clear message about yourself, and about others. Since all that God has made is very good, what part of your life or the world is not sacred, or not worthy of your care, your best thought and action? In other words, we are partners not only with one another but with all creation.

This understanding should leave us feeling great about ourselves. But we should also see the importance of treating others with the greatest respect. Too many boys, and men, feel that they are not worth much to themselves or to others, and they keep trying to compensate for feeling inadequate. Some men only feel good about themselves when they think they are better than women. Others only feel okay about themselves when they dominate or destroy others.

Consider this: you are a divine expression of God! And so is everyone. You are okay—and everybody else is okay, too.

O loving God, it sure does feel good to know how special I am to you. Teach me to treat others as you treat me. Amen.

Week 41, Friday **Reality Check**

Then the LORD God formed man from the dust of the ground, and breathed into his nostrils the breath of life; and the man became a living being. —*Genesis 2:7-8*

Without God no man can do anything.

Some men are blessed to discover early on in their lives that their very existence depends upon God. Others need reminders that come through problems and troubles, such as growing older, the death of loved ones, or terrible accidents. These can serve as reality checks that point us back to God as the very source of our existence.

I have been the officiant for many funerals, and it is always a reality check to say at the grave site, "Ashes to ashes, dust to dust." Our bodies will not last forever. But we are more than the ashes and dust that make up our physical bodies. Our physical form should never mislead us into thinking that what we see is the essence of life. Though we cannot see Spirit, we can see the fruit of the Spirit.

Unfortunately, some men stubbornly deny the existence of a spiritual Parent who has not only created them but also given them the breath of life. If we are to have a full life and a beautiful future, we need to acknowledge and be guided by the presence of the Holy Spirit. If you take the spirit out of any organic system, it will malfunction. If human beings ignore the Spirit of God, we will malfunction.

In order to remain focused on the essence of life, we men need to nurture our relationship with God. We must attend to the spiritual disciplines that include prayer, fasting, and Bible study. We need to spend time with God in order to let the Spirit fill us. The truth is, many of us spend a great deal of our time and energy trying to make a living. But none of us can live truly and fully without God.

O God of life, I don't want to be without your Holy Spirit. Lead me in the path of right and fruitful living. In Jesus Christ's name I pray. Amen.

Week 41, Saturday   **You Are Not Alone**

Then the LORD God said, "It is not good that the man should be alone; I will make him a helper as his partner."
—Genesis 2:18

Whatever task God has given us to do, we are not to do it alone. We are made for partnership and companionship. According to Scripture, God announces that human beings on their own cannot support the Spirit of God without some assistance. "It is not good that the man should be alone," God said. If a man gets tired, discouraged, weary, or is tempted to quit, who will help him to stay on course? Work, ministry is to be shared. No one person can do it all. Jesus understood this when he sent out his disciples two by two.

For one thing, men, we need prayer partners. We need to study the Bible with others, hold each other accountable through small groups and work on mission projects in teams. We are working against God's plan when we try to do any job for God all by ourselves.

Men of God, when we realize that we are children of the almighty, wise, and loving God, we begin to trust God for direction in all we do. The Bible teaches us that women are helpers and partners with men. Women are in the world and in our lives as a blessing from God. Women are to be valued and appreciated, not as our servants but as our equals. Partnership places men and women on the same level, and we should not allow our different gifts to make us treat women as less than men, for our gifts are from the same Spirit.

Living in God's plan encourages us to appreciate each other. As God's men, we cannot allow gender, race, or any other differences to deceive us into treating each other as enemies or inferiors—rather than as partners.

Thank you, God, for the wisdom of your divine plan that puts us with partners so that together we can do your will. Help me not to be stubbornly independent. Amen.

Week 42, Sunday   **What Does God Want?**

The LORD God took the man and put him in the garden of Eden to till it and keep it.   *—Genesis 2:15*

Take a minute to imagine what the Garden of Eden must have been like. Can you see the beauty of the garden and feel the peace that it offers? We are told in Genesis 2:9 that "out of the ground the LORD God made to grow every tree that is pleasant to the sight and good for food, the tree of life also in the midst of the garden, and the tree of the knowledge of good and evil." From the very beginning, God planned for us to live in the best environment, to have the best food, so that we could take care of the land and watch over the animals. We were made to live in a divine place without want, with the one job of keeping it going and adding to it.

What happened? Well we were selfish and disobeyed God and ate from the tree of knowledge. We destroyed God's first plan for us. But God did not give up on us. God wants us reconciled to the original plan that is laid out from the beginning. How God would have us to live is described throughout the Old Testament, particularly in the laws known as the Ten Commandments. However, it is in the life and teachings of Jesus that we are given the greatest and best model for patterning our lives. Our purpose on this planet is to glorify God by living in accordance with God's will. To assist in God's will being done we must become disciples of Jesus Christ. God wants a world that looks like Christ, and it is our job to help bring this image into reality here and everywhere.

O God Eternal, giver of all good and marvelous gifts, I thank you, I praise you and glorify you. May your will be done in me this day. In Jesus Christ's name I pray. Amen.

Week 42, Monday   You Must Believe

For God so loved the world the that he gave his only Son, so that everyone who believes in him may not perish but may have eternal life.   *—John 3:16*

Most of us won't do anything we don't believe in. One of the reasons good athletic coaches are so valuable is their ability to get players to believe in themselves, in the team, and in their ability to win. When players don't believe in themselves, they don't win games. We can see this same pattern in biblical history. The Hebrews had difficulty staying on course in the wilderness because they did not believe God. They did not believe they could defeat their enemies with God's help, so they were, in a sense, paralyzed.

Jesus reminds us over and over again in his teachings that faith opens the windows of possibilities to accomplish what we have been given to do. With faith all things are possible. Faith permits us to take action. We will not follow Jesus if we do not believe, and if we do not believe in him we will not work for God's purpose, which is made clear through Jesus. We must believe in Jesus Christ if we are going to help God's kingdom to come.

Because we are physical beings, we find it difficult to believe in the spiritual world God has created and is calling us to. We ignore God's way, seeking to do things our own way, making our own gods and establishing our own rules for successful living. With all the love found in the gift of Jesus as our Savior, we must still believe that he is our Savior and the model we are to follow if we are to fulfil God's purpose. Without faith we will not act.

Almighty and everlasting God, thank you for your gift of Jesus Christ, and your love for me. I step out in faith to be part of your kingdom and to respond to your will. In Jesus Christ's name I pray. Amen.

Week 42, Tuesday   **Why We Need Disciples**

Go therefore and make disciples of all nations.
—Matthew 28:19

From the beginning God designed the world with the idea that we would participate in the process of filling the earth with blessings (Genesis 1:28). God apparently wants us to be active in the world. God could have filled the earth with goodness without our assistance. Yet by his creative act, we have both the capacity and the purpose to work with him to reproduce goodness in the world— as his children, as extensions of his will in the world. God wants the world full of goodness, and it is our job to assist in this process.

How do we do that? By following Jesus and inviting others into a relationship with God through Jesus Christ. As disciples of Jesus Christ, we are extensions of Christ in the world—thus the name Christian. When we make disciples for Jesus Christ, we are filling the world with goodness. It is important to hear that Jesus commands his followers to make disciples of *all nations*. As men who believe in Christ, therefore, we cannot be satisfied with the status quo, either in our families, our congregations or our neighborhoods.

"Follow me," is Christ's call to his disciples, "and I will make you fish for people" (Mark 1:17).

O Holy God, I want to follow Christ and be part of filling the earth with your goodness, your blessings, and your love. Help me to begin right here, right now, with my own family. I pray in Jesus Christ's name. Amen.

Week 42, Wednesday   A Better World

And these signs will accompany those who believe.
                                                              —Mark 16:17

If you and I belong to Christ and his Spirit is in us, there should be signs of that relationship everywhere.

Though there are thousands upon thousands of Christians who witness to the goodness of God in the world and in their lives each day, it appears that there are many more Christians who haven't gone far enough in their relationship with Christ. They haven't put their faith into action. They don't understand that they are to participate in the transformation of the world.

How is it that so many congregations can coexist with slum neighborhoods, or neglect children who need love and care? What can be more devastating than for a child to struggle without ever learning that he or she is loved? According to scripture we are to participate in the wellness of the world. In order for this to happen there must be some connection with the Holy Spirit through whom we have access to power, love, and self control (1 Timothy 1:7).

Our congregations, that is, the communities of believers, must be places where people experience the love of Christ. If those of us who say that Jesus Christ is the leader of our lives do not show the kind of care and hospitality that reflects the way of Christ, we do more harm than good—we destroy the hope that is embedded in faith.

How are you demonstrating Christ's love?

O loving God, make me an instrument of your love, for Christ's sake. Amen.

And he said to them, "Follow me." —Matthew 4:19

If we are going to follow Jesus Christ, we must get to know Jesus so well that we can act in the way Jesus would act. The first disciples of Jesus watched Jesus pray, heal, and teach. They watched him in all of his interpersonal relationships and they listened to his words of instruction. When they started making disciples as Jesus instructed, they taught the new converts in the way that Jesus had taught them. Beginners must be taught. The new converts had to learn how to pray, to worship, to work together and share their resources. They were led into a relationship with God that would allow them to receive the Holy Spirit in their lives.

These are the same things that make for discipleship now. We men must not only invite men into a relationship with Christ, we must make sure that they are taught the same spiritual disciplines that we have received. We join fraternities and other clubs where we are required to know the club's history and rules, and to pay dues. But we can come into the church, be baptized and given responsibilities, and know next to nothing about the teachings of Christ, or the history of the church.

We must not only have models of the Christian life, we must also have classes and mentors if we are to live in the world as men of God.

Are you a disciple of Jesus Christ? I encourage you to seek out a class and a mentor who can help you learn and grow. Then reach out to invite other men to become disciples of Jesus Christ.

God, sometimes it is difficult for me to admit I need your help in following Jesus, because I don't want to seem weak. But I do want to be a faithful disciple. Please teach me. I pray in Jesus' name. Amen.

Week 42, Friday   **Get in the Discussion**

They devoted themselves to the apostles' teaching.
—Acts 2:42

Have you seen anyone wearing a wrist band with the letters WWJD? Over the last several years I have seen quite a few of them worn by both young and older people. What do the letters stand for? They are an acronym for the question "What would Jesus do?" That's a question I have encouraged congregations to ask themselves in every situation. It's vitally important that as God's men we must learn how to respond as Christians.

Asking that question, though, brings up another one. How can we align our behavior with Christ's if we do not know how Jesus talked or how he responded in situations? The point is, how will you know how to respond like Jesus if you do not know him as he is revealed through the Scriptures, if you do not know how he lived and acted when he was on earth?

As God's men, we need to read and study the word of God in our private meditative moments. But it is just as important that we also study it together, in study groups at church, or around the table in our homes, listening, sharing, and praying together for God to be made clearer to us through the Holy Scriptures.

Such groups are wonderful places for new and would-be Christians to learn what the Christian faith is all about. But because the Bible is intimidating for some people, when you invite others to Bible class, tell them that they do not have to bring a Bible unless they want to. And don't ask them to read out loud unless they are comfortable doing that. In other words, it is more important for them to be at the place where the Bible is discussed and personal thoughts are challenged than for them to feel anxious about reading from the Bible and therefore not to come at all.

Remember: WWJD?

Thank you, God, for laying out your plan for me in your Holy Scriptures. Through your Holy Spirit make your way clear to me and empower me to do your will. In Jesus Christ's name. Amen.

Week 42, Saturday **Something to Do**

Your Kingdom come.
Your will be done,
on earth as it is in heaven.
—Matthew 6:10

As God's men, we have something to do. We have a mission. We are the construction workers for the kingdom of God. If we are to follow Jesus we must be willing to work for the same things that he was committed to.

In the disciples' prayer known as the Lord's Prayer, Jesus instructed his disciples to indicate their support of God's will to be done on earth as it is done in heaven. In the remaining part of the prayer, we ask for help in doing God's will.

The Bible teaches us that we are not only to be hearers of the word but doers as well (James 1:22). We have been created to do, to act. We must again hear the message embedded in the question that Jesus asked Peter who had returned from fishing: "Do you love me? If you love me, feed my sheep." (See John 21:15-17.) Through us the gospel is to spread throughout God's world. Through us the kingdom of God is to be manifested in the world, beginning in our homes, congregations, places of employment and recreation. We have a job to do and it starts with you and me.

"You will receive power when the Holy Spirit has come upon you; and you will be my witnesses" (Acts 1:8).

Our Father who art in heaven, hallowed be thy name. Thy kingdom come. Thy will be done in earth, as it is in heaven. Give us this day our daily bread. And forgive us our debts as we forgive our debtors. And lead us not into temptation, but deliver us from evil: For thine is the kingdom, and the power, and the glory, for ever. Amen.

Week 43, Sunday   What Are You Going to Do?

Bear fruits worthy of repentance. —*Luke 3:8*

What a tremendous time we live in today. Our cars go faster, our planes fly higher, E-mail allows us to communicate with each other immediately and more cheaply than at any previous time. Through the Internet not only can we access a world of knowledge more vast than at any time in history, but we can connect with the whole world. But at what cost?

In spite of our increased speed, we seem to have less time for family, less time for trust and fellowship, less time for personal growth. In spite of our increased knowledge, we seem to have fewer values to guide our behavior. In spite of our vast linkage through computers, we seem to have less community and less peace. Why is that?

We are children of God, who is spirit and truth. The essence of our reality is spiritual. Until we begin to see and understand that truth is in God, we are lost and doomed to a way that has no future. John the Baptist reminds us that we cannot find life and all the fruits of the Spirit by following our own self-centered paths. We must repent—that is, we must turn our attention in another direction. Only then will we know true love, true joy, true peace, for these are manifestations of the Spirit.

Some of us are having a difficult time trying to find our way. We say we are part of God's kingdom, but our actions belie our words. For instance, what man can say he is health-conscious while he is still smoking cigarettes? Who would really take a man seriously who says he is going to lose weight while he goes back for seconds in a buffet restaurant? We say we are Christians but we measure our success by our material possessions.

In God's kingdom, success is measured by how we develop and employ our spiritual gifts to love and serve God and his creation, to love and serve our neighbors.

What are you going to do? Turn to God or remain selfish?

O God of love and grace, show me the areas of my life that need to be changed so that I can have a vital relationship with you through your Holy Spirit. For Jesus Christ's sake. Amen.

Week 43, Monday   Born to Change

Jesus answered, "Very truly, I tell you, no one can enter the kingdom of God without being born of water and Spirit." —John 3:5

He looked like Mr. Basketball standing there on the basketball court so very tall and slim, taking routine practice shots. As I watched, his coach said to me, "Look at that player. He will never be a good basketball shooter, no matter how much he practices. If he makes two points, it will be an accident."

"Why is that?" I asked. The young man's star-athlete physical attributes combined with the coach's comments had really aroused my curiosity.

"He has the bad habit of releasing the ball from the palm of his hand where he has no control," the coach said. "If he's going to be a good basketball shooter, he has to learn to let the ball come off his fingers, where he has more control. He can practice and practice forever, but unless he changes the way he practices, it won't change the outcome of his performance."

The same is true for us spiritually. Unless we change, unless we are born again, we will never be part of God's winning team. We will remain trapped in an endless circle of trying to find fulfillment in life by focusing on things of the world that cannot satisfy us. True life, true change, comes through a birth of the Spirit.

O God, I want to change my nonproductive ways and be born again into your kingdom, to be part of your winning team. Thank you for the gift of your Holy Spirit and your Son, Jesus Christ. Amen.

Week 43, Tuesday   Come Home

I will get up and go to my father, and I will say to him, "Father, I have sinned against heaven and before you."
—Luke 15:18

Television and radio news broadcasts bombard us these days with stories of small children locked in a bathroom or left alone at home for days. We hear of children searching garbage cans for food while their parents look for another opportunity to appease their addiction. We hear of parents killing their children to get attention. It is obvious that we are living in a sin-sick world where millions of people are hurting not only for lack of love but also for lack of spiritual direction.

At the same time, we must also recognize and honor all the men and women who, through individual heroics, congregations, and other organizations, are helping to reshape and retool many broken lives. Those who are faithful and responsive to God's will must be acknowledged and affirmed. Beyond their wonderful efforts, however, we are still called to hear the words of Jesus:

"The harvest is plentiful, but the laborers are few" (Matthew 9:37).

Men, what are we going to do to make sure that every child will experience enough love, fun, education, and affirmation that each one will reject a way of life that is not spiritually rooted and grounded? The prodigal son knew that the servants in his father's house were living a better life than his trash-filled life emptied of all meaning and purpose. Can we not put such a palatable taste in the lives of our young men and women that the bitterness of illegal drugs, gang communities, premature sexual activity, and poor study habits will be rejected? God is calling us to act for him.

Thank you, God, for creating in me a place that can only be satisfied by you. Help me to keep finding my way back to you so that I may experience your fulfilling life and help others to return to you. Amen.

Week 43, Wednesday   **Let Go and Let God**

So Peter got out of the boat, started walking on the water, and came toward Jesus.   *—Matthew 14:29*

What happens when we confront the world's problems and try to work on them? Too often the solutions we come up with create division, leaving us angry and hurt. We are so sure we are right and others are wrong. We hold so strongly to our views and plans that we won't listen to anyone—not even to God! We can do it ourselves, we think, so we don't ask for God's direction. But to put anything in place of God is to miss the mark—to sin. When we try to correct the evil in the world, we are too often full of ourselves when the solution lies in being full of God.

How do we change? We have to let go. Let go of our insistence on our own way, let go of putting ourselves in the place of God, let go of our pride that refuses to ask God for direction. We have to learn not to be self-reliant but to be God-reliant.

God has promised to always be with us. Will you rely on that? Can you let go and let God?

O loving God, I confess that I am not strong or wise enough to meet the world's problems in my own strength. I do need you every day and every minute of my life. Help me to trust you so that I will do what you want me to do. Amen.

Week 43, Thursday   Open Your Heart to God

> *Create in me a clean heart, O God,*
> *and put a new and right spirit within me.*
> *—Psalm 51:10*

The older we grow, the more apparent it becomes that people are imperfect, that justice is not evenhanded but is distorted by a variety of mitigating circumstances. The result can be a growing anger and bitterness. If we try to correct other people and change situations in our own strength, we will discover our solutions are quite inadequate. Before we know it we can get entangled in a web of inner and outer conflicts that make peace and joy appear to be a complex formula that has no answer.

If we keep insisting on our own way, trying to create our own happiness, we can't really serve God. Because we are filled with the stuff of the world, we need a clean heart. All our thoughts and deeds are too clogged up with our own self-centeredness for the Spirit of God to flow through smoothly. Therefore, we need to open our hearts to God and ask Jesus to come into our lives right now and allow us to be made whole. Only when we are able to yield to God, the source of our existence, will we become clear about life, find meaning for our existence, and be useful to God.

God's grace can change our trash to treasure, our pain to gain, our hurt to hope. With God, all things become possible.

O Holy and Righteous God, only you can make me well. I open my heart to you right now that through your grace I might find myself forgiven of my sins and filled with your Holy Spirit. In Jesus Christ's name. Amen.

Week 43, Friday   Faith Works

Come and lay your hands on her, so that she may be made well, and live.   *—Mark 5:23*

If we live long enough, we will come to situations where it is obvious that we have no control over our circumstances. Your doctor may give a gloomy report regarding surgery, or you know that the funds are not available for college, or the business that you work for has filed bankruptcy and you do not know how you are going to make it. I have met with many congregations and families who have lost all their physical possessions in a flood or a tornado or in some other natural disaster.

Jairus, whose story is told in Mark 5, had encountered such a situation. Jairus was a leader of the synagogue in his town who probably had a great deal of influence and respect in the community. But he had come to a mountain that he could not move. His daughter was dying. He could not heal her and he did not know anyone who could. Jairus discovered that success in worldly matters is not enough, that there are some things in life we have no control over.

Jairus heard that Jesus could help and he believed the report. His faith in the power of Jesus made him act. He went to find Jesus, to plead with him to come and heal his daughter. Jesus rewarded his faith.

Your faith in God will make a world of difference. Do you believe?

O God of Life and Spirit, help me to open the doors and windows of my life to receive your blessings so that I might be used for your glory. Amen.

Week 43, Saturday   Grace

For God so loved the world that he gave his only Son.
—John 3:16

My father died a few years ago, but the wonderful relationship we had still lives on in me. His mother died before he had a chance to know her, making his relationship with his father and three sisters all the more important. He had to drop out of school during his elementary school years to help the family financially. As a shoeshine boy, he learned a lot just by listening to other men. Some years later he went into the dry cleaning business, owning and managing a store for over forty years. In addition, he opened a restaurant and had a real estate business.

My father and mother taught me the meaning of love and introduced me to my walk with Jesus Christ through baptism. My father was very involved both in the life of the church and in the community in which we lived. Many boys and men were strengthened through his wisdom and the model life he lived, although the odds were stacked against him.

It was during the planning of his funeral program that I learned from my mother what my father's favorite hymn was— "Amazing Grace." I still find it inspiring to know that a man who was able to overcome so much and who lived so fully carried in his heart the awareness that all that he was and all that he did were due to God's grace in his life.

When we recognize how good God has been to us, we just want to stretch out our arms wide with gratitude or fall to our knees with joyful hearts and say, "Thank you, God, for your love. Thank you, Jesus. Now, what can I do for you?"

Thank you, God, for your amazing grace and for the gift of Jesus Christ, my Lord and Savior. In gratitude I give my life to you for your service. Amen.

Week 44, Sunday   Let It Shine

You are the light of the world.   —*Matthew 5:14*

What do we do when we've been hurt? Most of us know people who react with hate. Jesus Christ shows us a different way, the way of healing. Nothing heals like love, for love encompasses grace, forgiveness, and justice. Love is the highest gift of the Spirit, the apostle Paul tells us.

Love—for God, for ourselves, and then for our neighbor—is how Jesus sums up the Law given in the Old Testament. Love is God's will for all of us. This understanding of love in all relationships is reflected from the beginning of the Bible to the end. Jesus lived it and asked those who would be his disciples to do likewise. Love like Christ is the goal of everyone who wears the name of Christian.

Not enough of us are living by this simple yet radical principle of love, or are teaching it to our friends, neighbors, coworkers, and congregations. It is the job of born-again Christian men to demonstrate this way of love. We are to put the light of our new-found way of life up high enough for others to see what God has done for us, so that they too may come to Christ and have their lives transformed. It is Christian to be humble, but it is a misunderstanding of God's will to hide our light. *Let it shine!*

O loving God, you have been so good to me, help me to demonstrate and tell the good news everywhere I go. In Jesus Christ's name. Amen.

Week 44, Monday   Stand Up for Jesus

Jesus said to Simon Peter, "Simon son of John, do you love me more than these?"   *—John 21:15*

In the movie *Forrest Gump,* the young boy Forrest was stricken by a disease that affected his legs and was fitted with braces. One day when Forrest and his playmate were on their way home from school, some of the boys in the neighborhood started to throw rocks at him. As Forrest innocently looked at the boys, his little girlfriend understood that all people are not kind and loving. "Run, Forrest," she yelled. "Run!"

Forrest loved and respected his friend, so he obeyed. He ran and kept running. Soon he found his braces a hindrance and abandoned them. With stronger legs than he could have hoped for, he was able to outrun his enemies.

Forrest offers us a lesson on the importance of being obedient. Doing what God tells us to do, even when we think it impossible, gives us the strength to keep on doing. But we can learn another lesson from this scene, about how we should treat one another. When we begin to look at life from a spiritual point of view, we understand that we are all children of God and the idea of throwing rocks at anyone because they are different is wrong. If we are living a repented life out of our new relationship with God through Jesus Christ, we must be willing to love each person we meet (to want God's best for them), and to teach that God is love. In the spiritual realm we are all children of God and to that extent every man is our brother in Christ. We cannot say we love Jesus and not find a place in our heart for one another. Stand up for Jesus, men of God.

O God of love and power, fill me with your presence so that I may do your will. Help me to actively seek your best for everyone I meet, for Jesus Christ's sake. Amen.

Week 44, Tuesday   Start at Home

The man from whom the demons had gone begged that he might be with him; but Jesus sent him away, saying, "Return to your home, and declare how much God has done for you."
                                                    —Luke 8:38-39

In a world that is more on the go than ever, more diverse and more polarized, those of us who know the Lord must always be prepared to offer the world the love of God through Jesus Christ. To offer the world Jesus is to offer them love. The world needs love. The Christian walk is one of love and reconciliation to God through Jesus Christ.

As soon as we repent, we are given the job of being Christ's ambassadors. Our new quality of life is itself a witness to God's grace and his capacity to save us from our sins. But we should also actively share the good news with others whenever and wherever possible. Our ability to do this comes through a life of prayer and Bible study, and through seeking the guidance of the Holy Spirit.

Where do we begin? Men who have turned the leadership of their lives over to the Lord must remember that every person who is a member of a congregation is not a believer or a follower of Christ. Therefore, one of the immediate tasks for Christian men is to introduce Jesus Christ to those who are in the church but have not come to know Jesus as their Lord and Savior. We must also strengthen our witness by making sure that those who are in the church are not in want, that we are extending Christ's love to them and meeting their needs.

When we start out to evangelize the world, a good place to get started just might be closer than we think. Witnessing begins at home.

O loving God, thank you for the new life you have given me in Christ. Give me the wisdom and courage to start sharing Christ with those who are close to me. Amen.

I am the Alpha and the Omega, the beginning and the end.
                              —Revelation 21:6

Here I am sitting in a theater watching a twenty-year-old movie again—*Star Wars*. Who would have believed that you could reintroduce an old movie to the public that would be a box-office hit? Old and new moviegoers are jamming the theaters to see a movie that was a success two decades ago. In some cities people waited in line for hours to get a ticket to see something that has not diminished with time.

This success of *Star Wars* led me to think about what it is in our society that has lasting value. What is it that never grows old or loses its value with age? We might list several items, like diamonds and gold, but even these earthly treasures need a culture or a government to set their value and identify them as fair exchange for bread and clothing. For us men of God, we have the timeless value of the good news found in the life and teachings of Jesus Christ. Thousands of years have passed since Jesus walked on this earth, but do you know a family that does not need the presence of Jesus Christ in their lives today? What man do you know who has so much of everything that he does not need Christ in his life?

It is fascinating that a twenty-year-old movie could still be a box-office hit. But it is far more wonderful that the gospel found in Christ is still as relevant for the world today as it was in the first century. Jesus Christ is the Alpha and the Omega, the beginning and the end, the source of eternal truth.

If you have come to the light of the truth found in Christ Jesus, you have something that the world will always need. If you are in Christ the world is hungry for what you have.

Almighty God, send me forth with the bread of life, that people of every age might be fed through your grace in Jesus Christ. Amen.

Week 44, Thursday   **Come to Jesus**

When he heard that it was Jesus of Nazareth, he began to shout out and say, "Jesus, Son of David, have mercy on me!"   *—Mark 10:47*

Have you ever been to a yard sale? When I was growing up I do not remember yard sales as a popular experience, but today there is an abundance of them in many parts of the country. Items that are no longer valuable to the owners, rather than being thrown away, are displayed in the yard for sale, hoping that they may be valuable to someone else. Sure enough, people stop by and pay for what someone else is ready to throw away.

As I was walking through a popular store the other day, I heard one woman say to another, "They sure do have a lot of nice junk in here!" Into a world where junk is deified, even nice junk, into this world God has sent a Savior for those who are considered worthless by some.

As Christians, we need to be like yard sale buyers. Some people find little value in others because of their race, gender, age, nationality, or social status. We Christian men will claim these marginalized persons as children of God who have been redeemed by the blood of Jesus Christ. We are called to seek the lost and the least, reclaiming them as valuable expressions of God's love.

Because God does not make junk, we are called to invite all men and women to come to Jesus, for he will save them. In the hymn "Come to Jesus," there is a verse that says, "He will save you just now." God wants the world reconciled. God wants the world to be redeemed.

O God of life and love, it is good to know that I am your child. Help me to see the value you place on everyone I meet, and to offer them your love. Amen.

Week 44, Friday   Plenty of Men

But that night they caught nothing.   —*John 21:3*

I was returning from checking for mail outside the church office door, when I heard a young man yell, "Hey!". I looked around to discover that he was yelling at the postman. The young man responded to my look by saying, "I was not talking to you. I was trying to get the attention of that mailman. He didn't bring me my check."

Drawn into the situation out of concern, I turned toward the postal truck almost a block away and started yelling, "Hey!" but to no avail. As I walked back into the church office, I thought to myself, *The mailman cannot deliver anything that he does not have, regardless of how desperate a person is to receive something in the mail.* Furthermore, I had allowed this man's misconception to involve me in shouting to the mailman.

Here's the point. Too often in our society we find ourselves blaming others when they are clearly not at fault, or when we are clearly the ones responsible for our condition. We can also get others to take our side on illegitimate issues that only serve to remove us farther from the growth opportunity that the situation provides.

Why are there not more men in our congregations and in our church organizations for men? Are our men invited to Spirit-led Bible classes? Are we sensitive to issues of childcare, attire, times of meetings, status, and ethnicity? Sometimes our old habits can block our witness for Christ and we end up touching the lives of very few when the world is full of men who are hungry for meaning.

In the incident recorded in John 21, the disciples had been fishing all night but hadn't caught anything. Jesus instructed them to cast their nets on the right side of the boat. When they obeyed Jesus, they caught more fish than they could have imagined.

O loving God, help me to listen to you and to find new ways to invite other men into the joy of your service. Amen.

Week 44, Saturday   **Work Together**

. . . and there are varieties of services, but the same Lord.
                                                        —1 Corinthians 12:5

Shaquille O'Neal, the basketball icon, recently appeared in a television commercial in which he received a basketball, "Should I pass it?" he asked the fans. "Should I shoot it?" Finally he asked, "Should I slam it?" When Shaquille asked, "Should I shoot it?" a person dressed like a nun appeared shaking her finger, implying no shooting.

Why, I wondered, would it be necessary to clarify the type of shooting you are referring to when it is obvious that the subject is basketball? I decided that so many men, young and old, have taken the value of life for granted, that this was a way of making a point. Too many men, and women, have not received love or been taught that life is sacred and should be appreciated and nurtured.

Even in the church, where there should be support, and a team effort, there is competitiveness and jealousy. These are obvious human failings, as the competitiveness and jealousy in the biblical record shows, but they are not the will of God for us. In fact, Paul reminds the church in Corinth that all the people in the fellowship are members of one body, the body of Christ. In other words, we are to work together not apart.

It is the Holy Spirit who helps us transcend our individual differences to create a united effort. When you see a group of men working together toward a single vision, you know that the spiritual influence is guiding them regardless of what they name that influence. God wants the world transformed and it will take all of us who say we know Christ working together.

O Heavenly Father, bind us together that we may model your kingdom as we reach out to others. Amen.

12
LEAVING HOME
TO DISCOVER GOD'S BEST

Bruce Fish

Read Luke 5:1-11.

When I first read the Gospels I was troubled at the way Jesus seemed to have selected his disciples—appearing out of nowhere, asking randomly selected people to drop everything and follow him. Their decisions appeared both instantaneous and irrational, and were often held up as perfect examples of "godly" behavior. Fortunately, other Bible teachers encouraged us to look at faith as a thoughtful process, not an irrational leap.

In time, as I reread the Gospels, I saw that the disciples were drawn to Jesus gradually. Take Peter, for instance. He originally goes to meet Jesus because his brother Andrew tells him that the Messiah has been found (John 1:29-51). Later, Jesus heals Peter's mother-in-law (Luke 4:38-39). Still later, when Jesus is teaching near the Sea of Galilee, he asks Peter for the use of his boat, so people can hear him.

Peter is caught off guard by Jesus' next request. While he doesn't want to say no, he is sure that looking for fish where Jesus has suggested is useless. His irritation and embarrassment are replaced with shock and awe when the nets come up full to the breaking point. He expects a rebuke, at least. But when Jesus suggests a radical career change, he is overwhelmed—and now his compliance is immediate.

Peter's path from curious observer to convinced disciple shows us that healthy spiritual growth is gradual. It also suggests that this process is far from predictable and will often catch us off guard.

When he decided to answer Jesus' call, Peter had to hang up his nets, turn his back on fishing, his lifetime career, and leave home. For us, too, real discipleship requires that we let go of the good and the familiar so we can embrace God's best.

Father, I don't like to be caught off guard. I'd rather have a relationship with you that's predictable and pretty tame. At the same time I'd like to find my life overrun, like Peter's boat, with flashing silver blessings that overwhelm me. So please carry me beyond the good and the familiar to your best.

Week 45, Monday   Family Matters

Read Luke 4:38-44.

Peter has always fascinated me. He could be brash, mulish, and mouthy, but he was also forthright, responsible, and capable of remarkable insights. Of all those traits, he gets the least credit for his responsibility. Today's reading shows us how Peter cared for a close family member at a critical moment in her life.

Jesus is coming to spend the evening at Peter's home. Peter discovers that his mother-in-law is sick, so he asks Jesus for help. When Jesus heals her, a private, restful evening quickly becomes a public event. Throughout a very unpredictable time, Peter sets his own plans aside and focuses on the needs of his family and guests.

This was the first of many visits Jesus and the disciples made to Peter's house, indicating that Peter maintained it even after he left to follow Jesus. His faith might have taken him way from the familiar setting of his life, yet an ongoing commitment to his family was part of his discipleship as well.

I saw this commitment to responsibility in my parents' lives during a period of my childhood when I was often seriously ill. In the half-light of memory I see the hospital room where an aching lethargy holds me in bed after a terrible tonsillectomy. My chest burns and my breathing is labored. Fear waits in the shadows— but is held at bay by frequent visits from Mom and Dad. Still, I can see the strain from my illness in their eyes. Their lives are demanding so much of them these days. They are planning to buy their first house. My father has just become chief engineer at

Sumner Iron Works. My mother is seriously involved with studies in painting and music. Yet even as they respond to these new and exciting challenges, they keep up with their continuing responsibilities to me.

Responding to new challenges doesn't mean we cut ourselves off from the past. We cannot embrace God's best until we have learned to properly manage the good and the familiar.

Father, make me a good steward of this present moment. Help me to remember that the present is the raw material out of which you will fashion all my tomorrows.

Week 45, Tuesday   **Through the Shadows**

Read Mark 5:21-43.

Jairus did not want to make the trip. Jesus was a new and controversial teacher—could he be trusted? But as death crept slowly toward his daughter, Jairus's choice became clear. He would leave the security of family, home, and traditional beliefs in order to find Jesus and beg him to heal her.

Sometimes, though, we don't *choose* to leave home. Sometimes circumstances snatch us from the comfort of our daily routines. It can happen very suddenly—or, as for the woman with the hemorrhage, with the slow brutality of a lingering illness. She had been isolated from normal society by her ritual uncleanness for twelve years, imprisoned in a world of pain and shame. With the last of her strength she sought Jesus out—a man of God who spoke old truths with new authority. She may not have understood half of it, but she knew the sound of hope.

Today Jesus still seeks out wanderers who are far from home, prisoners in the valley of the shadow of death. He touches us and brings us home through the shadows. We often return to familiar surroundings to find them transformed by God's grace.

That was my experience when I left home as a young child to have my tonsils removed. After the cold operating room, the cold anesthetic, and the slow count backward from 100, I woke up—on a pillow covered in my own blood. When I woke again, two male nurses were trying to put needles in my arms. "You're killing me," I screamed, wildly fighting them off.

"We really will kill you if you don't cooperate," one of the nurses said. I went limp, but I couldn't stop shaking, so they tied my arms to the bed and secured the IV lines.

In the days that followed that traumatic experience, the staff tried to compensate by treating me with great gentleness and consideration. God reached out to me through nurses, doctors, friends, and especially my parents.

When I finally returned home, everything I looked at seemed changed. The sky was bluer, the air was fresher, the sunsets all brought tears to my eyes. I slept soundly and awoke deeply refreshed, just thankful to be alive. Had I been a little older, I might have called it an epiphany. But I was only eight, so I savored each day of returning health and celebrated Christmas with a profound joy I had never known before.

Father, when I journey into the far country of suffering, touch me with moments of grace. May I learn, in the midst of the shadows, to trust you for a way back home from exile.

Week 45, Wednesday   Expectations

Read Mark 6:1-6.

As he comes to Nazareth, Jesus is hoping for the enthusiastic support of those who have known him the longest. He wants to explain his mission to his hometown before the wild rumors flying about Galilee completely distort it. Instead he finds that God's plans for him cannot be reconciled with the expectations of his friends and neighbors.

The people of Nazareth had watched Jesus grow up. They admired him for his decision to take over his father's business after Joseph's death. They were certain they understood his destiny. To them, he was "the carpenter," that is, a highly skilled craftsman who could build anything out of wood. He could fell trees, reduce them to small-dimensional lumber, and monitor the curing process that made the boards ready for use. He could design and build complex pieces of furniture as well as small household items and could manage large projects, such as the construction of a house, a commercial building, or a fishing boat.

When Jesus claimed a radical new identity, he demolished his neighbors' expectations, causing them personal pain. They took offense as much at that as for any specific teaching they'd heard. Because of their attitude, his work among them was severely limited.

For us, too, the long-standing expectations of friends or family members can imprison us in the past by denying us the right to claim new identities and live independent lives before God. In her last year, my mother became increasingly incapacitated, both mentally and physically. As I cared for her, I was forced to re-examine our relationship. She expected to still totally possess me, her only child, and to control me by any means. I was amazed at the power this frail woman still had over me.

With the help of my wife, Becky, and of a therapist friend, as well as the grace of God, Mom's expectations did not consume me. I fulfilled my mission—to care for Mom until she died—not because she possessed me but because I chose to gladly.

Father, release me from the prison of unhealthy expectations—both mine and others'. Help me to find healing, growth, and freedom in your dreams for my future.

Week 45, Thursday   **Sea Change**

Read Matthew 14:22-33.

Most of Jesus' disciples had grown up around the Sea of Galilee. At least four of them (Peter, Andrew, James, and John) had spent hundreds of hours on it as fishermen. They understood the sudden storms that blew down from the surrounding hills, and they could navigate after dark by watching the lights on the shore. But this evening they made no progress against the persistent storm. After spending most of the night battling it in their small boat, they were tired, disoriented, and frightened.

When Jesus walked toward them on the water, they thought he was a ghost come to carry them off to the world of the dead. Even Jesus' assurance wasn't enough to completely still their superstitious fears. Peter said what the others were thinking. But then Jesus challenged him to step out of the boat into the storm.

This was the last thing Peter expected.

If the story weren't so familiar to us, it would be the last thing we would expect as well. Tough situations require careful, conservative responses, we say. We don't expect to escape from a crisis by taking on more risks. But to overcome this storm, Peter had to embrace it. He needed to stand where nothing protected him except the presence of Jesus.

Peter stepped out of the boat. As he moved toward Jesus, he understood that it was life, not death, that was waiting there for him.

And then he remembered the storm! Suddenly the waves and wind were more real to him than Jesus. Is it any wonder that he began to sink, overwhelmed by the surrounding fury that he believed must consume him?

Peter was trying to get home through the storm. Jesus asked him to be at home in it.

God still sends us into storms at times, to teach us about faith and to show us that we can be at home anywhere; because nothing can separate us from the love of God.

Father, when the storms of life come, may I have the courage to step out of the boat and stand with you.

Week 45, Friday   Clean and Unclean

Read Matthew 15:1-20.

The "Pharisees and teachers of the law," who had journeyed all the way from Jerusalem to see Jesus, were more interested in preserving the religious forms that gave them power than with matters of personal faith that required them to serve others. They actually believed that contact with ordinary people, during the course of a day's activities, made them unclean and therefore unworthy to approach God.

Though the best among them believed that external obedience led to internal change, they were more concerned with outward rituals and traditions. Jesus would not tolerate this nonsense. "You give a tenth of your spices," he told them at another time, "mint, dill and cummin. But you have neglected the more important matters of the law—justice, mercy and faithfulness. . . . You strain out a gnat but swallow a camel" (Matthew 23:23-24 NIV).

Internal change must come first, Jesus continually tells them;

lifestyle choices will grow naturally from such change. To focus on merely external actions leads to spiritual blindness and destruction.

The disciples' questions illustrate how hard it is escape the restrictions and legalism of our religious environment, the *dos* and *don't*s with which we grew up or that are part of our church tradition. It is not easy for any of us to understand the radical grace of the gospel that frees us to act from the heart, not merely to conform to outward standards. Our only defense against becoming legalistic is to remain focused on the difficult process of internal transformation. The heart is the birthplace of those paramount virtues—justice, mercy, and faithfulness.

Father, as I learn to surrender my life to Jesus, make me an advocate of justice, mercy, and faithfulness. Keep me focused on the issues of the heart.

Week 45, Saturday   **Firm Foundations**

Read Matthew 16:13-20.

Peter's forthright declaration that Jesus is the Messiah, the Son of God, shows us how far the disciples have come since they've been with Jesus. Now that they understand who he is, Jesus offers a simple presentation of the central truths of his message and the work he is calling them to. These truths are the firm foundation of our faith.

They begin with Jesus' identity as the Son of God. This is the focal point for life and faith. The surrender of our lives to Jesus Christ is a reasonable response to that discovery. Through this decision we become part of a new people of God, the church. Jesus tells us that the work of this community of faith is destined to succeed against all opposition. When we understand the identity of Jesus and embrace his mission, we will have both the power and the authority to shape the world around us to bring God's best into being. In fact, the things we allow or forbid will mark our world as though God were controlling them directly.

When Jesus proposes a completely new system of faith, based on a new vision of how the kingdom of God works, he forces the disciples to make a decisive break with their past. The need for this change of direction is clearly a shock to them, as we will see in tomorrow's reading. We, too, are regularly confused by the demands of faith in Christ. The uniqueness of Jesus and the power of the gospel are not things we can understand after only a few years. This is the work of a lifetime and even then we must rely on the knowledge and wisdom of many other lifetimes to make his path clear to us.

Becoming part of this community brings with it a responsibility to examine our own lives, the life of our community, and the larger structures of our society. The presence of Jesus, working in and among us, constantly looks for new ways to bring God's grace to people's lives. And the continuing presence of grace in our own lives is a powerful antidote for the legalistic fantasy religions that constantly crop up in every age.

This much is clear: after nearly two thousand years, Jesus is still building his church and there are still new things to discover about him and new miracles of grace to experience as we work with him to make his kingdom known in our world.

Father, in a world of rapidly increasing complexity and uncertainty, help me to maintain my connection to the roots of my faith in Christ, and to find there the power to change the world, beginning with myself.

Week 46, Sunday   The Kingdom of the Cross

Read Matthew 16:21-28.

Today we look at the cost of following Jesus Christ and becoming part of God's kingdom. For the first time, the disciples see the full picture of what Jesus means to accomplish. It contradicts everything they were expecting from their Messiah. They were looking for a warrior king who would throw out the Roman occupiers and fulfill their nationalist dreams. They longed for a hero who would keep them safe forever.

We who follow Christ today also want protection from the dangers and uncertainties around us. We expect our parents to be worthy of trust and admiration. We work hard to build marriages that are meaningful, supportive, and passionate. We guide our children toward their own unique paths in the world and in relationship with God. We plan for lives of reasonable prosperity and take aggressive steps to maintain our physical health. We try to make a positive impact on our world.

We also look to God for help, because we know instinctively that we cannot protect ourselves from all the threats of time and eternity. The biblical promises encourage us to look for a savior who will keep us completely safe and wipe away every tear from our eyes. It is easy to forget that the full expression of such promises belongs to the future and to heaven!

When Jesus talks about suffering, it frightens us just as much as it did the disciples. Denying ourselves and taking up the cross seems too much like a surrender to the raging uncertainties of life. But stop and think: losing our lives in order to find them is a reasonable way to live if we consider the frailty of what we are giving up. Gaining the whole world won't keep us alive, because the whole world is dying.

Though Jesus reveals here that he is on the way to the cross and that we must follow in his footsteps, death is not his final destiny, nor is it ours. All of us who face the peril of the cross are heirs together of the promise that we will "be raised to life" (v. 21 NIV).

Father, help me to press on toward the promise of eternal life. As I walk in the shadow of the cross, may my faith in Jesus, your Son, give life to your best dreams for me.

Week 46, Monday   **Promised Land**

Read Matthew 17:1-13; Luke 9:28-36.

The writer of the book of Hebrews assures us that Jesus was "tempted in every way, just as we are—yet was without sin" (Hebrews 4:15 NIV). It's important to keep the humanity of Jesus in mind when we read the Gospels. Much has been written about the impact of the transfiguration on the disciples, but it is just as important to consider how it affected Jesus.

He had just made one of the most difficult decisions of his life. He knew better than anyone else where it would lead. He sought God in prayer to confirm that decision in his own mind. Was it really the right thing to do? Was his assurance before his disciples justified? Did he have the courage and vision necessary to go through with this sacrifice?

Because he lived within the limitations of his humanity, Jesus could not foresee the results of his choices. That his sacrifice would change human history was a matter of faith for him, but without a certain vision of the future, he was left to wonder if the path to the cross was the right one, the only one. In response to his need, God allowed him access to the heavenly glory and conversation that he had left so long ago to become a human being.

Any journey is easier if we know where we are going. When the path is very difficult, a clear final goal is often the difference between completing the journey and turning back midway. The transfiguration makes very clear where faith in Jesus takes us. It gives us a small taste of what the kingdom of God looks like when it comes in power. It lets us see the place of Jesus in that final ordering of all things. It gives us good reasons to take seriously God's statement, "This is my Son, whom I have chosen; listen to him" (Luke 9:35 NIV).

Father, out of our humanness, you bring us to glory. Out of fear, you bring us to a place of security. Out of want, you create an abundance of life. I thank you that within us and among us your Spirit is fashioning a new promised land.

Week 46, Tuesday   That We May Not Offend

Read Matthew 17:24-27.

Of all the miracle stories in the New Testament, this is one of the strangest. Most of us have never been exposed to a religious tax of any kind. In Jesus' time, every Jewish male twenty or over was required to pay a yearly tax of approximately two days' wages for the upkeep of the temple in Jerusalem. This tax originated in Exodus 30:13. Those who brought this issue up with Peter were obviously trying to find a new opportunity to attack Jesus as a violator of sacred, national tradition.

Jesus clearly feels no obligation before God to pay this tax, but the issue is more complex than that for him. The key to understanding his underlying concern is found in the phrase, "that we may not offend them" (v. 27 NIV). The Greek verb translated "offend" is used in an unusual way in the New Testament. It describes not an affront to personal pride but an action that triggers moral compromise in another's life.

Even as he criticizes and redirects the spiritual life of the Jewish people, Jesus does not indiscriminately tear down institutions that still serve God. His new gospel of grace is meant to gradually draw people out of these institutions. In time, beliefs and structures that do not support grace will be discarded. Jesus is more concerned with creating a new kind of personal faith than with destroying those who oppose him.

There is a lesson here for any of us who may be frustrated with religious structures in the modern church. Moving forward to God's best is not incompatible with a careful respect for established methods and existing institutions.

In every new working of God's Spirit, some existing institutions are reformed and carried on into the future largely intact. Those that are truly incompatible with God's intentions simply fade away. There is no need to waste our time, wound our souls, or dishonor the name of Jesus by conducting witch-hunts to root out enemies of the gospel. Our job is to share the good news of forgiveness and hope in Jesus in such a way "that we may not offend."

Father, it is too easy for me to look for enemies, it is too much fun to hate. Listing the corrupt attitudes and outrageous actions of others makes me feel powerful and safe. It also sent Jesus to the cross. Forgive me and help me to seek out and work with those who can accept his gospel of grace. Help me to trust you to deal with its enemies.

Week 46, Wednesday   Peace with God

Read Mark 10:17-31; Matthew 19:16-30.

The man who approaches Jesus in this passage is on a mission. He longs for peace with God. He wants to be sure he has eternal life. He has grown up believing that God creates prosperity in the lives of those who keep his commandments. Since he is wealthy, he sincerely believes that he has obeyed God's Law.

His deep conviction of God's presence does not give him the security of a personal connection to God, but it does give him the courage to admit his inadequacy before God. Though society holds him up as an example of both personal success and intimacy with God, this young man refuses to be deceived.

No wonder "Jesus looked on him and loved him." Here is a great opportunity for life-changing repentance and growth, not only for one man, but for all who look to him as an example of godliness.

This man is drawn to Jesus with an irresistible force, because not only does Jesus speak of God as a gracious confidante but his security in that relationship seems complete.

In light of all this, it is shocking that Jesus tells him to make himself a pauper if he really wants eternal life. Jesus forces him to examine the roots of his belief system. Up to this point he has tried to find peace with God without surrendering to God. As he tries to manufacture holiness, the very attempt cuts him off from the relationship he seeks.

The disciples are shocked by Jesus' words. They wonder how they will provide for their families if material rewards don't flow from obedience to God. Jesus reassures them that God gives tangible rewards in both this life and the next.

Sometimes, we too are confused and frightened by the words and work of Jesus. As much as we long for a living faith, we feel just as great a need for a predictable, structured set of traditions and beliefs to define our spiritual experiences. We're caught, as the rich young man and the disciples were, between the promise of a living faith and the protection offered by religious orthodoxy.

Father, show me the path to a living faith. Teach me new steps in this dance called holiness, as I learn to embrace both the truth and the freedom of the gospel.

Week 46, Thursday   **Mountain of Shame**

Read Mark 11:11-26.

When real evil is at work, mercy has little impact, unless it is accompanied by judgment.

The payment of the temple tax was tied into dishonest money changing schemes. The tax had to be paid in shekels, but most worshipers arrived with other kinds of money. A fee, equal to about one-third of the total tax, was charged by the temple money changers to provide the "proper" coins.

Sacrificial animals were an important part of worship at the temple. But the temple administrators would only accept sacrifices from their own vendors, who charged twenty times the going rate outside the temple.

Jesus was speaking quite literally when he said that this house of prayer had become a den of robbers.

In spite of its drama, the cleansing of the temple was not the climax of Jesus' teaching about the dangers of religious corruption. That moment arrived shortly after dawn, on the steep road that ran up from the Dead Sea through Jericho and Bethany. Jesus and the disciples reached a place where it was possible to look west to Jerusalem and east into the valley of the Dead Sea, where God's judgment had fallen on Sodom and Gomorrah.

The sun was still low, illuminating the massive walls of the city rising up from the Kidron Valley. Above the topmost battlements, the temple reached farther toward the sky, glowing like a living mountain of light. Here Jesus stopped and explained that faith in God would allow the disciples to cast even this shining mountain of shame into the Dead Sea.

These words about the power of a purified faith give us great hope, but they have no meaning apart from his final words about the necessity of forgiveness. Twisted religious systems can only be straightened out by those who are willing to forgive. Ill will, even toward religious corruption, will block the effectiveness of our prayers for reform.

Without forgiveness, we become like those we want to remove, and the energy we expend battling "evildoers" will scar our own souls.

Father, when I am seized by burning visions of renewal, reform, and righteousness, help me to remember the words of Jesus on the cross, "Forgive them, for they do not know what they are doing."

Week 46, Friday   The Last Parable

Read John 13:1-17.

As Jesus bends over his disciples' feet, he shows them that spiritual and moral authority come from serving others. By taking on the role normally reserved for a household slave, he gives them important guidance for constructing a new community of servants who will bring God's grace into places where healing is needed.

The disciples barely understand the work Jesus is passing on to them. They may acknowledge him as Savior one moment, but they debate which of them will be known as the greatest disciple the next. Judas is about to betray him. Peter, who objects to Jesus' actions and is confused about their meaning, will deny that he even knows Jesus in a few hours. All the rest will flee for their lives when the soldiers of the Sanhedrin come for Jesus.

Even Jesus cannot dictate the responses of those he is trying to train. Should we be surprised if we have similar problems?

When we expend time and energy trying to make a difference in other people's lives, we expect to see results from our efforts. Unfortunately, not all whom we help cooperate with our need to feel successful. Perhaps they are unable to find ways of dealing with one crisis after another or they don't understand how to build patterns of positive change into their lives. Sometimes it may seem they are beyond the reach of even God's redemption. When, in spite of our investments of time, money, and personal passion, they remain spiritually unchanged, financially irresponsible, or chronically unemployed, we may feel betrayed, made to look foolish.

Jesus had a different view of success and failure. He shows us that each act of service has a unique power to transform lives and is not diminished by misunderstanding or even betrayal. The disciples' unthinking responses did not keep footwashing from becoming a standard by which spiritual compassion is measured.

Those who receive our help may never experience its full benefits, and that is a tragedy, but it is no reason for us to compound the loss by withholding our service.

Father, help me to remember that, in a fallen world, the feet I wash today will be dirty again by tomorrow.

Week 46, Saturday   Remember Me

Read Luke 22:7-38.

The terror comes on me most often early in the morning. Dreams of failure and despair leave me covered in sweat and choking on tears. It's particularly bad when I'm struggling to finish a project. It doesn't matter that I've already successfully completed dozens of them. I'm still haunted by a fear of failure. Those dreams have the power to make me forget who I am.

To defeat these night terrors, I must get up, turn on the lights, and remind myself of what Jesus Christ has done for me. In order to remember who I am, I must first remember who he is.

This is what Jesus does when, in this last supper with his disciples, he asks them to remember him. He wants them to remember him as a person, giving his life for them. But he is also pointing them beyond the impending suffering of the cross to what that sacrifice will accomplish, to the strength it will give them. They will know then who they are.

Today at the Lord's Supper, the Communion table, Jesus still asks us to remember him. And when we do, we are given the power to remember who we are, what God has done for us, and what we can still hope that he will do. That is the source for all our hope and strength. That is where the central meaning of our lives is to be found.

The Communion meal has the power to bring the light of God's truth into every corner of our lives and to transform them. Through the bread and the wine, Jesus is speaking peace to all believers, in all circumstances, for all time. "I am with you," he says to each of us. "Remember me."

Father, when the night terrors seize me, may I awake to the light of your presence and hold firmly to the self-giving love of your Son, Jesus Christ.

Week 47, Sunday   Betrayal!

Read John 13:18-30.

The shaking didn't start that Sunday until I approached the stone steps leading up to the front of the church. To avoid such attacks I had learned to walk with my head down, looking at the ground, the grass, the flowers, my feet, anything but the church building ahead. But when I glanced up at the double wood doors with their dark red paint and brass fittings, my upper back and lower arms began their rapid twitching. Within a few steps my stomach was in open rebellion, my head was pounding, and it was hard to breathe. I turned around and walked quickly back to the refuge of my car.

Even though it had been ten years since my character had been attacked and I had been betrayed by some of my closest friends at another church in the same town, I still often panicked when I entered a church building. The pain, fear, anger, and disgust from that experience still haunted me.

Few experiences are more powerful than betrayal, and Christians have felt its unique pain. Often, this violation of our souls comes from those who claim to be followers of Christ. Though most find a way back from these experiences, for some the devastation lasts a lifetime, leaving these haunted believers permanently isolated from the rest of the Christian community. Sometimes such betrayal ends a lifetime of Christian service.

Perhaps we should not be surprised that the Christian community is not a safe place, since Jesus reserved his harshest words for the religious leaders of his day. He warned that all who followed him would be mistreated by these same people. It was the "chief priests and the teachers of the law" who recruited Judas to hand Jesus over to them (Luke 22:1-6 NIV).

Jesus, however, is able to turn his betrayal into an object lesson. Even as he is preparing to sacrifice himself, he disarms the powers of darkness and dictates the course of events. Out of the tragedy of his betrayal comes the hope that the wounded areas of our own lives can be healed.

Father, when we are betrayed, we do not simply leave home; we are driven out. Seek us out in our lonely exile, comfort us and bring us to new places of refuge and renewal.

Week 47, Monday   **Light in the Darkness**

Read John 13:31-38.

Today's passage makes clear that Jesus' sufferings bring as much glory to God as his resurrection. Though that seems like madness to us, Jesus is saying that the process of redemption, whatever form it takes, glorifies God.

In our lives, that means that the struggle for holiness, more than its achievement, marks us as followers of Jesus. God is glorified by that struggle, even when we reach beyond ourselves and experience failure. We cannot achieve complete holiness in this life, and God does not expect that of us. God does expect us to continue the journey of faith. Both success and failure are part of that journey, and suffering as well as joy is a beacon that guides us along the path.

Not only does Jesus' suffering glorify God, but so does the betrayal of Judas and the imminent failure of Peter and the other disciples. It is important for us to reflect on this pattern, because it goes against everything we are usually taught about faith in Christ. We believe that only a strong faith will see us through the difficulties of life. While that is true, our understanding of what makes up "strong faith" needs some adjustment. We need a greater respect for the process by which our faith grows and for the role suffering, loss, and even failure play in that journey.

Even though Jesus knows that the disciples are about to be scattered, there are no words of condemnation here. He expects this crisis to overwhelm them. His only concern is that they find a way back to a meaningful faith beyond the trauma of the cross. He does not want them to remain at the foot of the cross, but to make their way to the empty tomb.

He wants the same thing for us. Even as we take up our crosses and follow him, he wants us to see the glory of God, both in the moment of our suffering and in the promise of our deliverance.

Father, when I am alone in the dark, speak to me of your glory. I want not only to hear the words, "Let there be light," but to come through the darkness into the light of your presence.

Week 47, Tuesday   The Shadow of Death

Read Matthew 26:36-46.

Jesus has already warned the disciples that they will fall away (v. 31). Is he now angry with them for showing their weakness here?

Jesus has come to the greatest crisis of his life, perhaps the greatest crisis of all human history. Here at the breaking point he cries out to God his Father. In the anguish of his doubts about his purpose, his path, his ability to endure, he cannot let his friends' failure pass without comment. The fact that his disciples are sleeping tells him that the night must go forward to the end he has foreseen. In their midst he glimpses the shadow of death.

With a lifetime of preparation behind him, he is still not ready for this moment. He is angered by human frailty. The frailty he feels within himself is reflected in the weakness of his disciples. When he sees them asleep for the second time (v. 43) and especially the third time (v. 45), he knows God has spoken.

Jesus does not want to die, he does not want to suffer, but he knows now with utter finality that he must. Somewhere within the mysterious unity of his humanity and his divinity he finds the strength to go on.

There is no three-step approach to guaranteed spiritual power hidden here. All such nonsense is burned away by the intensity of his struggle. Yet in the furnace of his suffering he finds a new source of tempering strength; it flows from a hope that is beyond the reach of all suffering.

Now he stands firm, with the certain knowledge that his Father has walked this road before him and has all things in hand. Now he takes the first steps down the last mile of his journey in this world.

Father, help me to find the strength I need to walk through the valley of the shadow of death, which is also the path of redemption. Give me the assurance that you have all things in hand.

Week 47, Wednesday   A Question of Authority

Read Matthew 26:47-56; Luke 22:47-53; John 18:1-11.

Power often comes to us quickly and with surprising ease; through a change in jobs, by an appointment to a committee, with the receipt of an award, or in some other way. Power gives us the right to act. But to actually get anything done, we also need the authority to act. Authority only comes when the people closest to us trust us enough to work with us for common goals.

Authority grows out of relationship. We acquire it slowly, over long periods of time, and it will disappear if it is not continually replenished. It is a gift given to us by our friends, family members, and associates at work. Where it is not given, we have no power to grasp it.

Today's passages are a study in power and authority.

As the Jewish officials came to seize Jesus and end his threat to the power of their religious systems forever, they could not understand that it was actually Jesus who controlled this situation. Jesus had given up power as he moved toward the cross, but he still retained all of his authority.

Jesus had chosen the time and place of this confrontation. He had the power to deliver himself from it by calling on God for direct intervention, but he choose to remain on the path to the cross, to achieve a greater goal. He reminded his captors that he had held the religious leaders at bay for years with his authoritative teaching.

After the resurrection, Jesus will appear to his disciples and send them into the world to preach the gospel with the assurance that "all authority in heaven and on earth has been given to me" (Matthew 28:18 NIV). When the kingdom of God comes in power, it will do so because it has risen up slowly out of the authority granted to Jesus, and to us his followers, lived out in our message and in the quality of our lives.

Father, I believe in your power. Help me to trust you and to live out the authority that you have given me through your Son, Jesus, and the presence of your Holy Spirit.

Week 47, Thursday   Guilty Verdict

Read Mark 14:53-65; Matthew 26:57-67.

Jesus often pointed out that the religious leaders of his day kept the law in a way that was convenient for them. The law was their servant, to be used to maintain their power and to confirm their view of themselves as God's chosen people.

Nowhere in the Gospels is their abuse of the law clearer than in the trial of Jesus. Matthew's account indicates that the official trial was held at night. It was followed by a very short morning session (27:1*ff*.) in order to satisfy the letter of the law and announce his condemnation. It was illegal to hold this kind of criminal trial at night, and in capital cases it was necessary for a night to pass after the day of the trial, before a verdict was decided upon. This was specifically designed to encourage those sitting in judgment to make room for mercy in the proceedings. Furthermore, no trials of this kind were to be conducted during Passover.

Guilt could only be established by the testimony of two witnesses, and the members of the court were responsible to make sure there was no opportunity for the witnesses to adjust their stories to agree with one another. Also, the evidence for the innocence of the accused was to be presented first.

The abusive treatment of Jesus at the end of this judicial lynching shows the real intent of his accusers.

Jesus had repeatedly condemned the religious leaders for their failure to make way for the kingdom of God. Now their self-deception is complete. When they condemn their Messiah as a blasphemer, they announce their own guilt. They seal their own doom even as they think they are proclaiming his.

When we are mistreated, we can take comfort in the fact that the methods they use against us stand in judgment against them.

Father, help me to learn to love justice and truth, even when they are not convenient and especially when they are not comfortable.

| Week 47, Friday | Acceptable Losses |

Read Mark 14:63–15:41.

From 1943 through May 1945, Allied bombers flew from bases in Great Britain, carrying out hundreds of daylight raids on targets in Germany and German-occupied Europe. These attacks severely disrupted transportation and industrial production.

Of all the aircraft flying these missions, the best known was the Boeing B-17, nicknamed "the flying fortress." Ten or more heavy machine guns, firing from at least five stations, allowed the crew to defend against fighter attack. Its ability to absorb tremendous battle damage and keep flying was legendary. Still, more than four thousand B-17s were destroyed by enemy fighters and anti-aircraft fire during these raids. To those determined to break the power of Nazi tyranny, these were "acceptable losses."

Today's passage gives us a vivid example of the losses God considers acceptable in the battle to redeem humanity. Part of the price paid by Jesus is easily seen—the long hours of personal indignities and awful physical pain. At the end of that ordeal, Jesus faced another kind of suffering that is largely invisible and very difficult for us to understand. As he atoned for the sins of the world, Jesus was cut off from the presence of his Father.

No living human being has ever been cut off from God in this manner. Neither those who are ignorant of God's existence, nor those who find belief in a personal God impossible, nor even those who resist surrendering to what they understand of God, are so totally isolated from God. Through the created world and even through our own humanity we are constantly surrounded by God's presence. Even in moments of suffering, despair, doubt, or anger we cannot escape the touch of God on our lives.

Sometimes, the losses God allows in our lives are frightening and truly terrible. God has never promised to eliminate suffering, but he has promised to take us through it and to heal the damage left behind. The bright light of God's presence emerges most clearly from the dark night of our own souls.

The road to the power of the resurrection leads through the dark shadow of the cross. But we have one remarkable advantage over Jesus; we are never separated from the love of God.

Father, thank you for the price your Son paid to set me free from sin. May the losses I accept in following Jesus set me free to experience the power of a resurrection relationship with you.

Week 47, Saturday   **Stumbling Toward Daybreak**

Read John 20:1-18.

Peter's name disappears from the biblical accounts of Passion Week after his denial of Jesus. There is no mention of him at the crucifixion, though he may have watched it from a distance, along with several other disciples (Luke 23:49). He did not take part in removing Jesus' body from the cross or preparing it for burial, though he did know where the tomb was located. Perhaps shame and fear kept him in hiding.

As Peter ran to the garden at daybreak Easter morning, in response to a strange message about an empty tomb, he did not know that new life waited for him there. And what he saw bewildered him. He did not yet understand it. He was still trapped in despair and suffering.

It is easy to stay trapped in a despairing past. My wife and I spent three years caring for my mentally ill mother after my father died. During the last year, in spite of our close attention to her needs, there were several times when she left desperate messages on our answering machine, accusing us of abandoning her. At times she got connected to the 911 operator while frantically trying to call us. On two occasions we rushed to her house only to find that the police or a city ambulance crew had gotten there first.

For a long time after Mom's death, we were still reacting to her illness. It took us weeks to get over the fear of finding incoherent messages on our answering machine and months to stop reacting with panic to the sounds of sirens in the distance.

For Peter, and for us, the resurrection, good news, is not something we can grasp all at once. A lifetime of careful examination and experience is required to even begin the process. In a world of pain and uncertainty, we will never entirely understand the freedom and joy it brings.

Like Peter, we will always find ourselves stumbling toward daybreak, the time of new beginnings.

Father, give me a new understanding of the power of the resurrection today. Let me stand by Peter's side at the empty tomb and rejoice.

Week 48, Sunday   Doubters Welcome

Read John 20:19-31.

As powerful as it is, the resurrection leaves us with doubts. What Jesus has done seems too good to be true. Like Thomas, we want to see it for ourselves, to touch it and to assure ourselves we are not self-deceived.

Even the definition of faith seems to demand the presence of doubt. As the writer of the book of Hebrews puts it, "Now faith is being sure of what we hope for and certain of what we do not see. This is what the ancients were commended for" (Hebrews 11:1-2 NIV). The things we hope for but do not possess, and the things we cannot see; these contain the seeds of doubt as well as faith.

Today's passage is for me the thematic center of John's Gospel. It is built around the story of someone who had doubts. Jesus went out of his way to accommodate the doubts of Thomas. He wanted all of his closest followers to be sure of what had happened. Either he could convince them that a whole new world of possibilities had been born or this new community of faith would end right there in Jerusalem. With so much at stake, we might expect him to begin by demanding belief and punishing doubt. Instead, he chose to begin by accepting doubt and encouraging faith.

We cannot manufacture faith, in our own lives or in anyone else's. It cannot be created by rhetorical tricks or theological rigor or spectacles of worship and praise. We cannot guarantee its appearance through relationships of unconditional love. Faith simply happens, when God brings it into being. To encourage it, we must make room for doubt; not just easy doubt or predictable doubt, but fearful, intractable doubt.

Jesus is always willing to prove himself, if we will only have the courage to doubt and the patience to wait for his appearance in our midst.

Father, help me to see my doubts as blessings, a rich mine of precious gems in which the living fire of faith can be discovered.

Week 48, Monday   **Identity Crisis**

Read John 21:1-19.

For our spiritual health we must sometimes go back to where our journey of faith began in order to reorient ourselves. In today's passage, the disciples are reminded of the time when they first met Jesus in Galilee, when they were confronted with another huge catch of fish. They reflect on their earlier decision to walk away from their nets.

The disciples had been told to go to Galilee, but no one told them to go fishing. That was Peter's idea. It was his way of escaping a painful and uncertain present by returning to a more familiar past. In response, Jesus gently pressed him to live with confidence in the future.

One of the most fascinating conversations in the Bible is recorded in verses 15-17, but the way it is usually translated obscures its dramatic nature. The first two times Jesus poses his question to Peter, he uses the Greek verb *agapao,* which means to love unconditionally and is often used to describe the love of God. Peter is only willing to respond with the verb *phileo,* which means he loves Jesus as a friend. In the third exchange, Jesus uses the word *phileo,* as if to say, "Are you really my friend?" Peter is upset because the quality of his commitment to Jesus is called into question. This is his deepest fear, the one he has come to Galilee to escape.

Yet, even in posing these questions, Jesus accepts Peter's assessment of his abilities. It is as "a friend" that Jesus asks him to "feed my sheep." Out of Peter's current uncertain loyalty, Jesus is sure a commitment will grow, one strong enough to face death with a courageous faith that will "glorify God." Jesus has no doubts about the course of Peter's life as he asks him to "follow me."

Jesus has great confidence in the work he is doing in our lives. Even during our predictable crises of faith, Jesus is sure we will continue to follow him and feed his sheep.

Father, thank you that, on the days when I am not sure that I love you or even if I am your friend, you have confidence that the work of your Son is still going forward in my life.

Week 48, Tuesday   **A Promise for Those Far Off**

Read Acts 2:22-41.

Fifty days separate Passover from Pentecost. During that time Peter has been transformed. He no longer sees faithfulness as the product of personal effort but understands that it always begins with God's promises and calling. He has known for a long time that Jesus was the key to a workable faith, but witnessing the resurrection has deepened his understanding of Jesus as Savior and Lord.

Surrender to Jesus Christ unleashes the power of the Holy Spirit, which is the power of God. All human weaknesses or limitations are irrelevant in light of that power. There is no minimum standard of spiritual health necessary to begin following Christ. Neither doubt or failure can separate us from the love of God.

Nor can holiness be the sole possession of a special class of people. God is interested in everyone and especially in those who do not feel they have any right to his attention. God's power is just as available to those who feel close to him as to those "who are far off."

In the wake of the crucifixion, Peter had been imprisoned by the shame and guilt of his own failure. A strong sense of his own unworthiness blinded him to the victory Jesus had achieved. Now he understands the power of the resurrection to set him free from this bondage.

That same power is available to all of us who follow Christ. It can release us from prisons of shame and despair, to discover the full potential of the lives God has created for us.

Peter has found his way home to Jesus by a path that did not fit the expectations of conventional religion. Now he calls upon everyone to walk a similarly unexpected path as heirs together of the grace of God.

Father, I am grateful that when I feel far off from you, you do not draw away from me.

Week 48, Wednesday   Victory in Jesus

Read Acts 4:1-22.

Peter had seen these men before, if only at a distance. They were present at the trial that condemned Jesus to death. Once again he was standing in the place where, just a few short weeks before, he had denied any association with Jesus. This time he had no hesitation in admitting his loyalties. As he proclaimed the gospel, his greatest moment of defeat was transformed into a great victory. Jesus through the Holy Spirit was with him in that victory.

And this victory was accomplished in the life of a man who was regarded as "ordinary" by the religious leaders of his day. Peter's only qualification was that he had been with Jesus. This is important for us to understand: God routinely raises victory up out of the painful ruins of defeat in the lives of ordinary people whose only qualification is that they have been drawn close to Jesus.

My first Christmas performance with the Concert Choir in Jewett Hall at Albertson College of Idaho is still a vivid memory, though it took place more than twenty-five years ago. That is because I can never think of it apart from a painful concert ten years earlier, when I was in grade school. Two weeks before the Christmas program I was removed from the choir. My changing voice was no longer up to the exacting standards of a choir director too intent on a "quality performance."

It was only after I came to faith in Christ, in my junior year of high school, that I began to think I might sing again someday. And only after God met me quietly during a fog-shrouded, moonlit walk on the Oregon coast at Cannon Beach did I have the courage to try.

The opening lines of Bach's *Magnificat,* which we sang that night in Jewett Hall, speak of an impossible victory having arisen out of a painful defeat: "My soul doth magnify the Lord, and my spirit hath rejoiced in God my Saviour. For he hath regarded the low estate of his handmaiden" (Luke 1:46-48 KJV).

Father, walk with me today and help me to dream of great victories where I have known painful defeats.

Week 48, Thursday   Holy Boldness

Read Acts 4:23-35.

What Jesus has done for us leaves us with an obligation to tell others about the new life offered through his death and resurrection. However, knowing what to say and how to say it can be difficult. We want to be bold but are afraid that our message will seem incomprehensible, insensitive, or irrelevant.

This first generation of believers had a similar problem. When they prayed for boldness, God showed them that any clear proclamation of the gospel must grow out of a compassionate lifestyle of service. They learned to make the grace and mercy of God visible by fitting the teachings of Jesus into their daily lives in new and unexpected ways. When they explained the facts of the gospel, their words were powerfully amplified by what was already on display in their lives.

We can also learn to practice this kind of holy boldness, as a lifestyle of intelligent compassion testifies to the presence of Jesus Christ within us.

Fortunately, most of us don't have to look very far to find compelling examples of this in our own day. Becky and I attend Trinity Episcopal Church, in Bend, Oregon. The church is located half a block from Thompson Elementary School, one of the oldest schools in Bend. Until recently, the building had seen better days and the teachers were chronically short of everything from supplies for their rooms to books for their library. Thompson serves an older neighborhood, with little political clout, so neither the teachers nor the parents were able to make much headway against these problems.

About five years ago, a few people at the church became aware of the problems at the school. They gathered a small group of people from the neighborhood, the school, and the church to create an organization called The Friends of Thompson School. Before long they were raising money and organizing volunteers to improve the quality of education and quality of life for everyone at the school.

Following in the footsteps of the first-century church, the Friends of Thompson School create opportunities to speak of the gospel with boldness, because they have chosen lives of compassionate and intelligent service toward others.

Father, I want to be someone who makes the good news of redemption in Jesus Christ visible through service to others.

Week 48, Friday   Unchained

Read Acts 12:1-17.

Peter was ready to die. He had endured the execution of James, who had been a fisherman with him in Galilee before any of them met Jesus. He remembered the warning about the circumstances of his death that Jesus had given him (John 21:18-19).

Most of us would expect the same thing. It is sometimes easier to suffer than to celebrate, and success is often as hard to endure as failure. Taking hold of God's blessings is definitely a learned skill.

Perhaps this is because there are so few clear victories in our lives. Most of the things that happen to us are a combination of good and bad. This ambiguity helps us to accept suffering as a part of the journey of faith, but it also makes us discount God's ability to deliver us from fears, frailties, or mistakes. Like Peter and those who were praying for him, we expect to remain in prison. When God sets us free in Jesus, many of us stand rooted in the open doorway, unable to take even one step forward to grasp the new opportunities waiting for us. Even after the chains fall off and the barred door swings open, we need someone to lead us out of bondage.

Peter was planning to die, but Jesus had plans for him to live. Every day, in dozens of situations, Jesus comes to us, removes our chains, and asks us to embrace the promise of a new redeemed life. Every day, he opens the door of another prison cell and asks us to walk free in joyful power so our lives will shine with his life and our world will be changed.

Father, help me to remember the words of Paul (who was no stranger to imprisonment) to the Christians at Thessalonica (who were afraid that Jesus had returned and left them behind): "Be joyful always; pray continually; give thanks in all circumstances, for this is God's will for you in Christ Jesus" (1 Thessalonians 5:16-18 NIV).

Week 48, Saturday   Eyewitness Account

Read 2 Peter 1:12-21.

Peter appears in the Gospels as a man who values honesty, who wants to know the whole truth about any situation, who insists on getting his information firsthand. He is not the kind of person who would ever perpetuate or even tolerate religious deceit. His faith in Jesus rests on the fact that he was an eyewitness to the events of the gospel. He doesn't want anyone else's faith to rest on anything less substantial.

Peter's commitment to accuracy is all the more important because the story of Jesus is like nothing else in human history. Parts of it are so remarkable that Peter himself might have been tempted to doubt their truthfulness if he had not seen them himself. Even in the case of an event as fantastic as the transfiguration, he can honestly testify that he heard the voice of God speaking from clouds and identifying Jesus as his Son. However, in his efforts to establish a firm foundation for the faith of these believers, he does not rely solely on his own experience to establish the truth of the gospel stories. He reminds his readers that "we have the words of the prophets made more certain."

These words refer first to Jesus, who fulfilled so many prophecies of the Old Testament by his incarnation and will fulfill even more at his second coming. They also point to the work of the Holy Spirit, who is the force behind all prophecy and the one who makes the character of Jesus live within us. Finally, these words apply to all who have committed themselves to Jesus Christ. It is through the church, as the body of Christ, that many of the words of the prophets find their fullest expression.

When the Christian community is doing its job, it is a living prophecy, written into the world through lives of compassionate service. Our lives, like Peter's, can provide eyewitness accounts of the majesty of Jesus Christ. Every day we have the privilege of embarking on a great adventure with Jesus, of embracing a lifestyle that is "the word of the prophets made more sure." And it all begins for us when we begin to let go of the good and the familiar, so our lives can be illuminated by the bright light of God's best.

Father, may my life this day be illuminated with your best. May I become for those around me "the words of the prophets made more sure."

13

A FEARLESS VISION

Tim Philpot

Where there is no vision, the people perish.
—Proverbs 29:18 KJV

I live in Lexington, Kentucky. Recently a Visioning Committee was formed to plan for the future of our city. Their job is to visualize the approaching progress and problems of Lexington, and to help the city grow purposefully.

One of the key events recorded in the book of Acts is Paul's life-changing experience on the road to Damascus. While he was "breathing out murderous threats against the Lord's disciples" (Acts 9:1 NIV), a flashing light from heaven physically blinded him. As he struggled in the darkness of that experience, he was given the vision that changed Saul of Tarsus into the apostle Paul. That vision became the focus of his life.

Today God is looking for men who have seen visions. Not spooky, mystical experiences, but genuine encounters with the Spirit of God that tell them what to do, where to go, and what to be.

Each person's vision is unique, but in Acts 26 Paul tells us that certain fundamentals always remain the same:

1. The vision is from God, not man.
2. The vision is given to ordinary, sinful people.
3. The vision benefits others.
4. The vision may encompass the world, but it begins at home.
5. The vision takes us to risky places.
6. The vision extends from one generation to another.

Lord, the world has been greatly blessed because Paul responded to the heavenly vision. Remind me that even tiny visions have significance and purpose and that my response affects other people. Amen.

Week 49, Monday   A Heavenly Vision

So then, King Agrippa, I was not disobedient to the vision from heaven.   —Acts 26:19 NIV

Paul never doubted that what he experienced on the Damascus Road was a heavenly vision. His personal plans were aborted and the rest of his life reflected that vision. As a lawyer, I spend my life helping clients unscramble the parts of their life that didn't go as they had planned. Life simply does not comply with mortal agendas.

Years ago, I discovered that my plans were fragile and unreliable. If I wanted my life to have any real meaning, I needed better plans. The university, the council of wise men, and even the church, tried to help me create new plans that were no better than the old.

Finally, I began to wonder if by chance God had a plan for my life. It didn't seem likely; I was such an ordinary fellow. Then one day I remembered that it was the fishermen, the tax collectors, the tent makers, even transformed harlots, that Jesus chose to be his disciples. So I began to seek God's plan for my life.

The heavenly vision given to me was a self-portrait. I saw myself as I really was—materialistic, harnessed to my job, stereotyped in the church, and empty inside because none of those things satisfied. I began to understand that the shams of life disappear in the light of God's will, so I surrendered to his plan for my life. Today, I have absolutely no plans of my own for my future.

Lord, send the vision and give me the courage to respond to the challenges and opportunities of your will. Amen.

Week 49, Tuesday   A Vision to Ordinary Men

I too was convinced that I ought to do all that was possible to oppose the name of Jesus of Nazareth. . . . I put many of the

saints in prison, and when they were put to death, I cast my vote against them.

—Acts 26:9-10 NIV

Who receives heavenly visions? Paul, the zealous missionary, was originally a vicious enemy of the church. The same zeal he used to proclaim the gospel was first used to stop the gospel. Paul believed himself to be the chief among sinners (see 1 Timothy 1:15), yet God chose to use him to evangelize the ancient world.

My father, Ford Philpot, rebelled against God until he was thirty years old. He was an alcoholic, a gambler, and a thoroughly miserable man. Like Paul, my dad struck out against all that is godly. Yet one autumn evening in 1947, at a cottage prayer meeting in Wilmore, Kentucky, he encountered Jesus Christ. His sins were forgiven, the peace came, and the vision was clear. He entered the ministry and served God for forty-six years, winning thousands of people to the Lord.

The vision is given to ordinary, sinful people. You and I are no exceptions. We're not too wicked, too stupid, too frail, too old, too busy, or too good to be touched by the blinding power of God. Seek the vision. Find the plan.

Lord, expose the hidden debris in my soul and cleanse that which is revealed in the light of your love. Make me a part of the solution instead of part of the problem. Amen.

Week 49, Wednesday   A Servant Vision

Now get up and stand on your feet. I have appeared to you to appoint you as a servant and as a witness.

—Acts 26:16 NIV

God's vision always involves our being a servant and a witness. If Satan can't prevent the vision, then his next tactic is to stroke our ego. Daydreams begin to foster egotism, and pretty soon our emphasis is self rather than others. We begin envisioning wonderful things for ourselves.

I know a fourteen-year-old boy who spends three Saturday afternoons each month volunteering in a geriatric center. He moves among the residents, reassuring them, calling them by name, helping them open a milk carton, reading their mail to them, and in general, making each person feel loved. When I asked him why he devotes so much time to these people, he told me that he enjoys hobbies and free time, but he is concerned that hobbies and free time are so seldom enjoyed by those elderly people.

Not many Christians of any age have the vision of this young man. The world tells us to be our own person, to find ourselves, to cultivate self-esteem. Satan and his evil spirits subtly suggest that we are special because the vision came to us. We have potential and God needs our help!

Satan's lies are nearly true. We *are* special because we are children of God; we *do* have potential, but it is God's potential in us. Beware, Christian! When God speaks, we are called to serve others through Christ. When Satan speaks, our emphasis will be self.

Dear Jesus, the agony in this world is easily seen. Make the vision clear enough that I can see beyond myself. Amen.

Week 49, Thursday   The Vision Starts at Home

I was not disobedient to the vision. . . . First to those in Damascus, then to those in Jerusalem and in all Judea, . . . I preached.
—Acts 26:19-20 NIV

Paul began preaching in Damascus because that is where the vision was given. Christianity begins at home. The vision may eventually take us around the world, but the service and the witness always begin at home.

I don't believe that I was "accidentally" born at Good Samaritan Hospital in Lexington, Kentucky. It was God's plan that I should begin life there. I grew up in Lexington. People there remember me from Glendover Elementary School, Tate's Creek High School, and the University of Kentucky. Today, my greatest chances for influencing others for Christ are in my hometown. When God does something to significantly change a man, the home folks notice.

Unfortunately, many people want to serve the Lord in other places before they serve him at home. A foreign mission is not an option until we've made a difference in our own neighborhood. We shouldn't even think about ministering in "Judea" until "Damascus" has benefited from our efforts.

The number one priority for Christian service and witness in the life of a married man should be his wife and children. A truly godly man is first a godly husband and father. If the Lord cannot depend on us to be faithful witnesses to those we love best, how can he expect us to be effective among strangers?

Lord, help me to discern the needs in the lives of those closest to me and give me the grace to be a good witness to them. Amen.

Week 49, Friday   A Long-Term Vision

You then, my son, be strong in the grace that is in Christ Jesus. And the things you have heard me say in the presence of many witnesses entrust to reliable men who will also be qualified to teach others.   —2 Timothy 2:1-2 NIV

Where does the vision end? Geographically speaking, it encompasses the world; relationally speaking, it goes from one generation to the next. Paul instructed Timothy to be strong in grace and to teach others as he had been taught.

That's how it works. God gave Paul many spiritual children to carry the message after his death. Paul's vision is still being shared by those of us who read and live by his epistles.

My dad's vision began in an obscure prayer meeting in 1947. In 1955, he held a tent revival in his hometown, Manchester, Kentucky. Irvine Arnett was converted in that meeting. Recently, Irvine's son, Billy, wrote to me concerning that night. He said:

My father has told me many times about his conversion in 1955 at a tent revival conducted by your father. I was a newborn baby at the time. When Dad gave his heart to the Lord that night, he also surrendered the most precious thing in his life. He dedicated me to God.

Today Billy Arnett is a singer and songwriter who continues to share the vision on behalf of his father and mine.

Thank you, Father, for the Christian heritage that is mine. Grant me the vision to pave substantial spiritual pathways for those who follow me. Amen.

Week 49, Saturday   A Risky Vision

I will rescue you from your own people and from the Gentiles. I am sending you to them to open their eyes and turn them from darkness to light, and from the power of Satan to God.
                                                    —*Acts 26:17-18 NIV*

Playing it safe is not a part of the vision. There comes a day when dedicated disciples are sent by the Spirit into places where rescue is going to be necessary. Paul went from Damascus into the hostility of Jerusalem and Judea and finally into the paganism of Rome. After Damascus, Paul was in danger for the rest of his life, but God rescued him time and again from the powers of Satan.

Unfortunately, many Christian men cannot imagine serving God in risky places. Risky places geographically, risky places emotionally, risky places politically. But God intends to send us into areas where we will need to be rescued. It is only men of clear vision and deep faith who respond to such a call.

Leaving home is always risky. In the 1950s Jim Elliot and four companions were martyred while sharing the gospel with the Auca Indians in Ecuador. They gave their lives—and God used their vision to redeem the Aucas, who ultimately accepted Christ.

Christian vision is not for cowards.

Lord, at times my life is scary and I must rely on your strength and courage. It is that same strength and courage that calls me to risky places and makes me willing to go. Use me. Amen.

Week 50, Sunday   Personal Risks

I will rescue you from your own people.
                                                    —*Acts 26:17 NIV*

Our families provide the riskiest emotional terrain. There are dangers in strangers, but there are few things more treacherous than presenting the gospel to families or friends in crisis if there are those involved who are hostile to the faith. Emotions boil, tempers flare, and hearts break. Guilt, anger, fear, and resentment that might be controlled in casual situations seem to explode when families and friends are in a critical situation.

It's risky to bare emotions, to speak the truth, to ask difficult questions that must be asked, to say "I love you." Yet, sometimes, as faithful witnesses, these are risks that must be taken. God has promised to rescue us and to use all circumstances for our good if we are obedient to him. (See Romans 8:28.) Paul's former friends, now his enemies, "formed a conspiracy and bound themselves with an oath not to eat or drink until they had killed Paul" (Acts 23:12 NIV). Friends and family misunderstand, and it hurts, but *no risks* would indicate *no family, no friends*.

Sometimes, the Lord needs to rescue us from ourselves. In 1985 I decided to go into politics and ran for County Attorney—thirty-four years old, full of ego, a real hotshot. I lost the election, but I won, because God rescued me from a potentially dangerous position. The person who beat me is currently serving a prison term.

Jesus, help me to love enough to take the risks that will demonstrate what your love actually means in my life. Amen.

Week 50, Monday   **Approaching Battle**

Some men came and told Jehoshaphat, "A vast army is coming against you from Edom. . . ." Alarmed, Jehoshaphat resolved to inquire of the LORD, and he proclaimed a fast for all Judah.
                                                    —*2 Chronicles 20:2-3 NIV*

Life sometimes gets perilous. We are overwhelmed by the "vast army" of the enemies that come against us. It may be illness, addiction, a broken relationship, financial stress, trouble with the kids, pressure at work, or any number of other seemingly insurmountable problems.

The Old Testament story of Jehoshaphat provides a formula

for victory. When Jehoshaphat, the great, great, great grandson of King David, was warned that a "vast army" was coming against him and his outnumbered people, he had no time to prepare an adequate defense.

Just as we struggle with panic and despair when tragedy and adversity unexpectedly invade our lives, Jehoshaphat was greatly alarmed. Alarmed to the extent that he "resolved to inquire of the Lord" and he "proclaimed a fast." He had no option but to seek divine help. The battle was upon him, so prayer and fasting became his weapons of defense.

The enemy hasn't changed since the days of Jehoshaphat, and neither has the defense. When life becomes a battlefield, and we fear we will be destroyed, we have access to the same powerful defense as did Jehoshaphat. God is both available and able to strengthen, protect, and keep us in the worst of circumstances.

Father, I constantly attempt to fight battles that are greater than my resources. Teach me to rely on you. Amen.

Week 50, Tuesday   **Prayer: The First Option**

O LORD . . . Power and might are in your hand, and no one can withstand you. . . . We have no power to face this vast army that is attacking us. We do not know what to do, but our eyes are upon you.   —2 Chronicles 20:6, 12 NIV

When he realized that a war was about to begin, Jehoshaphat brought the people together to pray. Many of us would form a committee, seek a government program, or just throw up our hands and forget it! But Jehoshaphat knew where success begins. He acknowledged that they had no power to face the enemy. He didn't know what to do, but his eyes were upon God. Good thinking!

Prayer is not the last resort. It is the first option. But Jehoshaphat did not pray alone. It is significant that "all the men of Judah, with their wives and children and little ones, stood there before the LORD" (2 Chronicles 20:13 NIV). There was unity among the people, including the children.

The prayers of children are powerful. In 1989, my wife, Sue, and I went on a mission trip to India with a number of business and professional people to volunteer our services at Bethel Agricultural Fellowship, which also includes a hospital and a large orphanage. Every member of the team received a prayer partner. Two little girls at the orphanage, Subha and Mumtaj, became my and Sue's partners and agreed to pray for us every day. We have been the beneficiaries of their awesome prayers ever since!

Awesome? Yes. In the years immediately following that visit we were very conscious that we were being prayed for, and many things changed in our family for the better. For one thing we were able to get out of debt. As a result I was able to run for and get elected to the Kentucky Senate, a position I feel God has called me to. Subha and Mumtaj are still praying for us.

Lord, when the war is raging, remind me that prayer is not the last resort but the first option. Amen.

Week 50, Wednesday   **Don't Be Afraid**

Do not be afraid or discouraged because of this vast army.
—2 Chronicles 20:15 NIV

While we were in India, I discovered that the ultimate and pervasive problem there is fear. The highways are dotted with Hindu temples engraved with countless images of gods. There are elephant gods, two-headed gods, scary idols thought by the people to be gods of protection for travelers. People stop and give money to these idols, hoping to buy protection for themselves. The Indian people live in constant fear that these gods will do something horrible to them.

We Americans are equally bound by fear. We are afraid of failure; afraid of going broke; afraid of rejection; afraid of death; afraid of certain people. Fear saps our strength and inhibits our productivity. Some people are actually paralyzed by fear.

God knew we humans would be afraid, so he provided the gift of faith. The opposite of *fear* is *faith*. Faith casts out fear and restores our minds as well as our physical bodies. We're told in scripture to live by faith. Fear is a large part of the enemy's arsenal, and only our confidence in the love and power of God can deliver us from the false gods of doubt and fear. Believe God! He *will* take care of his own.

Lord, when I surrender to fear, I put myself on equal ground with the pagans of the world. Help me to live by faith, even when I feel afraid. Amen.

Week 50, Thursday   Fear of Confession

Because of the Pharisees they would not confess their faith for fear they would be put out of the synagogue.
—John 12:42 NIV

Nearly thirty years ago, a Supreme Court case in California, *California v. Miranda,* declared that every person arrested for a serious crime in America has, among other things, "the right to remain silent." These are known as the Miranda rights, and everyone who is arrested is read these rights.

Today our churches are filled with people who also believe that they have the right to remain silent! They are what I call "Miranda Christians." They claim that their faith is a "personal thing" and therefore a private matter. They are hesitant to confess either their sins or their faith.

In 1970, when I was a freshman in college, God met me on February 6 at 1:00 in the morning in the Asbury College chapel. I knew that something very real had happened to me because the next morning, I could not wait to make some phone calls. I wanted to tell my parents, my brother, my friends that Jesus Christ had died for my sins.

In the night I had confessed my sins in the chapel and when morning came, I wanted to confess my faith in the world. You see, when you *really* experience God, there is something inside that does want to testify, even if you are the strong, silent type.

Lord, give me courage every day to confess my sins to you and my faith to the world. Amen.

Week 50, Friday   Confess for Salvation

If you confess with your mouth, "Jesus is Lord," and believe in your heart that God raised him from the dead, you will be saved.
—Romans 10:9 NIV

Believing Jesus Christ to be the Son of God is not enough to get us into the kingdom of God. Confession is a part of salvation. Romans 10:8-10 provides Paul's best explanation of saving faith. The two key elements to salvation are confession and belief. We need to believe that sin, unconfessed, is deadly and will cost us eternal life in heaven. We need to believe that Jesus Christ "is the atoning sacrifice for our sins" (1 John 2:2 NIV), and that when we confess our sins, he "is faithful and just and will forgive us our sins" (1 John 1:9 NIV). Paul says, "for it is with your heart that you believe and are justified, and it is with your mouth that you confess and are saved" (Romans 10:10 NIV).

When I fell in love with my wife, I believed it. I felt it in my heart. But it was not until I confessed it with my mouth—told her that I loved her and wanted her to marry me—that she accepted me as her husband. She still likes for me to occasionally "confess" my love for her.

Fuzzy, warm feelings toward wives are not enough. Fuzzy, warm feelings toward God are not enough, either. He wants us to speak *to* him and *for* him.

Lord, I am grateful that confession brings peace as well as salvation. Confession is for my good and your glory. Thank you for forgiveness. Amen.

Week 50, Saturday   No Spectators, Please

Meanwhile a large crowd of Jews found out that Jesus was there and came, not only because of him but also to see Lazarus.
—John 12:9 NIV

Rupp Arena, where the University of Kentucky plays basketball, seats 23,500 spectators. We fans sit comfortably in our seats munching nachos and sipping beverages. We cheer and yell, shouting advice to both the coaches and the players. We do none of the work but all of the criticizing.

Down on the floor, the players sometimes get so tired that they signal the coach to take them out of the game so they can catch their breath. They are exhausted from making every effort to win the game. We fans are still critical. I've never seen a fan raise his hand and offer to trade places with a player.

This reminds me a lot of church members I have known. They are church "spectators," people who leave all the blood, sweat, and tears to the pastor and other laity. They watch; sometimes they root; often they criticize, but they seldom volunteer to get in the game.

Thank God for our pastors and for men like Chuck Swindoll, James Dobson, and Billy Graham. They are mighty confessors of the faith. But God is looking for people like you and me to step forward and take part in the game. We may believe in our hearts that Jesus is the Son of God, but are we confessing with our lives and with our mouths that he is Lord?

Other men are watching you and me. Do they see a player or a critic?

Dear Lord, I'm too often in the bleachers instead of on the bench. Help me to be more involved and less critical of the church. Amen.

Week 51, Sunday   Attracting Curiosity Seekers

Jesus arrived at Bethany, where Lazarus lived, whom Jesus had raised from the dead. Here a dinner was given in Jesus' honor. . . . Lazarus was among those reclining at the table.
—John 12:1-2 NIV

We are familiar with the story of the Last Supper, but how many of us know the details of the next to the last supper? It was a dinner given in honor of Jesus by Simon the leper. A large crowd gathered for several reasons. First of all, Simon was himself an item of interest. Jesus had cured him of leprosy!

But more fascinating was the presence of Lazarus. A man dead and buried for four days, alive again and attending a dinner party! And, of course, the fact that Jesus, the Man behind these miracles, was present caused a naturally irrepressible curiosity among the people. Something truly marvelous had happened to both men while they were with Jesus.

Let me ask you a question. Are people ever curious about what happened to you while you were with Jesus?

Several years ago, when little Jessica McClure was being rescued from an abandoned well, most of us sat glued to our televisions, breathlessly awaiting the outcome of that ordeal. Why? Because we thought she was dead—but she was alive.

A "resurrected" life always attracts the attention of others.

Lord, may the same power that raised you from the grave be evident in the way I live my life. Amen.

Week 51, Monday   The Domino Effect

So the chief priests made plans to kill Lazarus as well, for on account of him many of the Jews were going over to Jesus and putting their faith in him.   *—John 12:10-11 NIV*

After Jesus raised Lazarus from the grave, Lazarus became a real problem to those who were seeking to destroy Jesus. John 12:17 tells us that the crowd who was with Jesus when he raised Lazarus continued to spread the word. When news got out that both Jesus and Lazarus were having dinner at the home of Simon the Leper, great crowds gathered to see not only Jesus, but Lazarus.

People were being saved because Lazarus had been saved. That's the domino effect. As God's confessors, we do not have to preach sermons, we simply need to (a) be ready to answer questions, and (b) pray.

One day after Easter, I ordered a sandwich in a Lexington deli where I often go. The waitress knew I was "religious," and that day she asked me, "Tim, nobody can tell me why the day Christ died is called Good Friday. Do you know the answer?"

"It's simple," I answered. "Because of my sin, I'm not good enough to go to heaven. I understood that and that I needed to pay a penalty. Instead of making me hang on the cross, God sent his only Son to pay the penalty that I owed. It was a very bad Friday for Jesus, but a very Good Friday for me, because I accepted Jesus' death for me."

Confessors may not know all the answers to life's tough questions, but they know where to go to find them. Indeed, confessors know The Answer, Jesus Christ.

Lord, I thank you for every confessor who influenced me to live my life for you. Make me a part of the "domino effect" that others might know you, too. Amen.

Then an angel of the Lord appeared to him, standing at the right side of the altar of incense. When Zechariah saw him, he was startled and was gripped with fear.

—Luke 1:11-12 NIV

Perhaps Zechariah, a priest, should not have been startled when God sent an angel to answer his prayer, but the Bible tells us that he was "gripped with fear." The angel came with good news. A son, John—who would become John the Baptist—was to be born to him and his wife, Elizabeth. Even though Zechariah was a righteous man, deep inside he was afraid of answered prayer.

I understand that kind of fear. While preaching in India a few years ago, I asked for testimonies from those who had felt God's healing touch in the service the night before. Twelve-year-old Raji, crippled by polio, spoke, saying that he was thankful that God had sent me to minister to him, and that he hoped to walk like other children.

I called for someone to bring Raji to me, and as you might expect, I silently began to beg God to heal that little boy. But as I held the boy in my arms and prayed that he would walk, I was trembling. I've never been so afraid in my life. My fear was not that he wouldn't walk, but that he would walk. The thought of such a miracle terrified me. How could I handle that kind of responsibility, that display of power?

I don't know if it was because of my fear or not, but Raji wasn't healed. Since then I have tried to find orthopedic help for him, but he is too crippled. He's a happy boy, though, and I keep praying for him—and about my fear of miracles. Such a fear is self-serving and limits God.

We must not be afraid of answered prayer.

Dear Jesus, make me brave enough to pray expecting an answer. Amen.

Week 51, Wednesday — Don't Be Afraid of Greatness

The angel went to her and said, "Greetings, you who are highly favored! The Lord is with you." Mary was greatly troubled at his words. . . . But the angel said to her, "Do not be afraid, Mary, you have found favor with God."

—Luke 1:28-30 NIV

There are three good reasons why God's call on Mary's life alarmed her. First, she was face-to-face with an angel sent from God. Second, Gabriel called her by name. Third, the message that she was to give birth to the Son of God was enough to frighten any young girl. No wonder the angel assured her that she had no reason to be frightened!

God told Mary that she was special and that he would accomplish great things through her. It's easy to understand why she was scared. The magnitude of the message and the mystery of what it would mean throughout her life were, each in their own way, terrifying matters.

The same kind of terror that clutched Mary's heart has, through the ages, frightened many Christians, men and women. We're afraid that the call is too great and we are too small. We're apprehensive about what the call will mean in our future. We'd rather not. We're unworthy, we say; we're unable; we're likely to fail; we can't do it! And we are right—apart from God we can do nothing. But when we are obedient, God can do anything through us.

Don't be afraid of God's greatness in your life.

Lord, help me remember that surrender and obedience are my part, and any great works are your part. Amen.

Week 51, Thursday   **Don't Be Afraid of Disgrace**

Because Joseph her husband was a righteous man and did not want to expose her to public disgrace, he had in mind to divorce her quietly.   *—Matthew 1:19 NIV*

Joseph feared that his reputation as a religious and righteous man would be destroyed by his marriage to Mary. Let's face it. Mary was pregnant and Joseph looked guilty. He was embarrassed. Under the law he had the right to "divorce her quietly"— that is, he could cancel the engagement and find another girl.

Did you ever think what it would have meant to our world if

Joseph had done what the law allowed? History would have recorded Baby Jesus' birth as illegitimate. Think about that!

Again, God sent an angel, to place a call on Joseph's life. God told Joseph not to be afraid. The situation involved much more than reputations and righteousness. It was about saving the world, and being *religious* wouldn't help. God needed Joseph to be *obedient*.

We Christians tend to guard our religious reputations fiercely. But God says that if we are to be useful to him, we can't worry about public opinion when it opposes his will for our lives.

When John Wesley was thrown out of the Church of England as a heretic, he stood on his father's tomb in the churchyard to proclaim the gospel. God honored his efforts by sending a great spiritual awakening throughout England and beyond.

We must always honor God's name above our own.

Lord, teach me to glory only in your name. Amen.

Week 51, Friday   **Don't Be Afraid of Enemies**

When he heard that Archelaus was reigning in Judea in place of his father Herod, he was afraid to go there.
                                        —Matthew 2:22 NIV

Because Joseph realized that Herod had massacred scores of baby boys in his attempt to kill Jesus, he was afraid of Herod's son, Archelaus, who was also an enemy.

Enemies can be scary things. Some time ago, I was warned that if I engaged in a certain debate, there were forces at work to harm me. I received two telephone threats against me and my family because of a stance I had taken. For the first time in my life, I began to fear for my safety. I kept on with the campaign, but with a watchful eye out at all times.

Then I thought about soldiers caught in the terrors of battle. Frightened, surely, but they respond to their duty despite the odds. The night I went to the debate, I decided that whatever it is that motivates men in times of battle must motivate me. Danger might be a reality in my life, but fear was an enemy that might cause me to abandon my stand against those things that I consider wrong. I wasn't harmed that night, and God has kept me and my family safe since then, though the battle still goes on.

God tells us not to be afraid. He sent his Son to deliver us from all evil. Christ came as the only Light in a great darkness. The angelic message to the world on the night of Jesus' birth was, "Do not be afraid. . . . I bring you good news. . . . the Savior has come."

Lord, fear itself can be the worst of my enemies. It's one of Satan's greatest strategies against me. Deliver me from fear. Amen.

Week 51, Saturday   Don't Be Afraid of the Real Jesus

And they took offense at him. . . . And he [Jesus] did not do many miracles there because of their lack of faith.
—Matthew 13:57-58 NIV

The gospel is good news, if we accept Jesus Christ as the good news heralded by the angels in the Bethlehem skies. The shepherds were frightened, but they believed the message, sought the Child, and spread the tidings through the streets of Bethlehem.

The people of Nazareth were not so wise. When Jesus came to their village, he could work few miracles because they feared his powers and rejected him. How tragic!

I had a friend in college who was wild by anybody's standards. He had a beautiful wife, who appeared to be a deeply religious person, and they had two little daughters. Things were fine in their lives—until my friend met Jesus. His life was completely transformed by his conversion experience.

Though she claimed to be a Christian, his wife was unable to accept her husband's transformation. She was threatened by his childlike faith and his surrender to Jesus Christ. She demanded that he choose her or his "religion." When he refused to reject Jesus Christ, she packed her bags and took the little girls and left. She sacrificed her marriage because she feared having the real Jesus involved in her life and marriage. Her fear robbed that family of God's rich blessings. How tragic!

Lord, become so real in my life that my fear of you becomes an absurdity. Amen.

On the evening of that first day of the week . . . the disciples were
together, with the doors locked for fear of the Jews.

—John 20:19 NIV

Following the crucifixion, we find the disciples huddled away
in an upper room with the doors locked, afraid of the Jews who
had killed their Leader. They were terrified that Jesus had left
and they were now alone to face the consequences of his ministry.

Most people are critical of their cowardly conduct, but I
believe that their behavior is actually a positive attribute. They
were literally afraid to leave the house without Jesus.

So am I. If I thought I had to live today without Jesus' intimate
presence, I'd stay at home, too.

I can remember as a child being frightened of a great many
things: the dark, bullies, big dogs, to name a few. But when my
mom or dad was with me, none of those things were a threat. I
find similar circumstances in my life today, except now it is the
presence of the Lord that takes away my anxieties and helps me
meet any threat with courage. Just think about it. We have no
reason to be afraid, because Jesus is always with us through his
Spirit (John 14:15-18).

Before Jesus was born, the angel told Joseph that Mary's child
was to be called "Emmanuel," which means "God is with us"
(Matthew 1:23). So don't be afraid! God *is* with us.

Dear Jesus, I realize that when I am afraid, I am living
below my privileges as your disciple. Teach me to cast my
fears on you and live in the reality of your presence. Amen.

The battle is not yours, but God's.

—2 Chronicles 20:15 NIV

What a wonderful promise! The battle is not mine, but the
Lord's.

It is almost comical to envision a mere mortal at war with the devil and his foul spirits. The whole idea reminds me of a small child lost in Daddy's battle fatigues, crooked helmet covering both eyes, boot tops nudging his knees, dragging a saber half his own length. What a joke it is to imagine that you and I could ever, in our own battle gear, beat the devil.

But what, exactly, does it mean for the battle to be the Lord's? The simplest illustration that occurs to me is my law practice. A lawyer's purpose is to relieve the client of his or her problems. I encourage all my clients to do their best to leave their troubles in my office. It is the lawyer's responsibility to fight the enemy or meet a legal challenge on behalf of the client.

This is exactly what Jesus Christ wants to do for us. He is not only our Advocate with the Father, he is our Defender, our Counselor, our Advisor, and our Mediator. Jesus Christ beat the devil on the cross, but he left the armor for us to wear—the girdle of truth, the breastplate of righteousness, the sandals of the gospel, the shield of faith, the helmet of salvation, and the sword of the Spirit. (Read Ephesians 6:10-17.)

We are protected by the armor while the Lord fights our battles.

Lord, when I struggle with Satan in my own power, I lose; when I surrender to you, I win. Help me to remember that. Amen.

Week 52, Tuesday   It's a Battle for Souls

What good will it be for a man if he gains the whole world, yet forfeits his soul?   —Matthew 16:26 NIV

What's the nature of the battle? It's not a political battle to lower taxes or stop crime. It's not a '60s war on poverty or a '90s war on big government. We're not promoting the Democrats or the Republicans. The battle is for the hearts and souls of men and women, boys and girls. Humanity's eternal destiny is at stake.

My mother's brother, Neil Robinson, became a colonel in the U.S. Army and has always been a hero to me. It was Uncle Neil's job to plan funerals for political and military dignitaries. Mom recently gave me an old copy of *Life* magazine whose cover pictured Uncle Neil escorting the widow of Douglas MacArthur to MacArthur's funeral.

The article included MacArthur's final speech at West Point. He closed the speech with these words: "I want you to know that when I cross that river [speaking of death], my last thoughts will be 'the Corps, the Corps, the Corps.'"

When I read those words, it occurred to me that when it's my turn to cross that river, my last thoughts will be "the cross, the cross, the cross." It's our only hope of heaven. We mortals are absolutely doomed without the great love and sacrifice of Jesus Christ on Calvary's cross.

The battle is for souls.

Lord, Satan has come to wipe out mankind. Jesus has come to save us. Give me a clear vision of what the battle is about, and help me to live my life for the cause of Christ. Amen.

Week 52, Wednesday   Stand Firm

Take up your positions; stand firm and see the deliverance the LORD *will give you.*   —2 Chronicles 20:17 NIV

God did not allow Jehoshaphat and the people to avoid the battlefield. He told them to face the enemy, even though he would do the fighting for them.

Several years ago, a young man in my political party was running for the state legislature. He looked good in the media, but I knew he was not the right man—for many reasons. I contemplated publicly exposing his faults, thereby creating a real battle within the party, as well as producing a lot of messy accusations about my motives, along with negative publicity.

Then I considered the story of Jehoshaphat and remembered Joshua at the battle of Jericho. Instead of speaking out against this young man, I decided to drive around Lexington for two hours, praying that God would intervene and stop him from being elected. It seemed a crazy thing to do since we were three weeks away from the election and he was ahead in all the polls.

Two days after my "crazy" prayer, the newspaper wrote a story about him that revealed much of the truth. He not only lost the election, he spent time in jail for domestic violence.

It's not easy to "stand firm" when fighting seems the logical thing to do, but the *supernatural* can overcome the enemy only when the *natural* stands firm in faith.

Dear Jesus, standing firm is difficult in most situations. I need your strength when it's my turn to stand. Amen.

Week 52, Thursday   **Sing Praises**

After consulting the people, Jehoshaphat appointed men to sing to the LORD and to praise him for the splendor of his holiness as they went out at the head of the army.
                                          —2 Chronicles 20:21 NIV

How interesting that the song leader led the battle! Who would ever think of sending George Beverly Shea or Bill Gaither instead of Norman Schwarzkopf to take control of a war? Yet Jehoshaphat appointed men "to sing unto the Lord" as they went into battle.

Praising God through music is not a lunatic reaction to spiritual emotion. It is evidence to God that we truly trust him to fight our battles. The enemy is not too great and the battle is not too difficult. Through prayer and praise all battles can be won.

The enemy forces differ from one country to other. The enemies in third-world countries are often poverty, illiteracy, and religious systems that tell people they can never improve their lot in life. The enemies prevalent in the United States are greed, materialism, violence, drugs and alcohol, and complacency. The tactics used by the enemy do not determine the outcome of the war. It is our reaction to the enemy's tactics that makes the difference.

God has given us a formula for victory:

1. Pray.
2. Don't be afraid.
3. Stand firm.
4. Let God fight the battle.
5. Praise God before the victory!

Praising God is the formula's most vital element.

Lord, give me the confidence and grace to praise your name in the best of circumstances and the worst of circumstances. Amen.

Week 52, Friday   **Real Leaders, Not Poll Takers**

Day after day men came to help David, until he had a great army, like the army of God.
—1 Chronicles 12:22 NIV

I've had great admiration and respect for the Salvation Army ever since I spent four weeks ringing their Christmas bells in New York City when I was a college freshman. I especially like their name—the Salvation Army. Indeed, all Christians should consider themselves to be a part of such an army.

Paul told Timothy to endure hardship like a good soldier of Christ Jesus (2 Timothy 2:3). Victorious armies, however, need dynamic leadership as well as valiant soldiers. Who are these real leaders? I'm not sure who they are, but I know who they are not.

A real leader is not a poll taker. Few politicians ever say or do anything without first polling the people to see what everybody thinks. People controlled by polls are followers and not leaders.

The standard for Christian living must always be the Holy Word of God, the Bible. Real leaders are not illiterate concerning God's Word. Popular opinion, politically correct ideas, yes, even the polls that are taken by experts, are not adequate data for establishing the moral fiber of our world.

The "Salvation Army" will ultimately win the war between good and evil, and it is the Sword of the Spirit, God's Word, that will be the authority in the victory.

Dear Lord, your Word is precious, but so often I don't spend adequate time studying its mighty truth. Give me a new hunger for its teachings. Amen.

Week 52, Saturday   **Declare the Truth**

Then you will know the truth, and the truth will set you free.
—John 8:32 NIV

Real leaders are not afraid to stand for the truth. God's Word clearly states that right and wrong exist in the mind of God. Debating matters of morality will never alter God's rules and regulations. A true leader knows the rules and respects the authority of God.

In 1991, I spoke at a prayer breakfast in the Hungarian Parliament. There I met Gabor Roszik, the first freely elected member of the Hungarian Parliament since World War II who was not a Communist. Roszik, a thirty-five-year-old Lutheran pastor with no title but Reverend, had stood against the Communist regime. He held no office, but he knew the difference between right and wrong.

A small band of citizens stood with him, and eventually the pressure from this group increased until a free election to select members of Parliament was permitted. Ten Communists opposed the young pastor, but Gabor Roszik received 70 percent of the votes.

Gabor Roszik left the Hungarian Parliament after serving a term, but he still preaches the gospel, and is recognized today as one of the most influential men in Hungary. Why? He didn't take a poll; he didn't have a title; but he had the courage to stand for the truth.

Our world needs leaders, as well as foot soldiers, who have the same kind of courage as Gabor Roszik. Are you such a soldier? Such a leader?

Lord, give me the courage to take my place in your army. Amen.